£1.9ac

STRIPPED

D1340663

SAMANTHA BAILEY

Stripped

A LIFE OF
Strip
&
Tease
IN CLUBLAND

**MAINSTREAM
PUBLISHING**

EDINBURGH AND LONDON

Copyright © Samantha Bailey, 2012
All rights reserved
The moral rights of the author have been asserted

First published in Great Britain in 2012 by
MAINSTREAM PUBLISHING COMPANY
(EDINBURGH) LTD
7 Albany Street
Edinburgh EH1 3UG

ISBN 9781845967840

No part of this book may be reproduced or transmitted in any form or by
any other means without permission in writing from the publisher, except by
a reviewer who wishes to quote brief passages in connection with a review
written for insertion in a magazine, newspaper or broadcast

This book is a work of non-fiction based on the life, experiences and
recollections of the author. In some cases, names of people, places, dates,
sequences or the detail of events have been changed to protect the privacy of
others. The author has stated to the the publishers that, except in such cases,
not affecting the substantial accuracy of the work, the contents of this
book are true.

A catalogue record for this book is available
from the British Library

Printed and Bound by
CPI Group (UK) Ltd, Croydon, CR0 4YY

1 3 5 7 9 10 8 6 4 2

Contents

Author's note

This is the serious bit where I tell you that some of the names of the people and establishments mentioned in this book have been changed. It won't take you long to understand why: I like having kneecaps. By taking these stories out of the actual clubs they happened in, I hope it shows that these stories can happen in any club, in any city, maybe in a street not so far from wherever you are right now. The important thing for you to know is that everything you are about to read really happened to real people.

Introduction

When I tell people that I used to take my clothes off for money, there are usually three questions they want to ask. The first is 'Why?' The simple answer, and the answer that a lot of people don't want to hear, is that I enjoyed it. I liked showing off, I liked being desired and I liked earning a lot of money. Simple as.

The next question is, inevitably, 'How did you get into it?' That's pretty easy to answer too: I was 17, I had a shit job earning shit money and I couldn't bear the thought that that was all there was. If you give me two options – the boring one and the dangerous one – I will choose adventure. If you tell me something's forbidden, I'm going to try it. If you tell me I can't do something, I will prove you wrong. I'm pretty nosey about life, and if I sniff that someone's having a barbecue on the other side of the fence, I am going to jump over that fence and introduce myself. That's just who I am.

The third question is usually asked with a glint in the eye: 'So, Sam, what was it like?' Well, that's why you picked up this book, isn't it?

Samantha Bailey
London, 2011

LA DOLCE VITA

Bye bye Essex, hello adventure

The first person I want you to meet is my auntie Nya. Once you get to know her, a lot of what happens next will make sense.

I loved my auntie Nya. Absolutely adored her. She wasn't my real aunt – the best aunts never are – but at big family occasions, she would turn up in the latest designer clothes, looking immaculate from head to toe, with armfuls of exciting presents. Even as a kid I knew she was stunning. She knew it too, of course, but that just made her even more gorgeous. The guys looked at her, the women looked at her; it was like she was the greatest movie star who never made a film. *When I grow up*, I thought to myself, *I want to be like that*.

Ten years later, my cousin Heather (my *real* cousin) decided to give me a bit of a pep talk. I was a year out of school by this stage and was telling anyone who would listen that I hated my job at Next on Oxford Street. The family was a bit worried about me because I'd been getting moody and they had started to think I might be about to go off the rails. Cue the not-so-subtle pep talk from my big cousin.

Thankfully, Heather knew me pretty well and knew better than to tell me to go and get some A levels or secretarial qualifications.

'Do you know what Auntie Nya does for a living?' she asked.

It was a simple enough question, but it was one that changed my life. It suddenly occurred to me that I'd never asked. I'd been so caught up in Auntie Nya's hair and her nails and her fabulous clothes that I'd never thought about how she paid for it all.

Heather narrowed her eyes, the way people do when they're about to reveal a secret. 'Well,' she said, 'she might be able to get you a job.'

'What kind of job?'

'You know Auntie Nya always travels?'

'Yeah.'

'Well, how would you feel about travelling?'

What an odd question. 'I feel OK about travelling. Where are you going with this?'

'And, um, how would you feel about dancing?'

'I feel OK about dancing. Heather, you know I like dancing.'

Heather paused for a second. 'And how do you feel about dancing . . . in a bikini?'

Something clicked in my head and I just knew where she was going.

'In a bikini? Yeah, yeah, I could dance in a bikini.'

This might be the point where most people would say *No thanks, not for me*, but the thing is, I just knew it *was* for me. All my life I had looked at women like Sam Fox and Linda Lusardi and thought they were the height of glamour. If you'd grown up in Essex in the 1980s, you'd have thought Sam Fox was classy too. Trust me. I looked at those girls on Page Three, or the girls on TV with huge perms and skimpy tops, and I knew I wanted to be like them. They just seemed so grown up. And so like my auntie Nya.

Heather called Nya there and then and we had a chat. She explained that she supplied dancers to clubs in Denmark where you could earn good money.

'Are you interested, Sam?'

'You know I am.'

'You know what we're talking about here, don't you?'

'Pole dancing, that sort of thing.'

'And you're OK with that? You're really OK with taking your clothes off?'

'Yeah. Yeah, I am.'

'In front of men?'

'I'm not stupid, Auntie Nya.'

That night I lay on my bed and thought, *This is it. This is my ticket out of Essex and out of retail. Good money. An adventure. Bring. It. On.*

There were two things I instantly knew for sure. The first was that I couldn't tell my parents. They didn't know what Nya did for money and they weren't going to find out from me. My dad is a very proper guy. If you bring a burnt DVD into the house, he believes there'll be a helicopter over your roof and men in black on ropes in your back garden in minutes. He would not approve, and he would think he had failed as a parent. I wasn't going to have him thinking that. Besides, I'd already left home a couple of times in the past, so they wouldn't be asking too many questions. The second thing I knew for sure was that I was not going to go alone.

The Thelma to my Louise was my mate Alison. She worked in the warehouse at Next and hated the place as much as I did. The next morning, I couldn't wait to talk to her.

'Ali, how do you feel about travelling?'

'I feel OK about travelling. Why are you asking?'

'And how do you feel about dancing?'

'Sam, where are you going with this?'

I used exactly the same questions Heather had used on me and about two minutes later Alison had decided she wanted to go to Denmark too. We went out into the loading bay at the back and called Auntie Nya.

The deal was this: we'd get an apartment paid for and £50 for every night we worked. Nya also said we could earn more in commissions. I didn't really know what she meant by that, but at £250 a week and no rent to pay we didn't really care.

The next day we resigned, with immediate effect. The day after that we shopped – a pair of six-inch glass heels, some bra-and-knicker sets and a handful of outfits to wear on stage – and the day after that we got on a plane. Sayonara, retail. Adios, Essex. We are outta here.

When we boarded the flight, I noticed two other dancers straight away. The stripper equivalent of gaydar, I suppose. Their presence was really important to us because Nya had told us that two of her other girls would be on the same flight. If they were there, then it meant everything Auntie Nya had told us was true. Part of her deal was that she would pay for two trips home a year, and knowing these other girls a) had been home and b) were choosing to go back to Denmark meant that everything would be all right.

Alison and I had hit it off from the moment we'd met on a tea break at work, but as I sat next to her on the plane I realised just what an important friend she had become. If she had come to me with such an outrageous plan, if she had been the one with an Auntie Nya, would I have gone? Probably, but I might not have been so confident it would all work out. Knowing that Alison trusted me, and trusted my judgement, really meant a lot to me. Right at that moment, she became my best friend.

As we ordered another drink from the stewardess, I felt like the most adventurous, most glamorous person on the plane and there was nothing not to love. I mean *nothing*.

The set-up

Auntie Nya met us from the flight. The way she sashayed into the airport with her hair all groomed, wearing a long fur coat and swinging a Chanel bag has never left me. She was just as I remembered.

'Samantha, Samantha, come here, babes.' It was like being hugged by a teddy bear. 'And you must be Alison. You just got yourself an Auntie Nya too. Come here and give me a hug.'

I really respected Nya for that. She made the effort to put Alison at ease and let us know that we were going to be looked after. We needn't have any worries. Cos our auntie Nya had it all locked down.

She took us to our apartment. Even though it was very basic, and very small, the last time I'd left home I had moved into the YMCA, so this was definitely a step up. Actually, it was several steps up: it was on the fifth floor and Ali and I had a lot of luggage. A lot of heavy luggage. We had blown our final pay cheque from Next on way too many clothes.

After a quick tour of the flat, Nya took us out for dinner to a Vietnamese restaurant. In the bit of Essex where I grew up, we didn't have restaurants with cutlery – it was KFC, or McDonald's if it was your birthday – so that instantly felt glitzy, but this wasn't about having fun: Nya wanted to talk seriously. She needed to be absolutely sure that we knew what we were getting into. We talked about what *exactly* was involved, and only when she was sure we were as serious as she was did she take us to our first club.

La Dolce Vita, like half the strip clubs I've ever been in, was on the first floor. The other half are all below ground because there are too many prying eyes at ground level. We followed Nya up the stairs and through a pair of double doors – don't ask me why, but there are always, *always* double doors in strip clubs – and straight away the club was just as Nya had described it. Down one side was a long bar and opposite it were a number of tables and booths. The air was thick with cigarette smoke, but at least the constant fog muted the effect of the red flock wallpaper that would have been too OTT for a curry house. There were a few girls sitting together at a table, and at the bar a couple of guys were talking to hostesses. In front of each couple was a bottle of champagne. The champagne was important: Nya had told us in the restaurant that we could make commission every time a guy bought a bottle.

The three of us took a table and observed what was going on. Nya wanted us to see how things worked, but she also wanted other people to see us with her. We were her girls: harm us, and she'd see you got repaid. I felt safe with Nya and as long as the visuals in the club matched the verbals she had given us over dinner then I was happy. Of course, it also meant I wasn't looking out for anything she didn't want me to see. My auntie Nya's very clever like that.

The waitress brought over our drinks and Nya explained how the hostessing side of things works. Let's say a punter comes into a club and I'm his flavour. He would then come up to me and ask if he could sit with me, and the only way he can do that is if he buys a bottle of champagne. Depending on the size of bottle, and the brand he chooses, the hostess gets more or less commission. However, the cheaper the champagne he buys, the less time he can talk to you for.

'Your job,' Nya told us, 'is to get him to buy another bottle. The quicker you both drink, the more money you make. If you can make all your money from one guy, great, but some nights you're going to have to talk to a lot of guys.'

Now I might have been an Essex girl, but there was still a limit to how much booze I could handle. So Auntie Nya showed us several new ways to manage our liquor. The first trick was The Swap.

The Swap works like this: the punter fills your glass, you both take a sip, then you make your apologies because you need to go to the bathroom. You promise you'll only be a minute. Then you nip into the kitchen where a girl is ready to give you an identical glass filled with lemonade that looks exactly like champagne. It sounds ridiculous but I'm completely serious: there are girls who are employed just to swap glasses. You return to your customer and suggest you get the evening off to a good start with a little drinking game.

'Down in one?' you say casually.

And of course the quicker he drinks, the slower he is to realise all the other tricks we had. The guys were so fixated on our boobs that they failed to notice us tipping our drinks away into plant pots behind their head as we leant seductively over them! I tell you, we had to empty those pots three or four times a night.

My favourite trick was Auntie Nya's own personal invention. She had got hold of some colostomy bags – I am not kidding – and had customised them so that she could keep one in her handbag. When the customer wasn't looking, she would whip out the tube and blow her champagne into the bag! Nya was smart: she also sold those bags to her girls.

When Nya had told us about these tricks in the restaurant, Ali and I had split our sides laughing.

'You cannot be serious.'

'Honey, you just wait.'

It was even funnier to see it in action. Were men really that stupid? Were they really that distracted by a pair of breasts that they couldn't tell that the girl in front of them was just acting drunk? Sometimes I had to remind my face not to follow what my brain was thinking. There would be many times in the next few years when I wanted to laugh so hard because the guys in front of me were so dim. I wanted to drag them into the light and shine the torches in their eyes until they saw reality. But if I'd done that, I'd have been doing myself out of a whole lot of money, and so I just kept filling those plant pots. You wouldn't have thought that the promise of seeing some boobs could lead to all that money, but it does. I swear.

To a couple of teenagers, the idea of knowing about champagne was pretty exciting. I saw it as another thing to throw in the knapsack of life, and Nya encouraged us to become knowledgeable about vintages and brands. After all, we were going to be living off our champagne money. Pretty soon we learnt to gauge a punter by the bottle he bought. Just as Columbo looks at the shoes someone is wearing, or the paper a suspect is reading, to figure out if they're a murderer, I got a bit Miss Marple when it came to champagne. I discovered you could always test a guy out by seeing what brand he chose and how much he was prepared to spend. If all you could get him to buy was a Piccolo – barely enough for a glass – then you knew not to waste too much time with him because he wasn't suddenly going to turn into a big spender later in the evening. If, on the other hand, he wanted one of the better brands, then you knew to keep him talking. People think working in strip clubs is all about taking your clothes off, but it's what you do when you've got them on that earns you the money. I got very good at making conversation.

So far, our first night in Copenhagen had been thrilling. I had so much adrenalin flooding through me that I didn't think I'd be able to sleep, but then the three of us took our drinks and made our way to the back of the club where the stage was. Now obviously I knew I was in a strip club, and of course I knew why I was in a strip club, but until we got to the stage part of the club, the closest I'd ever come to seeing a striptease was on TV. Seeing actual real live strippers doing actual real live stripping – odd as it may sound – took me by surprise and it got me a bit flushed. Was it the booze? The excitement? Or the fear?

All night long we'd heard a DJ call girls up to take their turn, but now I really listened to him for the first time. His voice was strange – like a Butlin's bingo caller bigging up his part – but despite the sleazy drawl, the accent was unmistakably English. It turned out most of the people who worked in clubs weren't local. They were either running away from something, or someone, or they were desperately looking for something. Me and Alison were in the second category, but Poco the DJ – we quickly started calling him Pokol, as in Poke Hole – was in the first. He was like something from *Shaft* with his shiny brown suit, platform shoes and sleazy voice. We decided his picture was definitely pinned to a notice board in a police station somewhere in Britain. But as long as you put a drink in his hand, Pokol would prove to be completely harmless.

We watched the dancers come out on stage, and I was transfixed. I wanted to see what worked, who was good, who was rubbish, who got the biggest round of applause and why. I wanted to see how little you could do. For some, a sultry look and a pout seemed to be enough. Some strutted up and down, and some really worked the pole. One girl was so supple she could practically hang off the light fittings by her toes. Of course, what I was really looking to see was if a good dance equalled coming off stage and making good money. If those girls were my competition, I wanted to understand what I was up against.

Each girl danced to two songs. They kept their clothes on for the first one, but undressed during the second. By the middle of the second track, Nya told us, you had to be topless, that was the only rule. Apart from that, every performance was as different as the girls who got on that stage.

Nya impressed on us that it doesn't matter how you feel, it doesn't matter what's going on with you, when you get on the stage you put on a good show. Not for the punters, not for the managers, but for yourself. When you dance, it's your only opportunity to get the attention of every man in that place. You may not have been his flavour when he walked into the club, but by the time you come off that stage you owe it to yourself to be everyone's flavour. You want every guy in that place to want to buy you a drink.

The hot flush I'd got when we'd started watching the show slowly got hotter and flushier. I started to sweat. *Maybe I'd got a bug on the plane? Maybe I just needed my bed?* It wasn't either of those things. You know how sometimes you're in an air-conditioned building and you walk out into hot, hot sunshine and the heat just engulfs you? It was like that, only instead of hot sunshine I had just stepped into hot, burning fear. *I can't do that.*

In the abstract, the thought of stripping had been fine. Sitting in the warehouse in Next it had seemed like fun. On the plane it had felt like an adventure. Even when we'd come into the club it had been a laugh. But all of a sudden it was real. I wasn't some globetrotter who knew her champagnes, I was just a 17-year-old girl who'd barely been out of Essex. *What are you doing, Sam? What have you got yourself into?*

I looked at the dancers' moves, their clothes, their long, lean legs: there was no way I would be able to do it.

'Nya . . . I . . . I can't.'

'Don't worry, honey. Nobody's that good straight away, but you'll learn.'

You've misunderstood . . .

'You'll pick up ideas, you'll practise and you'll get good.'

Did she know I'd been about to pull out, that I was going to promise to repay her for the airfare? Had she worked out that by telling me I didn't have to be good straight away I'd end up agreeing with her and calming down? Cooling down. I don't know how she does it, but my auntie Nya always knows the right thing to say.

By the end of the night I'd figured out it wasn't about being the best dancer anyway. Nor was it about wearing the most provocative clothes. Girls in full-length dresses were getting just as much of a response as the girls with the tiniest bikinis. Every girl had her own style, her own persona, and the more of it she brought to the stage, the better the response. It wasn't about being good at ballet or being the most beautiful girl in the club. It was character that got you the money. So that was fine. Cos character is something I have plenty of.

Do you wanna dance?

The next night, Ali and I started work. We must have been excited because we got there so early that the girls on the day shift were still working. We went into the changing rooms and got into our little outfits. I'd gone with a halter-neck dress because I thought it would be easy to get off.

There were girls in the changing room from all over the world. There were quite a few Brits – most of whom were Nya's girls – as well as Jamaicans, Thais, Koreans, Poles, Russians, Swedes and Norwegians. It was like the United Nations or something. I instantly wanted to know what everyone's story was: how come they had ended up in Denmark? What choices had they made, what paths had they taken, to be working in La Dolce Vita?

Although they all smiled at us, none of them came over and introduced themselves. Changing rooms are weird like that: you're all naked, you're all exposed, and you can see each other's flaws, but at the same time you're all in competition with one another. It's a place where there can be no secrets, and yet it's where we can be very guarded. Everyone is always looking to see what everyone else is wearing, or how the next girl is doing her make-up: over the years, I have developed the ability to look over my shoulder while simultaneously – and expertly, I might add – applying mascara.

At 17, I didn't really have any body issues. I'd never been fat or thin; I'm pretty average height, pretty average build – C-cup, nothing exceptional – and at that age everything was still perky and in its proper place. Even if I had been worried about how I looked naked, I think I would have found being in the changing room quite reassuring, as up close you can see the pockmarks and cellulite and saggy bits that professional dancers know how to hide with make-up and accessories. The myth that dancers all have perfect bodies was busted right from the start.

If there was one aspect that made me feel new and inexperienced, it was the clothes they were all wearing. Their dresses – embellished with sequins and diamanté – and accessories seemed so much more sophisticated than the Camden market dress I had on. But then I remembered what Nya had told us: you'll look around, and you'll learn, and you'll get good.

Once we were as tarted and titivated as we could get, Ali and I went and gave Pokol our CDs. Nya had told us that our music had to be something that, no matter what, we couldn't help but move to, something that was guaranteed to put a smile on our faces. I knew Ginuwine's 'Pony' would get me up on that stage, and 'Do You Wanna Dance?' was the kind of music I could take my clothes off to.

'What are your names?' Pokol asked.

'I'm Toni,' I said.

'And I'm Blue.' It was Nya who'd suggested we use stage names. At the time I didn't really ask why, probably because I thought it sounded glamorous. I chose Toni after a girl I'd known at school. I think Blue came from the title of a film Alison liked. The name change would turn out to be one of the many little ways in which Nya was looking out for us: by protecting your real identity, you were protecting yourself from some of the worst things the night can throw at you.

'Which track do you want first?' Pokol asked.

I barely had time to answer him before those double doors swung open and a stag group of six came in. Nya had explained that as soon as there's a customer on the premises, even if it's just one guy, the show starts. By now, the day girls were already in their civvies, which meant it was just me, Ali and two other girls who were ready to go on stage. And when I say ready, I mean scared, unsure, panicked. That kind of ready.

'OK,' Pokol's drawl oozed out of the speakers. 'The show is gonna start.'

The two more experienced girls went first, but when they left the stage there was only me and Alison left. Ali's not much paler than me, but she was looking pretty ghostly. One look at her petrified little face made it quite clear that I was next.

Right then, Sam. This is it.

I started to sweat like I was in a sauna. *You can do it. It's gonna be your favourite song. You are wearing the kind of shoes you've wanted for years. You've got a great outfit. You'll be . . .*

'And now, coming onto the stage . . . it's Toni.'

I stood in the doorway to the stage. You couldn't see the audience from there, but you could hear them, and the sound of the stag party started to amplify in my ears. They were probably only whispering, but inside my head it sounded like they were shouting. The only other noise was my heartbeat. Ba-dum. Ba-Dum. Ba-DUM. Then the first few beats of 'Pony' pulsed out of the speakers. Yet again, Nya was right: some songs always get you moving, and I took my first steps out onto the stage.

My focus was the pole. *Get to the pole, Sam, then you can just hold on.* There's something about your heart pounding so hard that makes it difficult to balance, but I managed to stagger to the pole. For the next minute it was all about the pole and nothing but the pole. After a little while, my heart stopped thumping quite so hard and I started to hear the lyrics. I tried out a few moves I'd seen the girls use the night before. I might have even sung along a bit, but I still couldn't let go of that pole.

At the back of the stage were two large mirrors and I could see that some of the poses I was trying out looked pretty foxy. *Oh, that's a nice move. How about I try this? What if I just hold my arm like this? Or like this?* I found I had about four silhouettes that got a reaction and so I just kept repeating them. When one hand left the pole, the other hand grabbed on. In the mirrors, I could also see the stag party. Six pairs of eyes were staring at me. *Well, I must be doing something right.*

Pokol brought 'Do You Wanna Dance?' up in the mix. My heart started to beat harder again. This was it. It was tits-out time. I'd chosen my dress because it was pretty simple to take off. It was a halter-neck. All I had to do was pull it over my head and then peel it down. As I started moving to the music, I realised I was going to have to let go of the pole cos there was no way I could undo it with one hand!

Without the pole for support, I had a tiny moment of panic. Something wobbled inside and I lost concentration. In that split second, I got stuck. Like a kid taking its school jumper off over its head, I'd got my arm caught and I couldn't get it free!

Right, Sam, just get your top off. Come on, girl. God knows how, but I managed to keep dancing, pretending that one arm was meant to be stuck to the back of my neck. One breast was hanging out, but I just kept on moving regardless. The relief I felt at finally freeing myself might have been why I smiled so much when I eventually untied the dress and peeled it down.

The reaction of those six guys to seeing breasts was absolutely stunning. Amazing. It was like they had cartoon eyes that popped out of their heads, and their body language was approving, leaning back in their seats and nodding slowly. When a man puts his drink down, it's a sure sign you've got his attention. To be honest, they were so thrilled I half expected scorecards. I turned around and saw myself in the mirror. I gave myself a little wink. I had done it.

I ran into the changing rooms absolutely dripping with sweat. I was so pumped with adrenalin that I didn't notice how scared Alison was. I prattled on about how brilliant it was, not realising that she hadn't said a word. As I pulled my dress back up, I was already looking forward to doing it again.

'You're gonna be great, Ali,' I panted. 'You're gonna love it. I'm going to go out front and watch you.'

I had practically left the changing room when I heard her say something: 'I can't do it.'

What? I turned back. 'Of course you can. I had a great time. The guys out there are great. You have got nothing to worry about.'

Her face told me she didn't believe me.

'I don't want to do it. I *can't* do it, Sam.' She looked genuinely terrified. 'This is your bag, it's not my bag, and I don't even know why I'm here.' Words just came spilling out of her mouth. 'I don't know why I agreed to come along. This is not for me. I can't do this. What are my mum and dad going to think?'

The girl completely unravelled, but as she poured it all out I could hear that the filler track Pokol had put on was fading. She didn't have long.

'You can't bottle it now. Your name is Blue. You're gorgeous. You can do it and you are gonna love it.'

She wasn't convinced.

'Just get to the pole, Ali. If you get to the pole, you'll be OK.'

She nodded.

'I'll be watching you. It's OK. You're going to be great. Promise.'

I heard Pokol call Blue to the stage – though of course in his voice it sounded more like Bloooo – and went out front. The best man waved me over and I sat down with the guys. I can still see their faces very clearly. They were all in their mid twenties, pretty average-looking local lads who had come in early because they were doing the 'lap of honour': touring all the clubs in the city in one night. The best man's name was Rene.

'Where are you from?' he asked. Like everyone else in Denmark, his English was incredible.

'I'll tell you later,' I promised, 'but this is my friend, let's watch her.'

Only there was nothing to watch.

Ali's first song was 'One More Chance', the Biggie Smalls track, and even though it was blaring out, Alison wasn't on stage. I could see her hovering at the stage door.

Come on, Ali. I was willing her to move. *Just get to the bloody pole.* Eventually she tottered forward, and boy did she grab that pole. To be more accurate, she completely wrapped herself around it. One leg twisted in front of it, and both arms snaked up above her head. Every bit of her that she could get in contact with the pole was touching metal. And then she froze. Solid. *Come on, Ali. Just MOVE.*

But she didn't. She was too terrified to even wave an arm about. I knew that I had to do something: number one, she was my friend; and number two, I had put her in this situation. I was also going to get her out of it.

'Rene, how would you and your friends like a little double trouble?'

'Really?' His tongue poked out a little bit at the prospect.

I went backstage then ran out and joined Alison. And when I say joined, I pretty much mean it. I wrapped myself around her as tightly as she was wrapped around the bloody pole. Then I ran my hands down her body. When I worked my way back up, I grabbed her hips.

'Move with me.'

She swayed with me but still wouldn't let go of the pole.

I ran my hands over her body as we moved. Then I got hold of her hands and prised them off the pole. I grabbed her wrists and made her take a step back with me. I walked her over to the back wall, turned her around and – bam, bam – slapped her hands against the mirror. All she had to do was stand there as I felt her up and down like an X-rated cop frisking a suspect. The lads seemed to like the masterful act. I kept my hands on Alison's hips and got her to move her arse. And then, when it felt like she could finally hear the music, I stepped away. She kept moving her arse and I – sneakily – slipped off stage and left her to it.

Alison managed to get through her second song, strip and all, but when she came off stage she was distraught. She ran into my arms and started crying.

'I want to go home. I just want to go home, Sam. Will you take me home?'

The difference between our experiences was absolute. I felt like I'd found home, but she thought she'd just been in hell. Her face was terrified, her features were filled with doubt, and I felt awful for putting her through it. Terrible. What kind of mate does that to her best friend?

'Let's just get through tonight. Yeah?' I couldn't think what else to say. I couldn't make her any promises without talking to Nya.

'Just a few more hours, then we can sleep on it. Can you handle that?'

I detected a tiny, teeny nod.

'I've spoken to the lads out there, and they seem all right. I think I can get them to buy a bottle of champagne. Let's at least see if we can't earn some commission, yeah?'

Alison fixed her face and we went out hand in hand to sit with Rene and his friends. As I suspected, they were nice, normal lads who were fascinated to talk to a couple of black girls from Britain. In a country where everyone is pale and blonde, Ali and I were seen as something exotic. As we talked, they kept buying champagne. Alison needed the booze, so I didn't remind her about The Swap, but when she wasn't looking I tipped her glass into the pot plants. She was my mate and I was going to look out for her as much as I could.

The guys were obviously enjoying themselves. They just wanted a laugh and so Ali and I kept them talking. They forgot about their lap of honour and spent all night with us. They knew the deal. They understood we weren't there for free and they kept the champagne orders coming. Alison and I got through our other dances (we had to do four each shift), I worked out how to untie my halter neck faultlessly, and by the time the club closed we had both made about £300 in champagne commission. Plus the £50. Plus the free accommodation. That was more than we earned in a week in Next.

When Ali realised how much money we could make, her aspiration to go home quickly evaporated. I certainly never looked back. I never had any more doubts after that first night and felt absolutely sure that I was on the right path. I couldn't be quite sure where it was heading, but those first few steps had been amazing for me. That night, I barely slept a wink.

To Helsingor and back

Ali and I walked into the club on our second night in a fit of giggles. The nerves of that first night had been replaced with pure excitement – and acute curiosity. One of the girls in our apartment block had told us that two of the most beautiful dancers in the club were actually men. Kiki and Kimmie were absolutely stunning Thai girls, and Kimmie in particular was so petite and so feminine that we could not believe she could have once been a man. She looked like a porcelain doll. We just couldn't stop giggling about it – we had never heard of people having sex changes before – and when the first person we bumped into that night was Kiki we just couldn't hold it in. The giggles rose up like bubbles in champagne and fizzed straight out of our mouths. We might have felt like women of the world, but we couldn't stifle our teenage sniggers.

It was still not a week since we'd walked out of retail, and we had completely transformed our lives. We'd left home, left the country, changed our names, quadrupled our earning capacity and were wearing considerably shorter dresses while walking six inches taller in our fabulous shoes. We felt worldly. We felt invincible. I didn't realise it then, but we were in danger: I've since seen that mix of teenage naivety and cockiness do a lot of damage to a lot of girls.

We were wandering round with eyes bigger than Mr Magoo's glasses. One night we'd be talking to a gangster, the next night it'd be an American businessman, then maybe a transvestite, and throughout the club there was an endless parade of vice and glamour: girls would whisper that he was a pimp, she was a madam, he was a professional gambler or she was an escort. Our reaction to everything was 'Ooh, tell me more.' We thought these people had

27

fascinating lives and I just wanted to load up on as much gossip as I could get. In contrast to Essex and our jobs in Next, La Dolce Vita felt deeply, wonderfully, fabulously exotic.

I didn't know it then, but it takes a long time for your eyes to adapt to the dark. You think you're seeing things the way they are, you think you're getting the characters pegged and getting to know the lay of the land, but some things that go on in nightlife can't be seen by daytrippers. Even after a couple of weeks you'll still only be seeing half of what's there. The good thing about that is that if you can't see something, if you don't even know it's there, then you can't be afraid of it. Like I say, we were in danger, but we didn't have a clue.

The fact that our first night had gone so well, after Ali's panic attack, meant I started thinking that I was doing the job I was born to do. After precisely eight hours on the job, I thought I had got things pretty much sorted and thought I was already getting good at reading customers. I figured I could tell from the way they walked into the club, from the shoes they were wearing or the size of their watches, whether or not they were going to be a big spender. About halfway through my second shift, a good-looking guy in his early 30s with dark Mediterranean skin and shiny black hair came in wearing an expensive-looking camel coat and a jewellery shop's worth of bling. *Wey hey*, I said to myself, *Toni's about to make her money for the night*.

He said his name was Samir and he didn't take too much persuading to buy a bottle of champagne – not the most expensive, but not the cheapest either – and we sat down to talk. He told me he was from Turkey and imported sports cars. I got the impression he made a lot of money. When he found out that I had only just arrived in Denmark, he offered to show me around and gave me his card. I couldn't quite believe I was earning money just talking to this guy.

A couple of hours later, Ali and I were talking in the changing room and I was telling her all about Samir and how he was going to show us the sights. One of the Danish girls – a statuesque, athletic blonde called Karina – overheard us.

'Who did you say will show you around?' she asked.

I told her about Samir.

'Describe him to me.'

I got as far as the camel coat when she stopped me.

'That guy's name is not Samir. It's Mehmet.'

'No it isn't, he gave me his card.'

I showed it to Karina.

'Come with me,' she said.

Karina took us to the bar and asked the barman for 'the bad box'. She opened it up and inside were the business cards of all the customers who had caused friction. There were at least 11 copies of the card 'Samir' had given me.

'That guy is trouble,' Karina said, 'stay away from him. He finds out when the new girls have started and he targets them.'

I really rated Karina for that. She didn't have to say anything, but she had taken pity on the two new English girls and had taught me a big lesson: I couldn't read the customers nearly as well as I thought I could. I had also learnt that Karina was someone I could trust.

I also met an English girl that night called Paula, who was that little bit louder than everyone else and a proper good-time girl. Her moves on the pole were sensational and I thought she was someone I could learn from. I didn't know it then, but Paula was just about the biggest cokehead in the place.

It was a couple of nights after that when Good Time Paula came up to me at the end of our shift and said she had a regular who wanted to take us out for drinks. So when Ali went home to bed, I did one of the stupidest things in my life: I got into a car with Paula and her regular. George said he had a little house by the sea that we could go to for a smoke and a drink.

Once we'd got round the corner, George pulled over to let a mate get in. As soon as I saw the hand reach for the door handle I knew who it was: the bling on his fingers gave him away.

'Hello again.'

Samir slid into the passenger seat. I caught his eye in the rear-view mirror and he smiled. 'I said I'd show you around.'

At that point, I wasn't too fearful. Samir really did have a nice smile and it was possible that Karina might have been overstating the issue. Anyway, Paula seemed relaxed about it, so I decided to relax about it too.

After ten minutes or so, George turned the car onto the motorway. I had assumed his little house by the sea was somewhere near the docks in Copenhagen, but I realised now I was wrong. Really wrong. George put his foot to the floor and sped us away from the city. Samir lifted up the armrest between the front seats and pulled out a massive bag of white powder. It was a brick about the size of a tissue box, the kind of thing you see in *Scarface*.

'Let's get this party started!' Paula squealed as Samir passed her a book from the glove compartment and a platinum credit card from his wallet. I watched in a state of shock as she cut up the cocaine into neat lines and passed the book around the car. When I passed on my line, she was happy to take it.

I was so naive about drugs back then that I just thought people went to the toilet and came back happy! I'd never, ever taken them and had only seen them on screen. I didn't know what they did or how you took them, but I was finding out that cocaine could get my heart pounding just by watching others take it.

The cocaine made George go faster. I looked out the window to see if I could work out where we were going from the street signs, but unless a sign said 'Copenhagen' it wouldn't have meant anything to me anyway. On the horizon, it was getting light. I realised I didn't know where I was or where I was going or who I was with. If anything happened to me, no one would know where to look.

'Where are we going?' I asked, trying to sound laid-back.

'George has a summer lodge, right on the water,' Samir said.

'How far is it?'

'About a hundred miles.'

One hundred miles? Really? Oh shit.

Now I started to panic. I was hurtling along a Danish motorway with a bunch of cokeheads who were so high they probably thought we were flying. I was shitting myself. That good old rectal reflex was kicking in. *Samantha*, I said to myself, *one way or another you need to sort this. Wherever we get to, whenever we get there, you need to make sure that we turn this car around and we go home.*

One of the things movies had taught me about cocaine is that when people are high, you can pretty much persuade them to do anything. Deliver illicit packages, give you vital information, kill people: these are the kind of films I watched. I figured that as the only sober person in the car, I could make them do what I wanted.

It was almost light by the time we arrived in the town of Helsingor. It seemed fairly run down, not the kind of town where you had your summer house. George followed the coast road out of town and pretty soon we came to his lodge. It looked more like a fishing hut. Like a big version of a garden shed. This was not the playground of some rich wheeler dealer. This was just plain grotty.

If I hadn't needed the loo, I would have refused to get out of the car, but the call of nature meant I went inside. There was hardly any furniture, just a few children's toys lying around and a table and chairs. This wasn't anybody's holiday home. Paula and George headed straight for the bedroom with the bag of cocaine.

At that moment I just thought, *No, this isn't fucking happening.* I grabbed Paula by the arm and pulled her close to me. I started dancing with her and mucking around. The guys loved it, of course, and Paula was so wired she just went along with it. George put some music on and got ready for a party.

'We just need to powder our noses,' I said.

I took Paula's hand and led her to the dingy bathroom. It didn't look like it had ever been cleaned. I shut the door and looked Paula in the eye. She was delirious. I got hold of her other hand and made her look at me.

'Paula, you need to sort yourself out. I don't get a good feeling about this. I don't know why we're here. You do understand that we are in the middle of nowhere, don't you? We need to get home.'

I hadn't realised just how suggestible people are on cocaine, but her trippy smile turned instantly into dread.

'Listen. You need to go out there – I don't care what story you tell – but you need to tell George that you need to go. He wants to impress you. He wants you to like him. That means you are in control. You just have to tell him we need to get back.'

She nodded. And five minutes later, without any fuss, we all got back in the car and drove the 100 miles back to the city. It was as if they had all forgotten why we'd gone there in the first place. When I finally got to my bed at around 10 a.m., I knew I had been very, very stupid . . . and very, very lucky.

That road trip had been a big eye-opener for me and over the next few weeks I realised that Paula was by no means the only dancer using drugs. I also noticed that it was always the Turks who were supplying them. They would start by asking a girl if she wanted a couple of lines – it was always free at first – and then before she knew it she would need it and she would have to start paying for it. All of a sudden, girls found themselves with a habit. The more girls I got to know, the better I got at spotting a user.

Some girls would pay for it as they took it, but others ran up a tab, spending £500 or even a grand a week. It was the ones who bought it on tick that the Turks really got hold of. There was a really pretty Swedish girl who had been in Denmark a couple of years by the time we met her. At first we thought Sylvie was dating one of the Turks, but we later found out that she was sleeping with five of them. They were passing her around to let her pay off her drug debts. She was like a walking, talking neon sign that said, 'Don't do drugs. Don't end up like me.'

But that didn't stop me and Ali being curious – surely a little bit of sniff was all part of the Denmark experience, wasn't it? We knew that we didn't want to end up like Paula or Sylvie, but we were just so damned curious to know what all the fuss was about. Trouble was, since the road trip, no one had offered us anything. I realise now that word had gone round that we were Nya's girls and everyone had been told to leave us alone. However, one of the Turks was finally persuaded to sell us a bag of cocaine.

Now you've got to remember that at this point I had never

taken drugs before. I had no idea how much was a regular amount to buy and I had no idea how much it cost. That Turk saw us coming: we bought a ridiculously large bag – big enough for a rock star's rider at Wembley – that stayed in our apartment for a really long time because we only took tiny amounts at a time. We were still scared that if we took too much we'd go crazy. I liked the way it made me feel, and sometimes at the end of a shift, if I wanted to go on somewhere, getting a little snowed seemed to help.

One morning, I got back to the apartment at four and thought I might pop down to a diner that started serving breakfast at 5 a.m. A quick line, I said to myself, followed by pancakes while watching commuters start their daily grind. Only problem was I couldn't find the bag. Had we been robbed? Had Alison sold it? She was in bed, but I woke her up.

'Don't be mad at me,' she said, pulling the covers up to her chin as she sat up. 'But I took it.'

'All of it?'

She nodded. 'Oh, Sam, I have just *got* to tell you something. I think I will burst if I don't.'

'OK.'

'Don't shout at me, but I came back early last night and the bag was . . . well, it was like it was talking to me.'

'OK.'

'So I had a line. Then I had another.'

'OK.'

'Anyway, I could hear Orla walking around in her flat downstairs, so I asked her if she wanted to join me.'

'What happened?'

'We took it all, and, well, oh Sam . . .'

'What happened? Alison!'

'Oh Sam, we got so fucking horny.'

'Alison!'

'I know. I tell you, I had the bizarrest, weirdest, bestest sex I ever had in my whole life.'

'With Orla?'

'Of course with Orla! I was proper down there, and then we spun around and she was down on me . . . Sam, what have I done? What am I going to say when I see her again?'

As Ali told her story it became clear that, if she had had her way, it wouldn't have just been Orla she'd have slept with. They were so turned on that as soon as the newsagent's had opened at 5 a.m. they had gone downstairs and tried to get the guy who worked there to join them! The poor guy was too terrified to say yes. Their eyes must have been like overcoat buttons and their jaws would have been swinging like hammocks. He probably thought he'd get arrested.

'You know what, Ali,' I said through tears of laughter, 'that is such a funny story that I cannot be upset that you sniffed our entire stash, even if it would have lasted us till the end of the month. That is the best story. Ever.'

Ali was full of surprises. I haven't told you yet that she was a Muslim convert. She was really quite a proper sort of a person, and I don't suppose any of her other friends would have believed that she would have taken her clothes off in public, let alone taken so much cocaine that she got so horny she tried to get the guy from the sweet shop to take part in a threesome! That girl was awesome.

So much about life is who you travel with, and Alison was the best travelling companion I could have possibly had. We sat there for about an hour, laughing our heads off and crying our eyes out as I made her relive every sordid detail. When I finally got to bed, I realised I wasn't just curious about what she'd been up to: I was a little bit turned on.

La Vida Loca

As the months went on, I started to realise just how much weird stuff was going on, and Ali and I came up with a new name for the club – La Vida Loca. The thing most people don't realise is that a strip club is a place you can go where you will not be judged. Which means that those people on the margins of life, the people who don't fit in anywhere else, find themselves going through those double doors and finding themselves at home.

You very quickly get used to the freaks and their fetishes, but every now and then someone would come in who would make you redefine your notion of odd. Of all the weirdness I witnessed, out of all that strangeness, one man and one night stands out in my memory: the night Candle Man came in.

There's a bit of me that thinks me calling him 'Candle Man' is giving his fetish away, but another bit of me is so sure that his fetish was so peculiar, and so specific to him, that you'd never be able to guess what he wanted me to do to him. In fact, I am willing to bet that in the entire history of the human race, out of the billions of people who have walked the face of the earth, no one else has ever, EVER, had the same fetish as this guy.

Candle Man was from Thailand and a regular in the club. He'd probably come in once a month and always spent good money. When you are a good spender, everyone remembers your name and you are treated like a prince on your next visit. I'd never spoken to him before, but as his regular girl wasn't on shift I asked him if he would like a drink. He ordered Dom Perignon. Very nice.

Candle Man had brought a client in with him, a very posh English guy, definitely a public school boy, with smarmed-back hair and a pinstriped suit that was one size too big, like his mum had bought it for him. Of the two of them, you would have picked Tarquin to be the deviant one.

A pretty common fetish in Denmark was a penchant for black skin. It's one of the reasons Auntie Nya started her business. In a country where everyone is pale and blonde, black and Oriental girls do very well in the clubs – and Nya got a very nice commission every time she recruited a new dancer. So when Tarquin, or Peregrine, or whatever his ridiculous name was, asked if Ali could join us to make a foursome in one of the booths, this was a pretty standard request. This was going to be a good night: someone was going to pay for me to hang out with my best mate.

When a regular brings a client in, the name of the game is treating that client like he is the most charming, fascinating and virile man in the club. If you make the client feel great, the regular will always come back with other clients. Like the Danish boys who came in on stag nights, Candle Man and The Toff were fascinated by how two black girls from London had come to work in a Danish club, and the conversation flowed as easily as the champagne.

I loved these sorts of nights because where else, and how else, would I meet someone like Tarquin? Where in the Venn diagram of his life and my life would there be any crossover? Only ever in a club. One of the reasons I stayed in dancing so long was because I got to meet the most amazing array of people from the most extraordinary walks of life.

We'd been talking for about three hours when Tarquin unexpectedly announced that he had seen another girl who had really caught his eye and he was going to talk to her. As he left the table, he slipped a few krone on the table for me and Ali as a tip, which, if you ask any dancer, is a sign that he was a genuinely nice guy.

Throughout the evening, Candle Man had mentioned a couple of times that it was his birthday, and every time he did we toasted the happy day, waggled our boobs in his face and acted all girly. After Tarquin had left us, he ordered another bottle of champagne.

Believe me, a colostomy bag only holds so much, and there is a limit to how much you can get away with tipping into the plant pots: Ali and I were nicely lubricated, and I suspect that was exactly the way Candle Man wanted it.

'You know it's my birthday?' he said softly.

'Yes! Happy Birthday!!' Waggle, waggle.

'Do you think they would let you sing me happy birthday?'

Now, there was something in the way he said this that suggested he wasn't just asking for us to sing to him. So we said we didn't think there would be a problem with that.

'We can have a party?'

'A party? Sure, let's have a party.'

'And you think they would let me light a candle?'

At this point Candle Man reached into his top pocket and brought out a small felt pouch. He opened the pouch and pulled out a candle wrapped in a bit of cloth. Not the kind of candle you get on a birthday cake, but the kind you keep in your bottom drawer in case there's a power cut.

'I don't know,' I said, 'we might have to check about that.'

I left Ali with him and went off to find one of the managers. I didn't really think they would have a problem with us lighting a candle – health and safety and fire regulations weren't exactly high on their agenda – but there was something in the way he was making his requests that told me he was up to something.

I couldn't find a manager, so I asked Pokol the DJ.

'You got that Thai fella in?'

'Yeah,' I said, 'how do you know?'

'He's asked for that crazy stuff before. You are about to make some money, my friend.'

Pokol told me that the previous month, one girl had made over a grand from Candle Man when she had celebrated his 'birthday'. Then he told me what she had had to do for the money. I assumed what he was telling me was just one big joke. But then I thought about the candle in its little bit of cloth and knew Pokol was telling me the truth.

'Wow. Really?'

'Oh yeah.'

'Really? You're sure?'

Pokol nodded. 'One more thing, petal. Make sure you get the money up front.'

I went back to the table where Ali was still gallantly making conversation and told them both that the club were very happy for us to throw him a birthday party . . . in one of the VIP rooms.

Candle Man paid us both 1,500 krone, which was probably the equivalent of about £700 – it was easily the most money I had got from a customer – and we took him into the VIP room where he promptly stripped off. This guy was in his early 40s, but he worked out (martial arts, judging by the cut of him) and he was clearly proud of his body. You know something funny? In situations like these, guys always fold their clothes up! He made a nice neat little pile and then handed me his candle in its little pouch and a small pot of lube he had been carrying round.

I explained that I had spoken to the management, who had informed me that he'd been in before and had given me instructions as to what to do. 'So, if you would like to get on your hands and knees, we'll begin.'

Ali's face was a picture. 'What on earth?' she mouthed at me as Candle Man knelt down and presented us with his arsehole.

I gave Ali the candle and got some lube on my fingers and started applying it to Candle Man's bum. I could not look at Ali because I knew we would start laughing and never, ever stop. There are times in life when you do something and you think, *Am I ever going to be able to tell someone about this?* Well, I'm telling you now: I stuck my fingers into a strange man's arse crack and lubed him up. I can't quite believe I really did that. But I did. So there.

I then passed the lube to Ali, who put some on the candle. Now, I had never stuck anything up anyone's bum before. I didn't know the best way to go about doing it. Just pushing didn't work, and I didn't want to force it in case I hurt him. Ali had a go – seriously, I don't know how we kept a straight face – and we discovered that a gentle twisting action was required. The candle was duly inserted, and we took his special lighter out of his special pouch and lit his candle.

'Happy birthday to you!

'Happy birthday to you!'

As we started singing, he started crawling around on all fours leaving a little illuminated trail. Pokol had told us he liked a real fuss to be made, so Ali and I were stamping and clapping, and after three verses of 'Happy Birthday' we threw in a couple of 'For He's A Jolly Good Fellows'. Ali started to crack up. I slapped her, and she managed to choke down the laughter.

Pokol had told us that when he stopped crawling, Candle Man wanted us to kneel down either side of him and both blow out the candle together. Then we were to take it out, give it a little wipe with the cloth and put it back in its pouch so he could use the same candle the next time he had a need for a birthday celebration.

I can still see Ali's face as we looked across this guy's bum with a burning candle sticking out of it. Tears were streaming down her face.

'One! Two! Three!' We blew the candle out, and the funniest thing was that as soon as we took it out Candle Man was straight back to normal like nothing had ever happened. We left him in the VIP room to get changed and dashed into the loos to wash our hands, and to laugh our heads off. A bit like when you're desperate for a wee and you've been holding it in, we had been holding our laughter in so long that it hurt. We shut that bathroom door and we just howled.

'I cannot believe we just did that, Sam!'

'Me neither.'

But do you know what the strangest part of it was? We went back to our booth and waited for Candle Man to join us, and we carried on drinking as if nothing had happened. Then Tarquin came and sat back down, blissfully unaware of what had just happened, and we polished off another bottle of champagne.

I didn't know anything about fetishes back then, but I've since learnt that most of them are linked to an event that happened in childhood. I often find myself wondering what the hell the trigger was for that one. How the hell did this guy discover that the thing that did it for him was crawling around with a lit candle up his arse while he paid someone a lot of money to sing him happy birthday? Seriously, how does something like that start?

Candle Man was my first encounter with something that would normally be seen as deviant, or maybe even a bit nasty. But mine and Ali's experience hadn't been frightening, and he wasn't a nasty man, he didn't come in the shape of an ogre – far from it – and I started to realise that all sorts of people get down in all sorts of ways. I also learnt that so long as they don't hurt anyone, or force anyone, then that's OK. It's one of the things I love about strip clubs: so long as you pay, so long as you ask nicely, you can have whatever you want.

Except one thing. The first time I was asked for sex I knew – for sure – it was a line I would never cross. One of the things that had made working in the club so easy for me was the fact that the punters weren't allowed to touch us. If the rules had meant they could lay a finger on my flesh, I would have stepped right outside and hailed a cab for the airport.

One night, after I'd been in Denmark for about three months, I had been having champagne with an English guy who really reminded me of Rowan Atkinson. He probably thought I was a lot more tiddly than I was (I had got very good at the plant pot routine; my cleavage was proving to be very distracting to a lot of men) when he said that his hotel was round the corner.

'How much are you for outside of here?'

'I'm sorry?'

'How much for you to join me at my hotel?'

My response was 'Ha ha, let's get another bottle', but he was serious.

'I want to pay for your services for an hour. How much do you charge?'

'You know I can't leave here with a customer.'

'I'm sorry. What did you say?'

'I said you know I can't leave with you. You're only allowed to leave during your shift to get some food.'

'Of course you can leave.'

'Really?'

'Really. Why else did the guy on the door who I gave my coat to tell me to come back to him if I needed condoms?'

I must have looked blank.

'You really didn't know, did you?' He leaned back and smiled.

'No.'

He picked up his keys and very politely said that that was why he had come in and he was going to speak to a girl who would sleep with him. He left me alone in a booth with a glass of champagne and I just there, absolutely numb. I was truly stunned, but within a few minutes I knew he was telling the truth. I looked around the club and saw little negotiations going on that I had previously been blind to. I watched as a customer left, collected a discreet package from the cloakroom and waited five minutes until the girl he had been talking to followed him out.

My jaw dropped open. Had I really been that blind? And now that I saw it, I saw it everywhere. The girls who went out 'for food' and came back two hours later. I guessed that they had to pay for their drug habits somehow. I sat there slowly sipping my champagne and taking it all in.

Then, out of nowhere, I heard a voice in my head that made me laugh. It was a Jamaican aunt I hadn't seen in years and I could hear her telling me and a cousin that 'your middle wicket is private and you don't let everyone bat in there'! My aunt was so right, and the thought of any of the men in the club that night pounding away on top of me was just so disgusting that I knew I would never do it. I just couldn't.

For a brief moment, I was angry at Nya. *How could she have put me in this situation? She must know what goes on.* But by the time I had finished my glass of champagne I had worked out why she hadn't said anything: she knew that I wouldn't have come. So I had a word with myself: nothing had changed, no one was going to force me, and I had learnt that I could easily say no. I was enjoying myself, I was earning good money and I felt safe. That was good enough for me.

Lots of girls – most girls, I suppose – made a different decision, and they all told us that when they started in Denmark they had said they would never have sex for money either, but one by one they had all succumbed. Ali and I knew we wouldn't be like them.

'Give it time,' they all said. 'Maybe after six months, maybe two years, but everyone does.'

La Dolce Vita wasn't a brothel, it wasn't a place where guys came with guarantees of sex, but I discovered that most of the girls who worked there would occasionally sleep with customers for money. I called it opportunist prostitution. They didn't go into work each night and think 'Tonight I'm going to sell my bits.' But depending on their circumstances, and depending on the customer, and the amount of money he was offering, there were nights when they did sell themselves.

Of course, it was the girls with drug habits who were the most vulnerable, and very often it was the friends of the dealers that they owed money to who knew when to make a proposal. After a while, there really was no difference between some of the girls in the clubs and the girls on the streets. As my eyes adapted to the dark, I started to see that some of them needed the drugs so that they could go to work and do the things they did. A very vicious circle.

But not me. Not then. Not never. Not no how.

Den of iniquity

The girls who worked at La Dolce Vita were all trying to escape something. Some were in trouble with the law, some with debts. Some had fallen out with their families and had not spoken to them for so long that it was impossible to go back. They were all stuck. The question we were asked most often was 'How long are you out here for?' and when we said six months, maybe twelve, an eyebrow was always raised: 'You'll still be here in two years. Everyone is.'

When someone didn't fit that pattern, they stood out. Like Delia and Marilyn, two girls from Jamaica. I always paid close attention to other black girls because they were my competition. If a guy wanted a blonde, there was nothing I could do about it, but if he came in looking for dark skin, then I wanted to know why he didn't choose me. It wasn't easy getting to know the pair of them because they were always working. When we came into the club in the evening, they were always already there, but instead of leaving with the day-shift girls Delia and Marilyn also worked the night shift. Two shifts a day, seven days a week. I never knew them to have a day off.

And they worked their arses off. They would talk to guys for hours, get through bottle after bottle of champagne, and then they would – more often than not – take their client for a VIP. In a strip club, a VIP is how you really make your money. All around the club – and around every club – are little side rooms where you can take clients for private entertaining. The curtains are drawn and the two of you are left alone. As the client is taking you off the floor of the club – and reducing your earning potential – he has to pay to have you to himself.

The idea of the VIP is for the customer to feel like he's on a date. For an hour or so he can kid himself that it's just the two of you and that this beautiful girl in front of him is really interested in everything he's got to say. What goes on in a VIP is up for negotiation: you might just talk, you might get some food brought in or you might dance for him. Nya had told us that the rules of the club still applied – he still couldn't touch you and you couldn't touch him.

In those first couple of months, I had assumed that Delia and Marilyn simply had the gift of the gab. But after my encounter with the Rowan Atkinson lookalike, I realised that they were – almost certainly – doing something else with their mouths. And not just in the club. They would go pretty much anywhere with a customer to do pretty much anything. Eventually they had a night when they were not so busy and I finally got round to hearing their story. They weren't running away at all; in fact they were desperate to get back to Jamaica.

'Honey,' Delia told me as we finished her customer's leftover champagne, 'I am making £3,000 a week. Marilyn too. Do you know how far that will go in Jamaica? Another six months and we are taking it all home with us.'

'What are you going to do with it?'

'It is going to set us up for life. We are going to buy ourselves a little guesthouse. One day, you should come and stay with us.'

Delia and Marilyn had come to Denmark to make as much money as possible in as short a time as possible. They didn't care what they had to do for the money so long as, once they got home, they never had to do those things again.

On the one hand, Delia and Marilyn made good role models. They showed me that the money I was earning could be put to good use, but on the other hand they were doing things behind those curtains that I knew I never would. Not only could I not save up like they could, but I couldn't earn as much as them in the first place anyway.

There was a very good reason why I couldn't save – I was spending every penny I made. Ali and I were probably making a grand a week, maybe £1,500, and with no rent to pay, we felt very flush. On a trip back home, I took my two little sisters on a shopping spree to C&A and told them they could have anything they wanted. Can you imagine how fabulous that felt? I was only 18. I felt so grown up, but after a week in London, I was itching and scratching to get back to Denmark so I could earn more of the lovely stuff. I didn't realise it, but my addiction to fast money had begun.

I call it fast money because as soon as you've earned it you spend it. It's like you're just keeping hold of it for someone else. You make £500 a night, you spend £500 the next day, because you know you'll make another wedge the following night. When you eat out for every meal, when you take cabs, and when you get your hair done every week, your nails done twice a week and you have a weakness for shoes and clothes and handbags and make-up, fast money is easily spent.

I became fascinated by how customers had made their money. Did they make their money just as easily as we did? If they were happy to come into a club and spend £200, £300, maybe £500 on champagne and talking to girls, presumably they didn't have to work that hard to get it? Easy come, easy go. As I made my enquiries, I found out that some of the biggest spenders in La Dolce Vita were in fact gang members, and so I started to get to know some of the night's biggest characters.

No matter where you go in the world, the only place where gang members can meet up in big groups and sit at a table and talk business is in a strip club. In England, they're called 'coffee meetings'. In my early days in Denmark, I would often sit at the bar and just observe the gang members as they came in. One group would go to one dark corner, and another group would go to the opposite dark corner, and every so often a negotiator from one gang would meet the negotiator from the other gang at a table in the middle to talk about shipments or payments or favours.

I found it fascinating. For them it was a very safe place to do business because everyone in the club had something they didn't want other people to know about. No one was going to grass, and, so long as they spent money on girls and champagne, no one asked any questions.

There's a pretty natural fit between gangsters and dancers. We keep the same hours, we don't like telling people what we do for a living, and we are used to money passing through our fingers at speed. Gangsters like to be seen with pretty girls, the girls like their money: it's not surprising that a lot of dancers end up dating the bad boys.

The two main gangs who used Dolce were a biker gang and a Thai protection racket. The negotiator for the Thais was a short, well-groomed English guy who used the name Chris. A disciple of Full Moon parties, Chris had spent a lot of time in Thailand, learnt the language and was completely trusted by his bosses. He was also completely trusted by the bikers' negotiator, a massive bearded mountain of flesh called Olaf. One night, Olaf had been in a fight. Somehow, someone had managed to knock him out and quite by chance it had been Chris who had found him in the gutter. Knowing that Olaf couldn't go to hospital in case he got asked awkward questions, Chris did the first aid himself and made sure Olaf got home. So despite being from rival gangs, Chris and Olaf were very good friends. Some gangsters are very nice guys, and Chris and Olaf were among the best.

For some reason Chris got it into his head that I was a lucky charm. I guess every time we had a drink, the deal he subsequently did went well, so he asked me if I would go with him and Olaf to the casino. I said I'd love to, so long as Alison could come along too.

Forget any image you have in your head of Las Vegas or Monte Carlo. The casino Chris took us to was in an apartment building. The gambling den was run by the Chinese and as soon as the elevator doors opened it was like walking into downtown Shanghai. We had to be patted down and checked for weapons, and were then offered a drink by one of the beautiful Oriental women in traditional dress who were all over the place. My eyes landed on a Chinese guy with curly nails, straggly hair and a long moustache. He looked like a hermit or a priest. Chris told me he was the guy in charge. Not just of the casino but of pretty much the entire underworld of Denmark. On the surface, Copenhagen seems like this really normal place, but dig just a few inches below and you can find yourself in some really weird places.

Ali and I weren't allowed into the den itself, so we stayed in the foyer area where lots of other lucky charms waited for their men. At one point, Chris came out with a deck of cards and handed them to me.

'Just hold them,' he said, 'for luck.'

He went right back inside and about 90 seconds later this huge cheer went up. Chris came back out with a massive smile on his face: he had proof I was lucky and asked the guy with the straggly hair if I could go in. I watched as they spoke. Chris's body language seemed different around this guy, subservient almost.

Chris came up to us: 'Jim wants to meet you.'

Jim? Really? Green Dragon seemed more appropriate.

When I got close to 'Jim' I felt very strange. This man had the most amazing aura. I suddenly felt relaxed, almost like I'd been drugged. You hear about spiritual men, and this guy was definitely connected to something most of us can't understand. It was like he was the centre of everything. Jim looked at the pair of us and nodded: we could go in.

The gambling room in this penthouse was like that scene in *Star Wars* where aliens from all over the galaxy hang out in the same bar. Except here, instead of interplanetary beings, there was just about every breed of gangster looking to move a bit of dirty money around. Chris told me to keep my eyes to myself, but I just couldn't stop staring. I have never seen so much splendour in all my life. Women in the most beautiful traditional robes, men in immaculate suits and waiters in a constant swirl of silver service. Oh, and stacks of money. Everywhere.

Despite the fact that there were people there from all the member states of the United Nations, there was only one language anyone was allowed to speak, and that was English. Anything else could be a code for something, so if someone said a word in their own language they were immediately 'asked' to leave.

I don't know how long we were in there for – there are never any clocks in casinos so you never know when it's time to leave – but the ashtrays were slowly turning into little pyramids of cigar butts. The gamblers sat round the tables like pigs round a feeding trough: heads down, voraciously hoovering up every cent on offer. Olaf won an enormous amount of money at one point, and just in case someone decided to take it for themselves a little Louis Vuitton bag appeared and the cash was taken outside for safe keeping.

The surprising thing is that although I was surrounded by gangsters I felt incredibly safe. I didn't have to have it spelt out for me that there was a code of honour among these men that wouldn't let an outsider see the other side of things. Our very presence was the thing that was protecting us. They didn't know me, so they wouldn't show me. Anything bad was kept from us, and the idea that we could have become innocent bystanders at a gangland meltdown was just ridiculous. Chris and Olaf would never have taken me and Alison to a place where there was potential for things to kick off.

Anything goes

Ever since Alison's cocaine-fuelled night of girl-on-girl action, I had been trying to work out what it was I was feeling. Eventually I realised it was jealousy: Ali had had an experience that, if I was honest, I had always wanted too.

I had gone to school in suburban Essex. Being the only fully black girl in the entire school made me stand out enough; there was no way I would have ever said to anyone that I might fancy girls as well as boys. But now that Ali had been on a day trip to Girl Town, I finally had someone I could talk to about it.

We had been working with some truly beautiful girls, and in the changing room – as well as trying to get a good look at Kiki and Kimmie's bits to see if they really were men – I would often find myself staring at one girl in particular. When I confided in Ali that I thought I wanted the same experience she had had, she knew exactly who I wanted to have it with.

'It's Karina, isn't it?'

'No, it isn't!' I felt hot with embarrassment. How on earth could she know?

'Of course it is! I've seen the way you look at her.'

Karina was the exact opposite of me. Tall, pale and blonde. She was one of the few Danish girls who worked in the club and only worked a few shifts a week to help pay her bills while she studied. She was also a real sweetheart – she'd been the one who'd warned me about Samir – and she just happened to be stunning.

'Well . . . maybe . . . all right. I do fancy her but don't you dare say anything!'

The chances that Alison wouldn't say anything were somewhere

49

between zero and none. And now that my secret was out I felt completely embarrassed whenever I saw Karina. Had Ali said something? Had she dropped a hint? It was excruciating.

One night, around the end of October, when the weather was so bad that even the die-hard regulars chose to stay at home even though we were having a 'bikini night', there were far more girls in the club than punters. I was actually relieved that I didn't have to work too hard as I had a stinking cold. I was so bunged up I could barely breathe. But as long as there was one customer in the club, the show had to go on, and so Ali and I spent a lot of time that night watching the other girls dance. We were still adding to our repertoire of moves, and when we saw a girl do something new, we made a note and tried to incorporate it into our own routines.

When Karina came out to dance, I paid particular attention, and while I was staring at her Ali was staring at me with a wicked smile on her face.

'Well?' She jabbed me in the ribs. 'When are you going to say something to her?'

I didn't answer; I just kept on looking at Karina move under the lights. Right at the end of her routine she moved to the front of the stage and struck a pose, just as the spotlight fell on her. It was like she was illuminated just for me. I suddenly understood exactly how the customers felt and I was seriously turned on. I had let the universe know that I fancied her, and that spotlight was the universe letting me know that she was interested. Ali and I got the giggles. Karina saw us laughing from the stage and flashed us an electric smile.

'You have got to do something, Sam!'

'But I can't. I'm scared.'

I know it seems daft to say that – I was adult enough to leave home, to take my clothes off and charm men out of champagne, but around Karina I was like some mute teenage boy. She had the most amazing effect on me.

'Do you even know if she's gay? Or bi?' Ali asked.

I shook my head.

'Right, I'm going to ask her.'

'Ali! You can't!'

Ali got up in her little polka dot bikini and took a step in the direction of the changing room.

'You can't just ask her!' I reached out and grabbed her by the string of her bikini and pulled her back down. 'You can't just run in there and ask her if she's gay! I will run out of the club and never come back if you do that.'

'Wearing that? In this weather?'

'Ali! I am serious.'

Except, of course, I wasn't serious. I was desperate for Alison to ask Karina because I knew I would always be too scared to do it myself. And at some point later that night, Karina came and sat next to me. Just from the way she sat down I knew Ali had said something. She was just that fraction too close. I was so embarrassed I couldn't look at her. All of my cockiness, all of my chat – it was all out the window. I saw Ali out of the corner of my eye sitting at the bar. She raised her glass to me as if to say 'Good luck', but I still couldn't say anything. I assumed chatting up a girl was just like chatting up a boy, but I wasn't sure, and I was petrified of saying the wrong thing. I was mute, my head was down. I had no game.

'I was wondering,' Karina said, 'if maybe you wanted to come back to my place and watch a video sometime.'

And what did I say? What did my terrified, embarrassed 18-year-old self say? I only went and said 'No.' I made some pathetic excuse – I was tired, I had a cold, or I had plans – and then Karina made a dignified exit to see if she could get a guy who had just walked in to buy her a bottle. I sat there and just slumped. I was such an idiot. I remember hugging my knees, I was practically in the foetal position, trying anything to make myself smaller and disappear. Alison sashayed over.

'Oh Samantha! How the mighty have crumbled!'

'Shut up!'

'I dunno, you give it all this chat, and look at you. You're a wimp!'

51

'Shut it!'

'You can talk the talk, but you cannot walk that walk!'

'Shut. Up.'

Ali thought it was hilarious that I was so floored by Karina, and I had no explanation other than I was actually quite seriously smitten. I even dreamt about her that night and when I told Ali about my dream she made me realise I had to do something about it. This was an experience I wanted, and Denmark – where anything goes – was the place I wanted to have that experience in.

When Karina turned up for work the following night, I knew I had to say something. I followed her into the changing room.

'Hi.'

'Hi.'

'So, um, is that offer of watching a video still open?'

'Sure. Of course.'

The rest of the night was a blur. The weather had improved and it seemed all the men who hadn't gone out the night before were in the club, plus all the customers who would normally be there. The place was packed and everyone was making money. Occasionally I would meet Karina's eye and would look away instantly: a sure sign I was attracted to her.

Towards the end of the shift, I felt a tap on my shoulder, and just from the way the touch of her hand made me feel, I knew it was Karina.

'My customer wants you to join us. He says he likes the way you look.'

Guys often paid extra for 'a double' so they could live out that classic male fantasy of having two girls fighting for their attention. If a guy was happy to pay for a double, it usually meant he was comfortable spending money and the girls he chose were in line for a decent tip.

'Will you join us?'

Karina took me by the hand and it was like being grabbed by a live electricity cable. She led me to her customer, an American businessman in town to do a deal, or so he said. Of course, it's also part of the standard fantasy that the girls who do doubles together have the hots for one another. Normally, you get into conversations with the customer about how you like the other girl's arse, or her breasts, or her eyes, and he gets really turned on by this. But when Karina and I talked about each other, I couldn't look at her face. I don't know if she was looking at me, nor do I know if the customer could tell the difference between faked chemistry and the real thing, but it felt to me like we were having foreplay in public.

At the end of the shift I did something I had never done before – I used the shower at the club because, well, because you never know what's going to happen, do you? Then I got dressed and put on the best underwear I had left in my bag (a dancer regularly gets through several pairs of knickers a night – you can probably guess why) and pretty much behaved as if I was getting ready for a date. My palms were sweaty, my hand wobbled as I applied mascara and my heavy cold meant my temperature control was all over the place. Were those chills I was feeling anticipation, or just a virus?

Karina was waiting for me at the bar. 'Wanna get a coffee?'

I suppose we had a date. We went to a place that opened early to serve breakfasts to lorry drivers and shift workers. Those kinds of places are always fascinating to hang out in as the people who are up at 5 a.m. usually have a story to tell. There are nightclub bouncers and policemen and office cleaners and nurses and the odd broker who works on Tokyo time. Karina and I sat there for an hour trying to work out what everyone did and wondering if they knew what we did. (Of course they did: we were wearing six-inch glass heels!)

Then we went back to her apartment, which was really just a room in her hall of residence. I have a very clear memory of sitting on the end of her bed clasping my hands. I was so nervous. I'd seen a few porn films so I had some idea of what women did in bed with each other, but I just didn't know how to reach out and touch her.

'So, you wanna watch a movie then?'

A movie? You bet! I instantly relaxed. I knew how to watch a movie!

She made me choose and I pulled *Dirty Dancing* off her shelf.

We'd both seen it tons of times before, but I think I just reached out for certainty. The problem with choosing a film I had seen before was that I knew when it was getting close to the end. Normally, I like the finale of *Dirty Dancing* but I could barely look at the screen. It didn't help that I was sober. As a judge. The credits started to roll and Karina was looking at me, and I was looking at her, and then suddenly she made her move. She reached out and stroked my arm. It was like being electrocuted all over again.

People talk about how women touching each other is different from when you get touched by a man, and now I knew why. It was a completely different sensation, something that just beckoned me to go with the flow, that pulled me in. We started kissing, then we undressed each other, then her mouth was on my nipple, then she went lower.

Oh. My. God.

I had had a couple of boyfriends back in England, but teenage boys – I was in the process of learning – don't know all that much about sex. Karina, who was an older woman at the grand old age of 20, knew *a lot* about sex. It was my first experience of oral sex and it was just amazing. I had never been in such a tender situation with someone before when it hadn't been love. I couldn't believe what I was feeling and how deeply I was feeling it. I swear she had to scrape me off the ceiling at one point. And, of course, this was my first proper orgasm, and it was so full-on I thought I would explode. In fact, I did explode. I lay there afterwards on a warm moist cloud of pure bliss. And then it dawned on me: it was my turn.

Now I really felt like a teenage boy. Thankfully I had two advantages over a teenage boy, namely that a) I was a woman and b) I was a stripper. In the past few months I had seen more pussies and fannies than a porn addict – it's not like I didn't know the terrain. But unlike a teenage boy, I had just received the most sensational tongue action and had something to live up to. I was massively intimidated.

Oh, well. Here goes.

I slowly made my way down her body and started getting down

to business. She began to make some soft moaning noises, so I took that as encouragement and carried on. However, there was a problem. A big problem. I had a cold. I had a severely blocked nose. I couldn't breathe.

I didn't want to stop, because I didn't want her to lose the feeling, but I couldn't carry on . . .

Atchooo!

'Oh my God, Karina, I'm so sorry . . .'

I had sneezed all over her belly. I could see globules of snot in her pubic hair. Karina didn't care. She just stroked my cheek then shoved my head back to where it ought to be and I carried on. She casually reached over to the bedside table for a tissue and wiped it all away. That was a very cool move.

In an odd way, the snot incident was somehow more intimate than the sex and as we lay in each other's arms afterwards I felt incredibly close to her. We cuddled and stroked each other and then sporadically pissed ourselves laughing as we remembered the sneeze. At some point, probably around midday, I finally fell asleep.

For the rest of my time in Denmark, Karina and I would occasionally get together. It wasn't a relationship, or even an affair, but it was much, much more than just fuck buddies.

A dancer's life for me

Part of the deal with Auntie Nya was that she paid for two trips back to London a year. On my second trip home, I met up with some old school friends in a pub in Essex and within half an hour of meeting them I knew it would be the last time I saw them. It was as if their lives had stood still and mine had been fast-forwarded. They still lived with their parents, still thought ordering Snakebite was the height of sophistication, and all they were worried about was if some bloke they fancied was seeing someone else.

If I'm honest, it's not as if I had ever got on with them that well when we were younger. I had always felt different from them and had always wanted more for myself than they seemed to want for their lives. Saturday nights at Hollywoods, Sunday lunch with their gran and parents at the local Harvester and a nine-to-five job. That was all they wanted and they already had it. I knew their lives weren't going to change for the next 20 years.

I sat there thinking, 'You have no idea what I've seen, you have no idea who I've met, you have no idea what I earn.' All my childhood I had felt that I'd never really fitted in, and that there was something more exciting out there. As my old school friends talked about some new jacket Dorothy Perkins was selling, I realised that I had found somewhere where I fitted in, that I had found the adventure I'd been looking for.

'You know what,' I said as I stood up, 'I just remembered that I have to be somewhere. It's been nice catching up.'

And so I left. When I got back to my brother's house where I was staying, I got straight on the phone to Alison.

'I'm ready to go back. How about you?'

'I'm so glad you said that. I'm going mad here.'

I met her at Heathrow the next day and we headed out to Denmark for what would turn out to be the last time. The big reason we were both so keen to go back was that neither of us could stop thinking about how much money we were missing out on. Our regulars might come in and get to know another girl, and then they would never ask for us again. Or a stag group might come in and spend thousands of pounds on girls who weren't us. And if we didn't earn, we couldn't shop. Looking back, I can see that I was already well on the way to becoming addicted to the money.

As soon as we walked back into La Dolce Vita in the fabulous new outfits we had just bought on Bond Street, we were very glad we hadn't stayed in London an extra day as there was something very unusual sitting at the bar that night: a good-looking man. It was a seriously rare event for the kind of guy who could get any girl he wanted to come into a strip club. This guy was tall, with cropped hair, fabulous cheekbones and a seriously fit body. If you'd told me he was a model for Armani I would have believed you.

'He's mine,' I said to Ali as we made our way to the changing room. 'Hands off! He is all mine.'

'May the best dancer win.'

Once we'd done our hair and make-up, we raced each other out of the changing room and clattered up to the bar. I just had to reach him ahead of Ali, so I kind of lunged at him and tapped him quite hard on the shoulder.

He spun round faster than the Tasmanian devil and stared at me with these wild, animal eyes. He took a deep breath and then his eyes darted from one side of the room to the other.

'Whatever you do,' he said between short intakes of breath, 'don't *ever* creep up on me from behind.'

OK, I said to myself, *interesting response. What's the deal with this guy?* Whereas most girls might have run a mile after a start like that, I was desperate to know more.

'That's easy to do. Why don't I stay right here in front of you all night?'

'OK then.'

'And why don't you order us a bottle of champagne so we can get to know each other? This is my friend Blue, by the way.'

After that odd start, John proved himself to be pretty easy to talk to, but whenever someone in the next booth let their champagne cork pop, John would jump up. At one point when the door to downstairs was open, a car must have backfired in the street and John looked absolutely terrified. He ducked under the table.

'It's OK, John,' I said, peering under the table, 'it was just a car, but it's gone now.'

He sat back on the banquette.

'Do you want to tell us what's going on?'

John explained that he had just been discharged from the army and had served in Iraq. He was suffering from severe post-traumatic stress disorder and any loud bang took him straight back to the battlefield. As the evening progressed, and he kept on jumping at the slightest thing, Alison and I started to feel really quite sorry for him.

'Listen, when our shift's over we're going to go and get a pizza. Do you want to join us?'

He was just so pleased to be talking to a couple of English girls – I think he found it comforting – that Ali and I forgot about earning money and just spent the night chatting to him. John, however, forgot that he hadn't yet checked into a hotel.

'Ah, don't worry about it, you can stay at ours tonight.'

Were we totally crazy? Um, yes.

Later that night, we left John at our flat while we went to order the pizza. We were quite a long way from sober at this point and as we were coming up the five flights of stairs to our front door Ali had an idea.

'You know what would be really funny?'

'Go on.'

'If we kick in the door, SAS style, and Frisbee the pizza in like a grenade.'

Like I say, we were a little crazy that night.

We turned the key in the lock as silently as we could and then flung the door open wide.

'Freeze!'

We thought it was so funny . . . until we saw how John reacted. He did a proper dive off the bed and rolled along the floor and then stood up flat against the wall, like he was pretending he wasn't there. We stopped laughing because we realised that John didn't have a clue where he was. He didn't know who we were. He was somewhere else.

He started muttering to himself and then, only slowly, did he start to take in his surroundings. When he saw the two of us looking at him, he broke down in tears. We realised we had scared the life out of him. He really thought he had been about to die and we were so ashamed of ourselves, especially when he told us afterwards that we were lucky he didn't think we were the enemy. He could have tried to strangle us.

For the rest of the night, John pretty much spilled his guts. He was too scared to sleep because he had terrible nightmares, but then the lack of sleep made his paranoia worse. This beautiful, brave man just crumbled before us and by the time the sun came up we couldn't believe we had ever found his behaviour funny.

In a way, we had judged John as quickly and inaccurately as most people judge dancers. When people find out you take your clothes off for a living, they immediately put you into a box labelled 'dumb'. What they never realise is that dancers meet people from every walk of life, and because we learn very quickly not to judge people on their appearances we actually get to know them pretty well over the course of an evening. We are a lot more intuitive than we are given credit for, and a damn sight sharper than people realise. Those school friends I'd been with in the pub the day before couldn't have coped with John, and at 18 I might not have had the language or the learning to talk about post-traumatic stress disorder, but I had the empathy and the curiosity to understand John a lot better than most people would have done.

When we'd first started at La Dolce Vita, I had been suspicious of every man I met. *What kind of man comes somewhere like this?* I had a pretty clear idea in my 17-year-old mind that every man on the premises was lonely, ugly, fat or unclean, but so long as they paid me money and it remained a laugh I never examined them too closely. However, as the only men I met were at work, as the months went on it started to seem perfectly normal for a guy to walk into a strip club: from my perspective, ALL men went to strip clubs. I no longer judged them, and once that stigma had dissolved I slowly started to see punters as individuals. And once you lose your prejudices, you even find yourself thinking that some of them are nice guys.

Another customer who taught me how wrong first impressions often are was a priest. When you see a guy in a dog collar in a strip club, your first guess is that he's the groom, but this priest was only with one other guy – it was hardly a stag do.

'Hello there,' I said. 'Would you like to buy a girl a drink?'

The priest smiled but didn't say anything.

'I would,' said the guy sitting next to him, 'but can you be quick because I've only got an hour.'

'What happens in an hour?'

The two of them looked at one another, then looked at me.

'I've got to go back inside.'

In Denmark, I learnt that night, prisoners on day release have to be accompanied by a member of the clergy. This convict wanted to visit a strip club before he went back to his cell, and the priest had agreed to go with him. I don't suppose he minded!

I was learning from girls in the changing room too, and not just about eyeliner and boob tape. Kiki and Kimmie stopped being freaks and became real human beings to me and Ali, and the more we got to know them, the more incredible it seemed that Kimmie in particular could ever have been a man.

When we'd first started, we'd probably been pretty crass trying to get a look at their bits and pieces whenever they got changed. Looking back, I can see they were used to the attention, but we were so fascinated by them – we didn't even really know that transgender people existed, and we certainly wouldn't have called them 'transgender' – that we must have been staring at them like kids at the zoo.

One night, when Alison had drunk way too much of her customers' champagne, she came up to me and said, 'Fuck it, Sam, I've just got to ask her. I'm going to ask her now. Are you coming with me?'

Someone had to stop her saying something insensitive. 'OK, but let me do the talking.'

We went up to Kimmie, who was waiting for fresh meat to walk through the door. She was so petite and so gorgeous that the words that were forming in my mouth felt ridiculous.

'Listen, Kimmie, do you mind if we ask you something?'

'Sure, baby, what do you want to know?'

'Well, we've heard a rumour . . . we've never heard of this before . . .' I just couldn't find the words. Meanwhile, a drunk Alison was at my shoulder about to ask her to drop her knickers.

'Ah, I know. You wanna see, don't you?'

Clearly this was not the first time she had been asked.

'Come on then, darlings. Let me show you.'

She took us to the changing room, flamboyantly lay down, pulled up her dress, kicked off her knickers and did the splits.

'See! Nice and neat like yours!'

While me and Ali were having a good look, Kiki walked in and before we could stop her she had done exactly the same! The contrast was amazing. They had both had the full chop, but Kimmie had seen a much better surgeon, because you could really see Kiki's scars. It looked so painful it gave me nightmares.

I adored them for that show-and-tell, and I was starting to adore La Dolce Vita for accepting them for who they were. Kimmie had a regular – a really good-looking Danish man – and at first we wondered if he knew about the operation. In the end we were pretty sure that he did, and just as sure that he didn't mind because Kimmie was more feminine than most of the women I've met in my life. And, of course, no one judged him for fancying a transsexual. It's one of the very loveliest things about nightlife – you can be whoever you want to be. So when a group of Japanese businessmen came in one night and all turned their backs to the stage when Kiki and Kimmie went on, I got really angry on their behalf. Who the fuck did they think they were to judge them? You come into our world, you play by our rules.

By the end of my time in Denmark I had acquired well-developed instincts about who I could trust. In that environment, when so many people are on the make or on the take, the good people really shine. When the new girls started, I could guess with a good deal of accuracy which ones would develop drug habits and which ones would eventually turn tricks. I became adept at spotting a big spender as soon as he walked in the door, and equally good at identifying the customers who thought any woman who took her clothes off for money was trash.

I had started out wide-eyed and innocent, but my very innocence had meant my eyes never saw the grot. My innocence had protected me, because you cannot see what you do not know. But once I had adapted to my environment, once my eyes had finally got used to the dark, I became all-seeing. I started to see, for instance, that Kiki and Kimmie were not the only transsexuals working in the club, and that the reasons transsexuals are attracted to clubs is because it is one of the most accepting environments you can work in. And it's also a place where you can save up quickly for your next operation.

I also started to see when people were about to crack before they even knew they were crazy.

Queenie was another of Nya's dancers who I had got to know quite well in the early days. I knew – for sure – that she was one of the people who would never take drugs, but it was clear that something had started to affect her behaviour. One night when I was on stage I saw her shout at a customer, and then she started refusing to wear make-up and her appearance nose-dived. I called Nya.

'I'm really worried about her. I don't know what's happened, but something isn't right.'

'Keep an eye on her for me, will you?'

'Sure thing.'

I think it was the next night when I found Queenie at the bar, looking like a crack addict and rocking backwards and forwards as she hunched over a book. As I got closer I could hear her mumbling, and when I stood next to her I could see that she was reading the Bible.

'Queenie darling, you all right? Shall I call you a cab?'

She turned to me, stood up and started preaching just a few centimetres from my face, her thick Jamaican accent blasting my ears as she shouted out a couple of psalms. Everyone else moved to the other side of the bar, but I calmly asked the barman for the phone and called Nya. Queenie was on a flight back to Jamaica the next day.

Stripping can get to you. It sure got to Queenie. The Bible stories she grew up with chastised her for the choices she had made and they drove her crazy. Others tried to escape into a fantasyland where the fact that they made their money stripping was forgotten: a rich man will marry me, the next guy who comes in here will offer me a job, the shares I bought on a customer's recommendation will make me a millionaire . . . One girl, an American called Jacy, was always coming in with an idea for a business that we could all start and that would make us rich. At first I got caught up in her enthusiasm, but I came to realise that she was just as addicted to the fantasy of getting out of stripping as some girls were to cocaine.

And yet, in amongst all these damaged people, I felt incredibly strong. I felt like my minerals had been tested and I'd found out who I really was. Unlike them, I was pretty sure I didn't have the demons that would see me go to a customer's hotel room or get addicted to whatever the Turks were selling. But then I couldn't quite forget the chorus of 'give it time' from the other girls. Was it inevitable that if I stayed I would end up in prostitution or on drugs? I looked around for an example of who I might be in a couple of years' time. Was there one girl who still enjoyed the work and the money without losing some vital part of herself? To my alarm I realised there wasn't.

However, there was one person in the club in whom I saw just a little tiny bit of myself, and that scared me enough to make me realise a year in Denmark was enough: it was time to leave. That person was Stella.

Stella was in her 50s, though she looked a lot older. She was always immaculately turned out, like she was going to a cocktail party or the opera. She had Cleopatra hair and enough make-up to sink the *Titanic*: she was clearly trying to hold on to something she had lost. I asked around and found out that she had once been a dancer and that she had actually realised the dancer's ultimate dream: she had married a customer and, not only that, her husband was a Swedish billionaire. Stella had all the money she could ever want, but two or three times a week there was nowhere she would rather be than the seedy surroundings of La Dolce Vita.

Even though she had lost her looks and lost her moves, Stella still needed to be in a strippers' environment. She still wanted to see who would come in those doors and see which girls had learnt new tricks on the pole. For her, stripping was addictive and she needed a regular fix.

Was that my future? I sure as hell wasn't going to turn out like Queenie, or Paula the coke fiend. But Stella? I had to admit, there was a chance that in 30 years' time I would be inappropriately dressed and trying to kid myself I was still one of the girls.

'Ali,' I said one night as we counted our krone on our bedroom floor, 'I think it's time to go home.'

'I've been thinking the same. I want to leave while it's still fun.'

'Shall I call Nya?'

'Yeah. We've done this now, haven't we?'

'Been there . . .'

'. . . done that . . .'

'Got the G-string!'

I called Nya the very next day.

DIAMONDS ARE FOREVER

Back on the pony

I'm scared to think how much money I earned in Denmark, because instead of saving it up I came back to London with two or three grand. It's quite a nice amount of money, but when you think that I probably made around £50k out there, it's pretty obvious that I had got used to spending. So when I started looking around at my employment options in London and saw that the salaries were £15k a year if I was lucky, it wasn't long before I started thinking that I wasn't done with dancing.

We'd been back a week when Ali and I met up for lunch in Soho. After seven days at my brother's house in suburbia it felt so good to be back in the centre of things where everything was just a bit more . . . flamboyant. A bit more *me*. I'd realised that I didn't have anything in common with the people I knew from before I went away, and I was finding that I couldn't bond with any new people I met because they didn't know what I'd been doing. I was starting to crave being with other dancers again.

'I don't think I'm done with dancing,' I told Ali. 'I really, really enjoyed working at La Dolce Vita.'

'You must have done. It's the only job you've ever had where you never phoned in sick!'

I had to laugh: she was so right. My bosses at Next would never have believed that I would ever turn up for any job regularly and without complaining!

'And not only that, but I've got all these shoes now and it would be a shame if they went to waste.'

'You know what's a shame? It's a shame we're not the same size because then you could have my pairs.'

'Really?'

'I've been thinking about it a lot, Sam, and I don't think I can do it here. What if someone I know walks in?'

My face must have fallen. I wanted to carry on having fun with my mate.

'But that doesn't mean you shouldn't do it. I think dancing is for you, it's in your character. And you are getting seriously mean with that pole. You can't stop now.'

We clinked glasses. We were about to take different paths – Ali got a job in the civil service and, believe it or not, ended up working in the European Parliament at one point – but our experience in Denmark meant we would be friends for life. After lunch, I went to a newsagent's round the corner and picked up a copy of *The Stage*. I'd read it quite a lot when I was younger – I'd been a Sylvia Young stage school kid until my mum had got too busy to take me to auditions – and turned straight to the ads.

Dancers Wanted.

I called the number and the very next day I found myself in the back of a minibus with about seven other girls being driven around by a guy called Damian who called himself 'an agent'. Every week, Damian took dancers to every club in London for auditions, and if a girl got hired he got a commission. I don't know if the commission covered the cost of the adverts and the van, but he got laid a lot, and that was all he cared about.

Some of the clubs he took us to I refused to audition in. They were sleazy, dirty, cramped little places where you could just smell the criminality. Then Damian drove us out to an industrial estate somewhere off the North Circular and I was beginning to think I was never going to find work. But to my complete surprise, this club in the middle of nowhere turned out to be a real gem. Don't ask me why, but loads of clubs are named after Bond films. Goldeneye, For Your Eyes Only, A View To A Thrill; this one was called Diamonds Are Forever. If I ever open my own place I'm just gonna go for it and call it Octopussy.

From the outside, Diamonds looked like a branch of Land of Leather without the windows. The inside was kitted out like a cruise ship and as soon as I walked into the foyer I thought I wanted to work there, even if it was miles beyond the back of nowhere. There were wood-panelled walls, chandeliers and fake brass portholes. It just looked like the kind of place where a girl could make money. In the middle of the foyer was a big central staircase that snaked its way up to the main floor where the auditions took place.

Eight of us went into the changing room – which was like something from a luxury health club, another sign that this was a nice place to work – and got into our outfits. I'd chosen a cute white dress and I put my hair in pigtails so I'd look really girlie. As I fixed my hair, I caught the eye of one of the other dancers. I thought she looked like a Photoshopped Jordan. She had this tiny waist, beyond-enormous boobs, skin the colour of carrots and lips so pumped up I feared they might burst when she walked up to me and introduced herself.

'Hiya. I'm TJ.' Her voice was like something from a comedy sketch: ridiculously high and more Cockney than the entire cast of *EastEnders*.

'Hi, I'm Toni.'

TJ was a complete caricature of what you think a stripper is like. Blonde, booby and stupid. Only, of course, TJ was far from stupid, but if you'd told me then that she would turn out to be one of my best friends, I would have told you to get on the first train to Barking.

Not only did TJ look the part, but she had some amazing moves. As I watched her audition, I realised that the standard of performance in Denmark had probably been a little on the amateur side. The girls in London seemed like athletes by comparison and I realised I would have to use every weapon in my dancing armoury if I was going to get a job.

'Hi, you must be . . .' A good-looking guy in his 30s with a Scottish accent glanced down at his list.

'Toni.'

'Right. Nice to meet ya, Toni. I'm Brad, I'm the general manager, this is your house mother, Theresa, and the guy on the end is Warren. He owns the joint, so always make sure you're nice to him. You ready?'

I nodded.

'Show us what you've got.'

Brad then gave me the warmest smile I have ever, ever had from a man in a strip club. I instantly knew that he was that very rare thing, a one in a million: Brad was a nice guy in nightlife. His smile put me at ease and as the first notes of 'Pony' pumped through the sound system I knew I was going to put on a good show for him.

At this stage, my routine was still pretty slow, a series of poses, but I was linking those poses together in more and more imaginative ways. And I was getting stronger too: a year of dancing had meant I could grip the pole with my thighs and lean right back, or I could hold on with one hand and fling myself around. I might not have stopped the show like TJ had done, but I was pretty sure I was capable of stopping a few guys in their tracks.

I struck my first pose and smiled. Catching the light all around the doorframe of the changing room door were fingerprints. It's the same in every strip club in the world: a dancer comes out on stage, strikes a pose while holding on to to the doorframe and surveys the room. A punter might think she's letting him get a good look at her, but an experienced dancer always takes a couple of seconds to see who's in. And more importantly, who's ordered champagne and who's nursing his pint to death. Those fingerprints told me I was home.

The fact that I was smiling helped me get the gig and Theresa the House Mother then took me and the other successful dancers on a tour of the club. I was beaming. It felt fantastic knowing I was good enough to work in a place like Diamonds.

Mother Theresa was probably in her early 40s and looked like she could have been a branch manager of a building society. I took to her instantly.

'I am your natural barrier between the dancers and any males in here. We're all women, so we can talk. If you're honest with me, I promise to always be honest with you. Common courtesy is all I want from the dancers, and that means being ready to work when the club opens. If you're not ready to start work at 8 p.m., you won't be working that night, understand?'

We all nodded.

'I organise your shifts, and if any of you can't commit to at least three nights a week then I'm sorry but this place isn't for you. We're not a place for part-timers looking for pocket money, OK?'

I nodded very vigorously at this point. I liked how businesslike she was about everything.

'If you're not coming in, I need to know so I can cover my arse. If you're ill, tell me. If you've dyed your hair and it's gone purple, tell me. If you've got your period, just tell me. The truth is always acceptable, but if you start telling me stories about why you're late or why you're not coming in, I will know that they are stories and I'll stop trusting you. Even if you think your reason is stupid and pathetic, just give it to me straight and we'll get along fine. Understand?'

More nodding all round.

Theresa also explained how the money side of things worked. Unlike Denmark, where we got paid just to show up, at Diamonds the dancers paid the club a house fee. You didn't pay it for your first three nights, but after that it was £65 a night, £45 at the start of your shift and the other £20 by midnight. The house fee was a little bit of a shock at first, but when I looked at the platform Diamonds gave me to make money I thought it seemed pretty reasonable. They took care of the premises, the advertising, the security, the sound system . . . they even had a limo to bring in stag groups and corporate customers.

The set-up on stage was pretty much the same as La Dolce Vita: first song in your outfit and strip during the second song. The difference here was that it wasn't topless, it was fully nude. I wasn't ecstatic about the prospect, but I told myself that I would give it a go and if I didn't like it after one night I would never go back. I knew from Denmark that you could get away with being topless for just the last few bars of a song, so I figured it would be the same at Diamonds. I knew there would be ways to play with my outfit, or pose in certain ways, to make customers think they were seeing a lot more than I was showing them.

Dancers made their money from customers when they came off stage. If a punter had liked what he'd seen on stage, he'd call you over – or if you were doing your job properly, you'd have spotted his interest from the stage – and you'd dance for him at his table for £20. The rules were very strict: he wasn't allowed to touch you and you weren't allowed to touch him. Each dance lasted for one song, around three minutes, which meant there was the potential to make a couple of hundred quid an hour.

'If this isn't for any of you,' Theresa said, 'it's been nice meeting you, but if it is for you, you can start tonight if you've got your paperwork – I need a passport, your National Insurance card and some proof of address – if not, I'll see you tomorrow.'

I went back to my brother Alan's that night and I remember telling him that I really liked the vibe at Diamonds. I liked Brad's smile, I liked Theresa's businesslike manner, I liked the cruise-ship chandeliers and I liked that I thought I could make money. I also was quite surprised to realise that I liked the idea of working on the edge of town.

'That doesn't sound like you, Sam,' Alan said.

'Yeah, I know, but there's something about being all the way out there that means a guy has made a special trip to get there. He's there because he wants to spend money, he's not just popped in for a cheap thrill after work.'

My hunch was right. Diamonds weren't just forever – they would also turn out to be a girl's best friend.

Defluffin' the muffin

After a year in Denmark, there wasn't much that could shock me, but when I walked into the changing room on my first night at Diamonds I was so stunned that my jaw fell open and my eyes bulged. G-strings and Tampax were being tossed around the room and bras and garters were strewn across the floor – the usual scene as dancers get ready – but in the middle of the merry-go-round of tits and pussies was a middle-aged man.

'Don't worry about him,' one of the dancers said to me, 'that's just Terry.' And just to prove it, she sat on his lap – she was starkers at the time – and started rubbing his belly.

'Don't get him too excited, darling, I want him to last the night, you know.'

I looked in the direction of the voice and saw an older woman in a zebra-print blouse on her knees sewing sequins onto a dress while the dancer who was wearing it glued on her eyelashes. The woman on her knees was Jackie, and I came to love Jackie and Terry like a second set of parents.

Jackie had been one of the original 'nugget in a jar' girls who'd made her money – when she was younger and thinner – in pubs by getting every man in the place to put some money in a pint glass, and when there was enough money in the jar she would get up on the bar and do a striptease. She'd briefly hit the headlines when critics declared her act was sexier than Madonna's Blonde Ambition tour. When she'd got too old to climb on the bar, she and her husband started earning a living by making outfits for dancers. Brad had heard about them and invited them to work at Diamonds.

Jackie and Terry's dressmaking was a fantastic little business for them because strippers need certain things from clothes that most women don't want. A stripper, for example, could get a lot of tips from wearing a dress that has a slit right up to the crotch, whereas most women would get fired for wearing the same outfit. Jackie and Terry were absolute geniuses at using Velcro rather than buttons, so you could just whip off your dress, and then just as importantly whip it right back on. They designed dresses that would pop open if you stuck your tits out with enough force, or skirts that would fall to the floor if you dropped your hip at the right angle. With the right squeeze of a buttock, or a deft push of a boob, Jackie and Terry's clothes flew off you . . . and the punters were so amazed and entertained that they would often tip you more than £20 or ask for another dance so they could see how you did it. It was the stripper's equivalent of the three-card trick.

The really amazing thing about Jackie and Terry's outfits was that they were ridiculously cheap. Maybe £25 for a boob-tube dress to perhaps £65 for a sexy cowgirl outfit with all the accessories. So, of course, we all ordered dozens of outfits from them so that we always had something in our locker that would match any man's fantasy. The only rule Jackie and Terry had was that you couldn't copy exactly another dancer's outfit, but with her consent you could have it made in a different colour or with a different finish. It also meant that if you started to earn a lot of money in one particular dress, you could get Jackie and Terry to make you a copy so that when your first dress was in the dry cleaner's you could still slip into your money-maker.

There was a really big emphasis on looking good at Diamonds. I remember, some time in my second week, overhearing Mother Theresa arranging shifts with one of the other dancers:

'And you won't be in on Friday, will you?' she said.

The dancer said she was available to work.

'No, you won't be in on Friday, will you, because you will be getting that seen to.'

Theresa was pointing at the dancer's pussy. Her stubble had got beyond what you could cover up with a bit of concealer and powder, which meant an enforced couple of days off to visit the bikini parlour and to let the redness die down. *Blimey*, I thought to myself, *I knew we had to look good, but I didn't realise our muffins would be subject to inspection!* From then on, religiously defluffin' the muffin became part of the job description.

We didn't just have to look good at Diamonds, we had to look like movie stars. Not necessarily leading ladies – it wasn't always the girls with obvious looks that earned the money – but we had to be immaculate. Guys were making the trip to the back of beyond to look at the kind of girls they couldn't pick up in a bar. Our make-up had to be flawless like a cover girl's, our hair had to be styled, our clothes had to be clean and new, we had to smell nice, and our body hair had to be plucked, shaved, waxed or bleached as required.

It's amazing what make-up and styling do: sometimes it's like wearing a disguise. I was once in a Tesco Express picking up a pizza when this woman came up to me.

'How are you, Sam? You working tonight?'

'How do you know my name?'

'Sam, it's me, Donna.'

'Oh my God! Really?'

I looked closely and realised that it truly was this girl who I had been working with for about six months. In her civilian clothes with no make-up and her hair tied back she looked so . . . well, so *ordinary*. Yet at work she looked like a supermodel, with make-up to hide her spots and give her cheekbones, and a wig to make her seem six inches taller (of course, the killer heels helped with that too). I just couldn't believe it.

Every month, new girls started at Diamonds who were nothing much to look at. Real ordinary girl-next-door types. And within a few weeks they had been transformed, first by Jackie and Terry's outfits, and then by picking up tips from watching the other dancers. Concealer wasn't just used to hide zits and stubble, it also covered up bruises and stretch marks. Theresa got in a couple of hair and make-up artists who had worked behind the scenes on TV shows to come in. For £15 they would give you a complete makeover and show you how to make the most of what you had. Once you'd paid them a few times, you learnt how to do things yourself. And, of course, we were always sharing tips about the best places to get your nails done or get a spray tan or get your hair styled.

There was one other advantage we had over any girl a guy might meet outside the club: we had Look Good Lighting on our side. I don't know how it works, but the lighting in strip clubs is filtered, or coloured, or has the UV turned down, or some other kind of magic; however it works, as soon as you step out into Look Good Lighting you don't just look good, you look *amazing*. Zits and blemishes disappear, dark circles evaporate, pores tighten up and eyes sparkle. I do not know how they do it, but every club has it, and if I had the first clue how to do it I would invent a visor that emits Look Good Lighting so I could walk around in it every day.

Out of all the dancers I worked with at Diamonds, the girl who took her grooming the most seriously was TJ. Her spray tan was so thick it was like she was a candy-coated orange Smartie. Her eyelashes entered the room before the rest of her. And her forehead was so stiff with botox it could have deflected bullets. But there was one part of her that was not so invincible. I was in the changing room when she went out on stage . . . and came back about 45 seconds later in tears and with her hair in her hands.

'Oh my God, babes. What happened?'

'I was on the pole . . . I flipped upside down . . .'

'It didn't?' I felt a giggle coming on.

'It did. My wig fell off!'

I could not stop myself from laughing. I was wiping away her tears while crying plenty of my own because the laughs kept on coming. I so wish I had seen her face when it happened. Soon TJ was laughing too, and then the entire changing room was in fits.

'You know what you need?' I said to her as we pinned her wig back on. 'You need a weave. That way it ain't coming off if you do a triple back flip out there.'

'Where do you get one of those?' Of course, white girls don't know about weaves.

'I'm gonna show you.'

A few days later, I went round to TJ's house during the day so I could show her the secrets of a good weave. Needless to say, when I got there she wasn't ready – no one, in the history of the universe, on any planet, from any species, has ever taken longer to get ready than TJ. So I sat in her kitchen and waited for her and I noticed that all over her fridge were photos of her friends. One girl was in almost every single photo – she was a bit plump, had a big nose and a purple mohican. When TJ finally came into the kitchen I asked her if the woman in the photo was her girlfriend.

'I'm not gay.'

'Then who's that girl?'

'Take a closer look.'

So I did. And there was something about the smile, a slight lop-sidedness, that made me realise who it was.

'No? No! It *can't* be. It just cannot be. *Really*? Truly?'

'It is,' she said with a wink.

'Never! I don't believe it. I *can't* believe it.'

The girl in the photos was TJ.

'You have got some talking to do. Tell me everything.'

While I took her on a tour of weaveries and wig shops, TJ told me her life story. A few years before, she had been plain old Tracy Jones with a plain old boring life ahead of her. Then she had got really into some band and decided she would follow them round the world, sleeping on beaches because she couldn't afford hotel rooms. She became the most devoted groupie and got her hair cut in a mohican to look like the bass player.

The band then split up while they were on tour and she was left stranded on the Costa del Sol with no job and no money. Girls in those kinds of situations tend to fall into the hands of someone dodgy, and although little Tracy Jones did indeed end up being befriended by the Russian mafia, she got a new life out of it. In exchange for a little courier work, she was offered a new identity. The police and any rival gangs would be looking for a girl with a purple mohican; meanwhile she was having tens of thousands of pounds' worth of surgery to look like Jordan. She started to list the things she'd had done:

> Boobs, obviously
> Teeth, about £25k's worth of veneers
> Cheek implants
> Chin implants
> Liposuction
> Nose job
> Brow lift
> Buttock implants

I didn't even know you could get buttock implants. I spent most of that day catching flies as my jaw dropped a little lower with every new revelation. I could not square the girl with the mohican in the photos with the walking, talking Barbie in front of me. TJ was now, officially, the most interesting person I knew.

Like most women, I'm always reading magazines where they have pictures of celebrities looking ropey and flabby, and of course we all gawp at them because we're used to seeing celebs looking made-up, styled and properly lit. When they're working, it's their job to look fabulous, and it's just the same with dancers – it was our job to look amazing, which is why we all took the grooming side of things very seriously. Perhaps not quite as seriously as TJ, but around two hours a day was spent in front of one mirror or another. I understand why some women feel threatened by their boyfriends and husbands paying to see us take our clothes off, but I wonder if it helps to know that any woman who has the time and money and inclination to groom herself would look just as good as us. Trust me, after a few too many drinks or too little sleep, we can look as ropey as those bloated and saggy celebs in their bikinis.

Gangsters' paradise

Theresa was very smart at doing her rotas. Around 30 girls worked every shift and she always made sure that there was the right balance of blondes, brunettes and redheads. She always put a couple of 'girl next doors' on the floor for the guys who were too intimidated to speak to the stunning girls, and she always rostered on a couple of Oriental girls (and – for some reason – always just the one Indian girl). I was one of two black girls who worked at Diamonds. My look was what I call American black and Sasha had the Nubian look, like a dignified African princess. She never wore any make-up – she was just so stunning she didn't need to – and always wore really simple, elegant clothes. We called her Sasha Bush Hut Woman because she looked like she had stepped out of a BBC2 documentary. On the nights when Sasha and I were both on, each of us still got a lot of dances because we looked so different. Theresa really knew her business. She knew that if there were 30 girls on shift, we would all make good money, and when the dancers made money, that money filtered its way through the rest of the club. Theresa also knew that if she put any more black girls on the floor I wouldn't make enough money, I'd get pissed off and I'd leave. There was just no point having more than me and Sasha because most men preferred to get white girls to dance for them. That was fine with me because there was nothing I could do to compete with them. I wasn't being rejected because I wasn't as good a dancer, or not as pretty. But if a guy came in who liked black girls, well then, that was a night when I was guaranteed to make my money.

Whenever a dancer had a good night, she always made sure she tipped Theresa because somewhere down the line our House

Mother would have made it happen – either she'd got the rota right, or she'd made sure you were in when your regular clients were due in, or she'd looked after your clients with a complimentary bottle of something while you got ready. You look after your House Mother, she looks after you. That was just the way it worked back then.

The tipping culture was what kept things respectful at Diamonds. If someone helped you make money, then you showed your appreciation. Another dancer might walk past you at some point in the night and let you know that a guy in the far corner was asking for a black girl, so you'd make a mental note to go over to him as soon as you got a chance. Or maybe one of the waitresses whose job it was to show customers to their seats and take their drinks order let you know that a guy had just put a platinum card behind the bar. Because of her, you now knew that he was in there to spend and so you'd approach him for a dance rather than hustling the guy who'd spent his last fiver. A good waitress often got more in tips from the dancers than she did from the customers. The security staff got tipped too if they took good care of your regulars, or let you know that someone had just pulled up in a Maserati. It was like paying for intelligence, or having informers, and if I profited from their tips then they got a share of my profits. So long as everyone stood to gain, we all helped each other out. If things still worked like that in clubs now, I might still be there.

That's not to say that the guys who worked on the door were the kind of guys you'd be happy to take home to meet your parents. They were generally the kind of men who were too fat, or too thick, or too criminal, to join the police, but because they were the only men who were still up at 4 a.m. and who understood what a dancer's life is all about, plenty of girls ended up dating the door staff. And to be honest, apart from Brad, I think every man who works in and around clubs does it because he thinks he can get laid a lot. And he probably can.

In every club, in every town, in every country, the guy who is in charge of security is not someone you want to mess with. If I ran my own club, I would want the biggest gangster I could get to run my door because then I would only have to deal with one gangster; the rest would be dealt with by him. If all the other players in town know that you have a big man on your door, they will not bring their squabbles to your patch or try to do something that would see you closed down, like dealing drugs. Of course, gangsters still want to come to a club: apart from the girls, they like the fact that they can't rock someone else's boat. If you're a gangster, a strip club is one of the few places were you can relax.

All of which you need to know because on my second night Theresa and Eric the doorman were both doing their jobs brilliantly well and that meant I could earn a nice amount of cash. Theresa had made sure I was the only black girl on the floor, and Eric had tipped off a mate of his who liked black girls that there was a new dancer for him to get to know. I'm going to call his mate Patrick, cos my nickname for him was Tricky. If I used his real name – that's of course assuming the name he gave me *was* his real name – I might get a knock on the door.

Tricky and his mate Jamie were two of the best-looking men I have ever seen in a strip club. Or anywhere for that matter. They were beautiful, black, extremely fit – you could see the muscles under their tight-fitting shirts – and wore very expensive, very trendy clothes. If you'd told me they were Premiership footballers, I would have believed you. You've got to remember that I had come back from Denmark with quite a game on me and I could hustle most guys. But I was still only 18 and I hadn't learnt how to stay in the zone when I fancied the guy I was dancing for. If you genuinely find a guy cute, you just can't be as cocky as you need to be. With Tricky and Jamie, it was hard to know which I fancied more. So when Jamie beckoned me over, I was nervous *and* excited.

'Do you want a dance?' I asked.

Jamie pulled out a £50 note from his pocket and put it on the table.

'Just sit with us.'

So long as he was paying me, I didn't mind if I danced or talked for his money. Tricky sat there playing with his phone, so I spent the time talking to Jamie. By my calculation, £50 got him about 15 minutes of my conversational prowess, and we got on so well it felt like being down the pub with a mate. Jamie and I just clicked, but – oddly – there was absolutely no sexual chemistry between us at all. Which was good, cos that meant I'd be able to dance for him and get some more money out of him.

'So do you want a dance from me?' I asked.

Then, from the other side of the table, Tricky looked up from his phone for the first time and said in a smooth, slow drawl, 'Do *you* want to dance?'

I was absolutely stunned, not by what he said or how he said it, but by his eyes. They were bright shiny blue. For years I had been having dreams about a black man with blue eyes – and I don't mean idle daydreams, I'm talking proper waking-up-in-a-cold-sweat-in-the-middle-of-the-night dreams – and all of a sudden here he was in front of me. The man of my dreams.

At this point I had a choice: I could not take the dance out of embarrassment, or I could give the performance of my life and get some of the power back. This was only my second night, and so getting fully naked just a couple of inches from a customer was still something I was getting used to, but I had already worked out that I could get away with taking my knickers off on the last word of the song. Tricky got out another £50 and I started to get chills spreading across my skin. Game on.

Women who have never danced find it difficult to understand that dancing for a man is actually incredibly empowering, especially for an exhibitionist like me. You and he both know that he can't touch you – Eric and his boys made sure of that – and I always got a guy to sit on his hands and spread his legs: that way, I was in control. I would then push him back against the wall so that I could put my hand on the wall and roll my body up and down so close to his face that he could feel my body heat. I would let my hair brush against his cheek and let out a long, slow breath down his neck.

Often I would hear customers breathing heavily, but just as often they were so fixated, so paralysed, that they forgot to breathe, and it was when I felt him take an uncontrolled, sharp intake of breath that I knew I had him. He'd have goose pimples, he'd have a smile, he'd be satisfied, and he wouldn't even care that he hadn't seen much more than a pair of breasts. Men are quite happy with a peek: a little bit of knicker, a little flash of a nipple is just as sexy, if not more sexy, than giving them an anatomy lesson. And when you see the hunger in their eyes to glimpse just a teeny, tiny bit more than you are showing them, you know you have total control. When you feel wanted like that, you feel sexy, and when your garter starts to bulge with £20s and £50s you feel as hot as can be.

The first time my knickers had hit the carpet the night before and I'd been standing completely naked in front of a guy, I had realised that it was OK. All I had done was take my clothes off, and it actually seemed pretty trivial to me. If I could dance like that for Tricky, this man made of dreams, then I would have just as much power over him as those magnetic blue eyes had over me.

So even though there was this fizzing chemistry between us, even though he made me feel incredibly shy, I gave him my best game, and when I sat back down he put £100 on the table, as did Jamie, and the three of us shared a few more drinks, and more than a few laughs.

The two of them came in again the next night. When we made eye contact, Tricky beckoned me over, got out a roll of notes from his pocket and peeled off £500.

'Sit down,' he said, 'don't take your clothes off. Let's just talk.'

'What do you want to talk about?'

'What do you like doing when you're not in here?'

He just wanted to have a normal conversation, the kind of boy-meets-girl stuff that happens around office water coolers and cinema popcorn stands every day of the week. Tricky was wooing me. And let me tell you, I was very happy to be wooed. I took that £500 as a gesture that he knew what I did, he knew where we were, and that meant I spent my time with men in exchange for money. By paying me enough money for the night, he had me to himself and we could carry on talking.

My shift ended at 4 a.m. and we were still yakking away.

'You wanna get some food?'

The three of us went to a place in Farringdon called Tinseltown that opened at five in the morning to serve burgers and shakes to shift workers and pilled-up clubbers. After we'd eaten – it must have been about eight in the morning – I was absolutely shattered and Jamie offered to let me stay in his hotel room.

This is an interesting dynamic, I thought. *It's clear there's something going on with me and Tricky, but Jamie's the one asking me to come to his room. And Tricky is OK with that? Curious.* Actually, the really weird thing was that it really, truly felt completely natural for me and Jamie to share a room.

It's pretty standard in nightlife for people to have hotel rooms. It's not a line a guy spins you to bed you: people work odd hours, they've often been drinking, so crashing in hotels avoids awkward where-have-you-been conversations with family members and makes life a lot easier. And if you slip the receptionist a few notes, you won't have to check out until the middle of the afternoon.

When we woke up, Jamie drove me back to my brother's house.

'You know what, Toni? I don't think I have ever shared a hotel room with a girl and not had sex with her.'

'Bet you've never driven a girl home before either.'

'You're right. But you're not like the other girls, are you? You're one of the guys.'

So that was it: Jamie and me had just become good mates and it was quite clear there was nothing to stop me and Tricky getting together.

Nothing, that is, apart from the fact that I knew he was a massive gangster.

The give-away was the ring he wore on his little finger: platinum encrusted with diamonds. When a gangster can't get his money clean he's got no choice but to spend it on status symbols and bling. That ring was probably £50k's worth. Even though I knew he was a gangster, I still couldn't shake the feeling that I had been dreaming about him for years and that we were somehow destined to be together. However, I was determined that I wasn't going to just be another dancer he slept with: I was going to make sure that I was special to him, and the way to make that happen was to get him to see me in daylight hours.

He took me to lunch, took me shopping, took me to the movies and after about a month he took me to bed. The sex was *extraordinary*. His appetite was matched by his ability. That guy was so strong that he could hold me in any position, and his stamina was so great that he could keep going for hours. There are still some hotels in London I can't walk past without blushing.

I'd usually be woken by him getting dressed. He had so much energy he hardly needed any sleep, but to make it up to me for leaving we used to play a game. Tricky usually wore cargo pants so that he could spread his money around in different pockets, and when we played Pick A Pocket I could keep whatever was in the pocket I chose. Sometimes it was £500, sometimes it was £5,000. And if I slept through him leaving, I would always find out when I checked out that he had paid for me to go to the spa or get my hair done. If the room was booked for another night, it meant he wanted to see me again.

I got quite addicted to the sex, and the money, and I liked it when Tricky came into Diamonds and everyone knew I was with him. He made me feel special. I knew he had slept with dancers before, but I was sure he'd never felt the way about them that he did about me. We had something really special going on. I was mates with his best mate. I was one of their special gang. Or so I told myself.

At 18, there are things you just accept, things that today you can't believe you ever did. For instance, whenever I got in a car with Tricky or Jamie we always had to have a particular conversation:

'What's your name today?'

'Desmond.'

'What club did I meet you in?'

'Chinawhite.'

If the police stopped the car, I needed to be able to say I had only just met them and our stories had to match. That way, the police would probably just let me go. In my 18-year-old naivety, I thought that made him a gentleman: a lot of gangsters would try to drop everything on the girl. One time, there was a whole gang of us going to a party in a convoy of four or five cars. As soon as we heard police sirens, the convoy instantly split up, each car going down a different side street just in case the sirens had been for them. Afterwards, Tricky told me what had been in the boot of the car: guns. I had assumed he was just a drug dealer. I hadn't realised he did firearms as well.

The thing about gangsters – and the reason why we all watch *The Godfather* and *The Sopranos* – is that, whether you want to admit it or not, they are glamorous. You know in your head that it's dangerous and seedy and illegal and very probably wrong, but in your heart you just want them to get away with whatever they're doing because they're so damn glamorous. Gangsters are like movie stars in that way.

One day, in some hotel room, Tricky threw down a holdall and asked me to count what was inside. Asking a dyslexic person to count a lot of money wasn't the smartest thing he could have done, but how hard could it be? I opened the holdall and the notes started spilling out. I counted – in my own bizarre dyslexic counting method – over £300k. Now I know he didn't get that money doing something worthwhile or socially useful, I know he got that money through menaces and promises, but, damn, if counting out hundreds of thousands of pounds in a five-star hotel room wasn't a sexy thing to be doing. Especially when he let me keep whatever I could hold in one hand.

It took me a while to realise that every hotel we stayed in – I never went to his place, he never came to mine – was near or on a main road. I found out why about 6 o'clock one morning when Tricky woke me up by yanking open the curtains.

'What's going on?'

'They've come for me.'

'What?'

I leapt out of bed and joined him at the window. We had a view of the Hanger Lane gyratory system, which I suddenly realised meant he could make his escape in any of five directions. It must be one of the busiest junctions in London, but it was completely quiet. Even at 6 a.m. you'd expect traffic to be building up. But there wasn't a single car on the road: the entire junction had been closed off.

Tricky was already pulling on his trousers. He was convinced the police had found out where he was and he was so panicked, so unbelievably mentally hyper, that I really thought he was going to have a heart attack. He grabbed a rucksack that he hadn't let out of his sight the night before and ran out of the room without even kissing me goodbye.

I went back to the window and waited for the sirens and the helicopters, but there was nothing, just an eerie, abandoned silence. Half an hour later, several vans pulled up and lots of men in white boiler suits jumped out, like the kind you see on the news at the scene of a crime. But they weren't the police, they were some environmental health officers investigating a strange smell. When I checked out later in the day, the receptionist told me they had suspected a mustard gas attack but that nothing had been found. No one had been after Tricky after all.

We'd been seeing each other for about three and half months when I turned round in Diamonds and saw Tricky at a table with another dancer. I don't know what look I gave him, but the one he gave me in return was 'deal with it'. He was bored with me, he wanted someone new, someone who wasn't as close as I was to seeing through him, and what really hurt is that he didn't want to keep that from me. There was no pretending that he had fallen for someone new, he was just bored with me. So as soon as Eric the doorman let him know that a new black girl had started, Tricky had waltzed in to make sure history repeated itself. He didn't care how I felt.

I was so hurt and I felt *so* fucking stupid. I had been kidding myself that I was different, that I wasn't like the other dancers he'd slept with, that I had meant something to him. But I realised that night that I was just like all the others, another silly girl who thought gangsters were cool. Tricky is the reason why – when I became a House Mother myself – I always said to dancers that they needed to hold on to their civilian friends. You need to have some people in your life who have got nothing to do with nightlife otherwise you will lose perspective on what is OK and what is and isn't glamorous.

The only way I could deal with the anger and the shame I felt about it was to dance harder, hustle smarter and start earning more: Tricky's generosity had left me with an even more insatiable appetite for money.

Nightlife

Very early on during my time at Diamonds, probably just my second week, I noticed a couple of very interesting men come in. One of them was short, black and muscular and wearing one of those little Muslim caps, and the other was a giant – 6 ft 6 in. tall, face like a mug shot, shaved head and a neck thicker than my waist. They made an odd couple, but what really made me notice them wasn't the troop of trench-coated foot soldiers who followed behind them, it was how everyone made way for them, like a parting of the sea. *Oooh*, I said to myself, *gangsters*. They then sat down at a corner table and waited for Sandy, one of the waitresses, to bring their drinks over. None of the dancers approached them. *Interesting*.

After half an hour, they still hadn't been approached by a single dancer, so I pulled Sandy to one side and asked her who those two men were.

'You don't want to know.'

Sandy had just made me want to know a whole lot more than I did before.

'Trust me, Toni, just give 'em a wide berth.'

Sandy was one of the people I had learnt to trust from my very first day at Diamonds. She was Brad's wife and one of the coolest women you could hope to meet. When Brad had landed a job at Diamonds, he asked Sandy if she was OK with him working there. 'Fine,' she'd said, 'so long as you get me a job there too.' She was completely relaxed about her husband working in a strip club and was confident enough in herself to work around a bunch of naked women. In a sea of muck and despair, Brad and Sandy's relationship was like a little beautiful yacht, merrily charting its own happy course. Sandy was a woman whose judgement I should have trusted. But, damn, I was just so curious.

I started walking towards the gangsters when one of the dancers stopped me. 'Toni, you can't go and speak to them.'

'Why not?' I asked over my shoulder as I carried on my very important, top-level fact-finding mission. I approached their table and signalled with my hands that they should all shove up and make a little room for me.

'Let me in, let me in,' I said as I squeezed in between the Hat and the Meat Head. 'So, who are you then?'

The look of the guys in trench coats was what you might call stunned anticipation. *Has she really just sat down? Is she really opening her gob?* You betcha.

'Who are *you*?' said the man in the hat.

'Nah nah nah. I ask the questions. Who are you, walking in here like this? I wanna know.'

The two of them looked at each other and started laughing.

'Listen, darling,' Hat man said, 'we're just having a bit of a meeting, why don't you come back in half an hour?'

I left their table with a little wiggle and saw that a group of dancers were now clustered round Sandy.

'What did you say?'

'How come you were sitting with them?'

'What did they want?'

I was really surprised at all the questions. 'I just thought they looked a bit juicy,' I said, 'so I went and introduced myself. Let me tell you, they smell of money.'

'Toni,' Sandy said, 'you really don't know who they are, do you?'

The girls explained that the man in the hat was called John, and he was pretty much the main man for the whole of London. As gangsters go, Johnny the Hat was London's answer to Don Corleone and he was also responsible for the protection of Diamonds. *Really? Oooh.* I was now even more intrigued.

'Well, I'm going to go back over there.'

'You can't go over there,' Sandy said.

'They come here to talk,' another girl said.

'You can only speak to them if you've been invited.'

'Well, I was invited.'

Big intake of breath from everyone.

'Johnny said I should go back in half an hour.'

'You were *invited*?' They couldn't believe it.

So when I went back over, every dancer who wasn't on stage or in a VIP room watched our table.

'So what's going on here, then?' I said cheekily as I squeezed in next to Johnny.

'Look,' he said, 'I don't do dances.'

He wasn't getting rid of me that easily.

'Here's £100,' he said, 'dance for him. And him.'

So I danced for the other guys at the table and went back to Johnny. 'Want a dance now?'

'I told you, I don't do dances.'

'How about a freebie? No? How about a group dance then?'

Johnny thought that was hilarious. No one had been that cheeky with him for a long time, so he pulled out his wallet and pushed back the table to make room for me to dance in the round. He was still laughing at me when I finished.

'Now, are you sure you don't want a dance just for you?'

'I don't do dances. But maybe if we get to know one another I'll have a dance.'

'Right, then, let's get to know each other then.'

And so I started to talking to Johnny the Hat, just about the biggest gangster inside the M25. Of course I had no idea just how serious a player he was at that time, but the reaction of everyone else in the club told me he was one of the bigger fish in the pond. I loved it.

Gangsters and dancers go together like toast and marmalade. We keep the same hours, we can't tell our parents where we get our money from, the tax man doesn't often hear from us and, if I'm honest, they fancy us and we fancy them. I know it ain't clever, but gangsters are just so damned attractive. None of them were as pretty as Tricky, but even Meat Head had his admirers.

What was interesting to me was that it wasn't just the girls who wanted to sit with the gangsters, the men did too. There was one guy, I'll call him Ashley cos he looked like Ashley Cole, who used to come in with his mate, and the dancers all paid them attention because they were two good-looking guys. Then I noticed that Ashley had started coming in on his own, and I watched as Ashley worked his way into Johnny the Hat's world over a period of months. When you come into the club often enough, even if you're not a big spender, people get to know your face. And when you recognise someone, you tend to smile, and the doormen would shake Ashley's hand and the barmen would nod a hello. Maybe the doormen would start letting him in for free, and maybe the barman might let him have a few on the house, and to anyone else it looked like Ashley was friends with these men. And when someone like Johnny sees a guy be friendly with people he trusts, people he employs, he might start to nod in Ashley's direction too. Just by coming to the club several times a week, Ashley was proving to Johnny that he had the right kind of minerals.

As should be clear by now, I completely understood Ashley's interest in nightlife. If you've not the talent to be an *X Factor* finalist, or the brains to be a City trader, then what's the next best way to get your hands on loads of money and loads of women? Ashley wasn't really there for the dancers, he was there to get himself a career, and night after night, week after week, I'd notice him move from table to table, talking to different associates and making sure everyone knew who he was. When I saw him sitting at Johnny's table, I knew he'd found what he was looking for.

Ashley became a foot soldier, collecting and delivering envelopes of protection money, all the time trying to show Johnny that he could be trusted. He wanted to earn his stripes and move up the ladder. He wanted the sports cars and penthouses and Rolexes, and he knew Johnny could give them to him.

By the time I had broken up with Tricky (OK, when he'd

dumped me), I had got to know Ash pretty well, and it was clear to both of us that there was some chemistry between us. I knew that after Tricky the last thing I needed was another gangster, but Ashley was such a good-looking boy that I couldn't be entirely sure I wouldn't crumble. Looking back, it wasn't a coincidence that it was when I was seen getting close to Ashley that I heard from Tricky again. We'd been broken up for a month, maybe six weeks, when Jamie rolled into the club.

'Hi, Toni.'

'Hey, Jamie.'

'Patrick says hello.'

'Does he?'

'Yeah, he's been talking about you a lot lately.'

'Really?'

'Yeah, he's on holiday in Brazil right now and I got a text from him about you the other day.'

'Really?' Brazil is famously home to the most beautiful women in the world. If he was thinking about me in Brazil of all places, then maybe I did mean more to him than just a dancer?

Over the next few days, I started to get texts from Tricky himself saying that he couldn't stop thinking about me. Then he started calling. Every day. I didn't want to take his calls. I didn't want to read his texts, but I started remembering how good the sex had been – surely it hadn't been *that* good with all the other girls? Then I started thinking that he was genuine when he said he'd made a mistake.

I knew I was skirting round the danger zone. I forced myself to remember that he had hurt me really badly. I made myself put the phone down on him and then simply refused to take his calls. I was stronger than that. I was better than him.

So then he started leaving me messages saying that he had bought me a ticket to Brazil and I should get on a plane the next day. I texted back saying I didn't want anything to do with him. He left another message. This time he said he had bought an open ticket for me. I didn't really know what an open ticket was but I asked around and found out that they are the most expensive tickets you can get – any plane, any route, total flexibility. It meant I could go home whenever I wanted to. Maybe, I thought, maybe I should go. I called Jamie.

'Is he serious?'

'Completely. He won't stop going on about you.'

'Really?'

'I swear, go and see him. He really wants to see you.'

I sat there thinking: *Free holiday in Brazil, probably a few treats to say he's sorry, how bad could it be?*

'All right, then, I'll go.'

'Great. Let me know what flight you want and I'll take you to the airport.'

So, two days later, like a lamb to the fucking slaughter, Jamie took me to Heathrow. We pulled up outside departures and he reached inside his jacket pocket and handed over an envelope. I looked inside. I remembered the stacks of notes I'd counted in various hotel rooms. I reckoned it was about £10k.

'Tricky's run out of cash. I said I'd send some over with you. You don't mind, do you?'

Well, of course I bloody minded! Ordinarily I would have said no, but I was at the airport, my flight was leaving in less than two hours and a fortnight on the beach was beckoning. Like a mug, like a mug who had been really well played, I took the envelope and got on the plane.

Tricky had promised he would pick me up from the airport, but when we landed he was nowhere to be seen. It was only after I'd been sitting there in tears for two hours that he showed up.

'Where the hell have you been?'

'Watching you.'

What?!!

'I had to make sure no one was following you.'

Fucking bastard. Fucking *fucking* bastard.

He had rented a penthouse on the beach, which was like something from an MTV video. While he made some pretence that we could rekindle whatever it was we had, I made it clear that was not going to be happening. No amount of presents would do it. He had used me one too many times and that it was it. Over. Finito. Done.

A few days later, Tricky left for the airport and came back with another girl. I found out that she had been muled-up with drugs, and I am ashamed to say that my first thought was, *Well, he must like me more than he likes her because he got her to carry the drugs.* I could hear myself and I was appalled.

Listen to yourself, Samantha, think about what you are saying. The guy is a gangster. He does not care about you more than the other girl. He does not care about you full stop. Got it?

But I couldn't get it. Somehow I had to know that he thought something of me, that I had been more than just a dancer, and so I stayed around the penthouse watching boys do capoeira on the beach from the balcony while he played his games with the other girl. I hardly saw him the whole time I was there.

When I got back to Diamonds, my pride meant I had to tell the girls that I had had a wonderful time, that Tricky had treated me really well, and that I was indeed special to him.

'Sam, honey, I have to tell you something.' TJ had a very serious look on her face. 'The whole time you were away he was calling Lisa.'

'I don't believe you.' Of course, I believed every word of it.

'And not just Lisa. Candy says he's been texting her too.'

TJ made me face up to reality: I had been mugged. I had been used and trampled on. I had been made a fool of. All my hurt turned to rage and I was consumed with the idea of getting my own back on him in any way I could. I heard a rumour that Jamie was planning a trip to Barbados and I hatched a plan: I should go with him. After all, what could hurt Tricky more than if he thought I was getting together with his best mate?

I wasn't the only one who had heard the rumour and by the time I got round to suggesting it to Jamie quite a few girls had already booked their place in his apartment. He was offering to pay for flights for a few girls and so my fake romantic break with Jamie turned into a bit of a girls' week away.

It was only when we got out there and Lex refused to leave the hotel room that I realised Jamie had muled her up. After a couple of laxatives, she handed over whatever it was he had made her take. Take it from me, nightlife is only glamorous from a distance. Up close, it really is dangerous. People disappear. They get scarred. They get framed. And if you went out with a gangster, you probably wouldn't even know the guy's real name. You could never say 'How was your day at work, dear?' cos he might have killed someone, or kneecapped them. And if he thought someone was onto him, he would turn a corner and leave. All you'd be able to give the police was a false ID. You wouldn't see what direction he'd run in, that's how swift he'd move to get out of trouble.

The problem is that, as a dancer, as a female, I felt very safe around the gangsters I met. I knew they would never let anything happen to me. If a customer stepped out of line, he would be dealt with. That felt nice. And if you don't ask questions and just count the money when they ask you, they might let you keep a bit of it. So even though I understood that the less I knew about nightlife the safer I'd be, nevertheless, the closer I got to it, the safer I felt.

Tricks of the trade

An average night for me at Diamonds was £500. And on an average day, I would usually spend every penny of it and not give it a second thought. I got taxis everywhere. I spent an easy £50 a day on cabs. I ate every meal out – I was sharing a house with another dancer and we didn't even have plates in the house – so £20 on breakfast, £50 on lunch, maybe the same kind of money on dinner. I'd get my nails done a couple of times a week, my hair done at least once a month, not to mention waxing and spa treatments to keep me looking my best – I easily spent a grand a month on grooming. And then there were the incidental purchases – a new handbag, a new lipstick, some perfume, a present for my little sisters . . . I never stopped to think how much any of it cost because if Sam ran out of cash I knew Toni could hustle hard that night and earn it all back.

By the end of my first year at Diamonds, I had become extremely skilled at making money. Whenever I had a good night, I went home and tried to work out why. Was it the dance I did on stage? Was it the outfit I wore? Or the perfume? Was I getting more money out of older guys or groups of guys? I forensically analysed my performance to work out how I could maximise my income. If I had an outfit that made me money, I became superstitious about it and would take such good care of it. If it started to look old, I would ask Jackie and Terry for an exact replica. I worked out what opening lines worked best, what time of night brought the big money, what days of the week equated to what level of earnings.

Somehow, in the middle of all that naked madness, I found a recipe that made money. And once I had my hustle on a lock down, the money started flowing in. As the months went on, the connection between earning money and feeling fabulous was made at some primeval level inside me: a man giving me £50 means he likes me; £500 means I've got something special; £5,000 means I *am* special. If men are throwing money at me, then I must be beautiful, I must be desirable, I must be bloody good at what I do. And, of course, the more confidence I had, the more desirable I felt and the more able I was to hustle for more money. Some nights I actually felt sorry for the customers because they had no idea just how well they'd been hustled.

From the moment a customer walked into Diamonds he became a cog in a very well-oiled machine. All he would know was that the door staff had been friendly and the waitress had been charming, but behind the scenes a massive intelligence-gathering operation was going on.

What the customer didn't know was that the doorman had been friendly because he had seen him pull up in a BMW. The guys who pull up in Astras and Transit vans don't get the same attention. When the customer was directed to the reception desk, the door boys would have radioed ahead to say this was a man who needed looking after. While the customer was filling in his details in the visitors' book, a receptionist would go and fetch a waitress and pass on the information from the door staff. As she showed him to his table, she would ask him what he was in the mood for, or if he had any special requests, and if it turned out that he liked black girls then the Diamonds grapevine would get that information to me or Sasha, and the DJ would instantly call one of us to the stage. The customer takes a seat knowing none of this: he just thinks Diamonds is brilliant because all he has to do is think about seeing a black girl, or a redhead, or a baby-doll cutey-pie, and lo and behold there she will be in front of him. It wasn't coincidence; it was cooperation.

When a waitress took his drinks order, she would also take his credit card and put it behind the bar. If it was platinum, gold, diamond or black, that information got circulated too. We were like extras in a Jason Bourne movie, passing intelligence from one highly trained operative to the next. By the time Toni sashayed over to him, I was fully briefed on his likes, dislikes, hopes and aspirations.

Some dancers were so fixated on landing a prestige customer that they overlooked the guys who pulled up in Fiestas and Mondeos, but I was becoming one of the top earners at Diamonds because I loved delving for my own intelligence. I might ask Mondeo Man if he'd like some company, or if he'd like to buy a girl a drink, or if he smoked – this was before the smoking ban – I might ask him to spare a cigarette. If I could get him talking, I was pretty sure I could get him spending.

'Oooh, this is my favourite song,' I'd say, no matter what the DJ had just started playing. 'I'd love to dance to it for you.'

So that was my first £20. I would then give him the most erotic dance that is humanly possible without two bodies touching. I would let my hair brush his neck, I would let him feel my breath on his cheek, I would slowly peel my clothes off, letting a flash of knicker make him wonder what was underneath for a minute or two before he actually got to see. And before I had finished, I would ask him if he wanted another dance. There was always a chance that, if he'd not been to a club before, he would think he was getting two dances for the price of one, but he wasn't, he was getting what we called a 'rollover' and some nights I would keep those dances rolling over so slickly that by the time I sat back down, the customer was handing over £100.

On the nights when I didn't get a tip-off from a waitress or another dancer, I had developed my own criteria for spotting a spender. When I was on stage, or walking round the club, or sitting at the bar, I was constantly assessing who was in and where the money was. I would start to zone the club. For instance, I would see that a lot of blonde girls were clustering around one table, so I knew to avoid that. If I saw a lot of girls walk past a customer, I knew it was because he didn't want any dances. If a bottle of champagne arrived on a table, then I knew to go over and introduce myself.

I wasn't there for fun, I was there to make money, and if that lovely stuff wasn't finding its way into my garter, then I was quick to make changes. I would try a different outfit or change my hair. I would keep tweaking my wardrobe or my banter until something clicked. And when I had danced for a guy, I always made sure that the position I sat down in to put my clothes back on allowed me to lean into the customer. He thought I was being seductive, but what I was doing was making sure that as soon as he got his wallet out to pay me I could take a peek inside. How many notes are there? What colour are they? What kind of credit cards does he have? Is there a business card, a holiday snap or a picture of his kids? I now had topics for about half an hour of conversation.

'You know, it's lovely talking to you,' I'd say, 'but I'm not allowed to just sit with a guy. If the management see me with you and I'm not dancing, they're going to want to know why I'm not moving on.'

So out would come the wallet. Maybe he'd want another dance, maybe he'd just want to talk. If I liked him, if I thought he was the kind of guy I could spend some time with, then I might ask him if he wanted a VIP. If he'd never been into a club before, I'd explain that there were private rooms we could go to.

'Five dances out here is £100. If you throw in an extra £50, we could go and sit in a VIP room for an hour and I'll give you unlimited dances.'

All the customer hears is 'unlimited dances' and calculates he's getting a bumper deal, so you go off to the VIP area. A dancer would usually pay the club £20 to use a VIP room for an hour, so it works out at £130-an-hour profit.

I really took pride in what I did. I didn't think that seeing a pair of tits was enough. I wanted my customers to see a level of performance that would blow them away. Sure I wanted money out of them, but I wanted them to think they were getting value for money and I never wanted them to feel hustled or harassed.

That didn't mean I didn't have a few tricks up my sleeves, though. For instance, I almost always elected to pay my house fee in instalments. It wasn't because I couldn't afford to pay the £65 at the beginning of the night (although, if it had been a hard day on Bond Street, I might be a little bit broke), it was because when Mother Theresa came round at midnight and asked for the remaining £20, I could always turn to the customer I was with and get him to pay. If I was with a group of guys, I'd get them to pay a fiver each.

'Oh, please would you pay my house fee? I'll get into trouble if I can't pay it.' They always got their wallets out.

If I had spent a lot of time with a customer and I knew he was satisfied with my service, I would always ask him for a tip. I couldn't believe it when I first heard another dancer ask for a tip, but it earned her £50. So I started asking – 'So, are you going to tip me then?' – and the customers started giving. There was clearly no shame in asking. The transaction of £20 for a dance I understood. The tipping thing I never quite got, but I learnt not to question it too deeply.

If a guy wanted to see me outside the club, I would tell him that I would love to meet him, but that management didn't let us take any cards or bits of paper from a customer. It could be seen as soliciting, and that was in breach of the licence.

'They check us for bits of paper. The only way I can take your number is if you write it on a £20.'

Those £20 notes were still perfectly spendable with a punter's phone number on. If he really liked me, it might even be a £50.

I was on my way to becoming one of the best dancers at Diamonds, but without a doubt I was also one of the best talkers. After a couple of years in the clubs there wasn't a bloke I couldn't talk to or a conversation I couldn't get started. If a group of guys came in and swore blind that they didn't want any dances, I would tell them they could have a dance for a fiver each. If there were six of them, that meant I'd got £30 instead of £20. I was learning that the more you talk, the more you earn. And I found the most ridiculous ways to talk myself into money. One night I made a bet with a guy that I could hang his jacket off my nipple.

'I'm not interested in having a bet.'

'What, you come into a strip club and you're not interested in looking at a beautiful girl's nipples? Is there something wrong with you?'

The rest of his stag party were in fits and one by one they decided that they wanted to know if my nipples really were as amazing as I was making out.

'OK,' I said, 'but you've all got to be in on the bet. What do you reckon? Fifty quid each?'

They thought I was hilarious and they forced their mate to join the bet. I was due for £300 if I could do it.

'Right, you, take your jacket off.'

I peeled down my top, got my boob out and gave it a bit of a rub until my nipple got extremely hard.

'Hand it over.'

I took his jacket, hung it on my nipple, got the noisiest round of applause six people have ever made and collected the money. Whether guys wanted girlie, or dirty, or funny, or dominating, I was alert to every angle and I had the cheek to ask for any colour of note they happened to have on them.

When money is that easy to make, you have to wonder why anyone works nine to five. There were days when I'd get home at 8 o'clock in the morning and from my taxi window I would see commuters with their collars turned up and their umbrellas turned inside out rushing for a train they didn't want to catch so they could do a job they didn't want to do. And as the seasons changed, I would see the same people putting on their lightweight suits or their summer skirts, but the weather didn't make a difference: they still looked miserable. I honestly used to laugh at them because I thought they were mugs.

When I got in, I'd flop on the sofa and money would literally fall out of me. All night I'd have been stuffing notes in my garter, in my bra, in my knickers, in my boots. If I took off a jacket, there were notes in the pockets. When I took off my boots, there were notes stuck to my calves. Seriously. I was like a tree dropping leaves: give me a little shake and something would fall out of somewhere. The notes were sweaty, they were crumpled, they had phone numbers scrawled all over them, but they were all legal tender, and they were all mine.

What a man really wants

Why does a man go into a strip club? Given that he could go to a massage parlour and have sex for £50, he's clearly not coming to a club to get laid. I think women find it hard to understand the real reasons why a man steps through those double doors, because it's never for the reason they think. There are men who don't understand it either: I have several male friends who would never go into a strip club because they don't see the point of getting aroused and having no outlet to do anything about it. A lot of men think that once 'down there' gets stirred there has to be some kind of release, but those are the guys who don't realise that there is a great deal of pleasure to be had from being teased. Unless they meet someone like myself who can take that look of hunger in a man and turn it into confusion, then relaxation and then satisfaction, they will never understand that the release they think they need isn't always necessary. Every night, thousands of men walk out of clubs feeling totally satisfied even though they haven't been touched.

For a lot of men, the very fact that there is a 'no touching' rule in a strip club is the reason to go there. What most people don't realise is that the no-touching rule means there is no pressure on the men to perform. They can have a sexual experience without worrying about their beer belly, their grey pubes, their bent dick or their lack of prowess. No one is going to laugh at them. No one is going to tell them they weren't good enough. They aren't going to worry that they didn't satisfy you. There are no misunderstandings about who should be doing what to whom. And for a lot of men, that is the real release and it's why they find the experience of a striptease so satisfying. It's a sexual experience that is just about them and their fantasies.

In my experience, I have found that most punters fall into one of six categories. The first is The Virgin. He might not actually be a virgin, but he's probably never seen a girl naked. His sexual experiences are fumbled, rushed and unsatisfactory. Coming to a strip club is part of his sex education and he'll probably make his first trip as part of his 18th birthday celebrations with one other mate. How they have the conversation of 'Oh, do you fancy going to a strip club?' I don't know, but the Virgins usually turn up in pairs.

The Virgin does not spend a lot of money, therefore dancers don't spend a lot of time with them, but when they do hand over £20 the Virgin will stare at the parts of a dancer's anatomy he's only ever seen in porn before. And he will stare at them with enormous, bulging eyes as if he is watching an alien invasion.

Because Diamonds was fully nude, we got more than our fair share of teenage gawpers, but as striptease is about teasing just as much as it is about stripping, those boys usually went away thinking they had seen a lot more than they really had. They might get a flash of something when a girl was on the pole, or posing on the stage, but mostly a well-dangled G-string or a thoughtfully placed hand protected our most private of parts from the most intrusive of stares.

Of course, not all Virgins are 18 years old. Some are in their 40s and 50s, and although they may have had moments of ladylove in their life, those moments have been fleeting and rare. These are men who find it very difficult to talk to women because they never got any practice at it. And, being a guy, they don't often talk to other men either, because men don't really talk, not about emotional things. They can't open a bottle of wine and pick up the phone and unburden all their angst on a friend – men just don't have that release. But they do have strip clubs, and quite a lot of the customers who come in on their own just want someone to talk to.

That goes for my second category too: Mr Trapped. There are

quite a few men, you realise when you talk to them for three or four hours, who never thought they'd go to a strip club, but they're not sure where else they can go. They've been married for a while, have got kids, a wife, a mortgage and a lot of pressure. They need some space for themselves: at home they get grief from their wives, in the pub they feel obliged to join in with a macho bragging culture they don't feel a part of and at work they feel they cannot show any signs of weakness. They don't want to leave their wives, but they just don't want to feel so trapped. Coming to a club where there is a no-touching rule is just what they need. Their actions won't be misconstrued, they won't get themselves into a situation they'll regret in the morning, they'll simply spend a few hours in the company of a woman they fancy who will let them talk about themselves for as long as they want . . . just as long as they keep paying for drinks or dances. In a complicated world, the simplicity of a strip club can be very appealing. A strip club is really just a big, gaudy men's therapy room.

The next category is The Pretender, and these men come to a club because it's a fantasy palace. For the Virgins, strip clubs are a Willy Wonka factory of exotic and unexpected delights; for the Pretenders, clubs are a fantasy palace for a completely different reason: when they walk through the double doors they can pretend to be someone they're not. Just as I liked walking into Bond Street shops with wads of cash pretending to be something I wasn't, Pretenders come into a club to get the respect they don't get in the real world. For a few hundred quid they can be a racing driver, a City trader, a Premiership footballer or a millionaire: whatever they say they are is who they are for the night. So long as they hand over the cash, no one is going to rain on their parade and confront them or take them down a peg. Spend enough money and the dancers and the security boys will treat you like visiting royalty. The boundary that means punters can't touch the dancers also means that the dancers can't touch the shabby truth of their real lives: all that matters in a club is what they say matters. Some Pretenders really need those few hours in a fantasy bubble making out they are successful, or rich, or connected. So long as what comes out of their wallet matches what comes out of their gob, it is not a dancer's job to pick apart the Pretenders' lies or decipher their deceit.

The Stags are obviously a big part of a club's clientele. On a Friday and Saturday night, maybe half the men in there will be on a stag night. There's always an interesting dynamic between the men in stag groups: they are always quite happy to pay for dances for the stag but not for themselves. Of course, they get to look at the dancer too, but because it's 'for the stag' they feel released to behave in a way they wouldn't normally.

It was my experience that in every single stag group there was always one guy who would say, 'I'm only here because I've known Malcolm for 20 years.' He wanted it to be known that he didn't have to pay for female attention and always made it quite clear not to ask him for dances. They were very vocal about it and indicated that the whole business was beneath them. It wasn't too hard not to be insulted.

The next category of punter is one that surprises most people. I call them The Homosocials. These are men who come into a club not to impress the women who work there but the other men who might see them in there. Homosocial behaviour can take many forms. First, you get the guys who bring clients in to do business in the clubs. They want their clients to see them surrounded by beautiful women and when they shower the dancers with money it's to impress their client with their generosity and wealth. These are the kinds of men who used to sit in school playgrounds and brag about how many girls they'd kissed. They didn't care about the girls, just about the look on their mates' faces when they told them the number.

That's not to say that these men don't get pleasure out of spending time with dancers. These men love the company of women, but just not quite as much as the admiration of other men. Heterosexual, but homosocial. One of the most extreme cases of homosocial behaviour I saw was a very rich Indian man who came in about once a month and always asked to see Mother Theresa. He would then explain to her the same thing he always explained: he wanted two tables reserved for him and every blonde in the place to join him. Every single blonde. He would pay very handsomely for this exclusivity and the blonde girls, naturally, all adored him. Most of the time all they had to do was laugh at his jokes and be giggly and girlie with one another. This guy just loved the idea that these little birdies were all tweeting and cooing over him. But the thing he loved more than being the centre of the girls' attention was becoming the centre of the entire club's attention when he decided it was time to move to his other table. He got up and his little blonde ducklings followed him to the other side of the club, where they carried on their clucking and chatter. That man was paying for every other man in the club to look at him. He was taking the blonde girls off the floor so that no one else could spend time with him. It was a bizarre variation of the 'see how big my dick is' contest that men play all the time.

There was a very good reason why the girls were happy to spend time with him: he paid them a minimum of £700 a time to sit with him. If he really liked you, you might get over a grand. And of course that was all part of his elaborate bragging: he wanted the other men in the club to see that he had that kind of money. Strange. Very strange.

The next category contains the men who come into strip clubs to try to get away with behaviour they can't get away with in their day-to-day lives. I call these guys The Chancers. Though I could call them Shits. Unfortunately, these guys need a chapter all of their own.

The chancers

When you work in a strip club, you get very used to guys propositioning you for more than a dance. It's standard, and to be honest you expect it. When you've been dancing for a while, you realise that most guys will get a little semi happening in their trousers. The funny thing is that when they've got a bit of a throb on most men will do exactly the same thing: they'll look at you, they'll look down at their crotch, and then they'll look back up at you, expectantly. When that happens, you just know they are going to say something as you lean in.

'Just touch it,' they whisper. 'Just put your knee on it, just brush up against it.'

Some guys will tell you that they are friends with the management and that it's OK if you touch them. Of course, you never knew if they were from the licensing department at the council or the police, and if you did touch them the club would be closed down within the hour. Some men can do this trick – probably all men if I think about it – where they can make it flick up and down, and you will see their trousers move like there's a little frog in there. Each flick is saying, 'touch me, touch me'. It always reminded me of a boy at school who used to do it during maths class, so it always made me laugh. It also made me think that all the men who did it were naughty little schoolboys.

When I first started at Diamonds, none of the girls would ever touch a customer. But as the climate in strip clubs slowly started to change, some girls would whisper back, 'Give me £100', and if the guy said yes then he might find an arm or a leg made contact with his groin. And as more girls said yes, then more guys learnt there was no harm in asking. They were just trailing their rod through the pond hoping someone would bite, and if that happened they didn't care that they had upset a hundred girls to get the one. Guys will always test you.

When guys asked me to touch them, I was always very clear with them. 'No. Shut up,' I'd whisper in their ear, 'lean back and just get your £20 out.' I reckon most of them liked the forceful routine, but it didn't matter how firm you were with some men, they would not shake their belief that a stripper is a worthless sort of woman. And a black stripper? It was clear that some men despised me. Some clearly got a kick out of making derogatory comments. And then there were the men who wouldn't even want you to talk to them. 'Shut up, you little bitch. I know you'll do anything for my money.' Some would kick your knickers away while you finished your dance so that you would have to bend over in front of them.

It's funny, most women think, 'What kind of man goes to a place like that?' And most of those men think, 'What kind of woman works in a place like this?' I guess everyone likes to think they're somehow better than the person in front of them.

Some Chancers come into a strip club because they don't know where else they can go. If they treated a woman badly in their workplace or on the street, they might get sacked or arrested. For those men who really do think that women who undress for money are some kind of sub-species who won't call the cops out of shame, then a strip club is a place to misbehave. And for other guys who know their tastes are deviant or criminal, a strip club is a place to try things out. A man might not know where his nearest brothel is, or which websites exist that can feed his fantasy, but the big strip clubs advertise on billboards and in national newspapers: for some guys, a visit to a strip club is a first step into exploring his unspoken – and unspeakable – desires.

What those guys don't realise is that if they tried something on with me, they would have Eric and his boys to deal with. One night – when I was wearing a baby-doll outfit and had my hair in pigtails – I had a customer who told me he had a fantasy he wanted to indulge in.

'Oh, yeah? Tell me about it.' After all, if I can make a guy's fantasy come true, I should be in line for a healthy tip.

'When you dance, I want you to tell me that you're thinking about having sex with boys.'

He meant young boys. My first thought wasn't that he was a pervert, it was that he was an undercover policeman, so after a bit of a chat I made an excuse that I was so turned on I needed to go and change my knickers. A quick word in Eric's ear and Mr Pervert was taken out the back way where there are no security cameras.

Of all my outfits, it was the baby-doll costume that brought out something sinister in punters.

'How old are you?' they'd ask.

Knowing that they wanted me to be young, I'd say 18 – any younger and you're not allowed to dance. 'You look 14,' they'd say. 'I've got this fantasy about younger women. How about a VIP?'

I negotiated a VIP with one customer for £250, but then he said that he wanted me to call him 'Daddy'.

'No, I don't want to do that.' I was firm but discreet.

'What do you mean?' He instantly blew his top. 'Of course you'll do what I say!' He then threw his money at me. 'Take it and do what you're told.'

At that point I just gave a little signal to the boys on the door and he was back in his car within five minutes. Eric's boys didn't beat him up, but they threatened to unless he handed over his wallet. In his wallet they found the guy's business card.

'Now, unless you want your colleagues to know what a pervert you are, you will never come back here. Understand?'

Of course, they weren't going to leave it like that.

'You have really upset Toni tonight. I don't think you meant to upset her, did you? I'm sure you'd like to apologise, wouldn't you? What do you think, is £250 enough compensation? I do.'

Security then gave me the money, and I gave half of it straight back to them as a tip. The way I saw it, if it hadn't been for them I wouldn't have seen any of it.

It was because you got so many Chancers coming into a club

that I was always glad that Auntie Nya had got me to use a stage name. I was like one of those Russian dolls with Toni on the outside providing a hard shell to protect Sam on the inside. Mostly, punters could throw what they liked at Toni because she wasn't real, but every now and then Toni's guard went down and Sam got hurt.

I developed a pretty good antenna for sussing out who was a Chancer, but occasionally my early-warning system failed. One night, when I'd been at Diamonds for a couple of years and was right at the top of my game, I was dancing for a guy who had come in on his own. A nondescript, average, middle-aged kind of guy – the kind of bloke who is invisible because he's so ordinary. He seemed to enjoy my dancing, so I asked him if he wanted a rollover. He said yes. At the end of the second dance I asked if he wanted another. Yes again. *Great, now I'm on £60 and if I play my cards right I might get a ton out of this one.*

When you do several dances in a row for someone, you try to mix up your routine a bit. So I turned my back on the guy, put my hands up against the wall and started wiggling my arse when all of a sudden I felt this extreme pain in my buttock. I whipped round and saw that he hadn't pinched me – he had bitten me. I screamed, partly out of shock, partly out of pain, but mostly out of rage. In the few seconds it took me to work out what to do next – give him my best right hook to the bridge of his nose – two security boys were on us. The doorman lunged in and pulled the chair out from under him, dragged him up by his collar and took him straight out to the back door. There are only two ways to leave a club: through the double doors at the front or the fire escape at the back where the security cameras were positioned so that Eric's boys could do whatever was necessary. We never saw the biter in Diamonds again.

The damage he did wasn't just to my skin. I was worried he might have drawn blood. Thankfully he hadn't, so I didn't need to worry about HIV, but his teeth had gone straight through Toni and sunk right into Sam. No punter had ever done anything like that before and there was no way it was an accident. He had planned it. He had picked on me to help fulfil his fantasy and I felt violated.

Humiliated. I realised that the whole rollover deal had been about taking my guard down. I felt played. I felt used.

The fact that I had misjudged him so badly threw me. I figured the best thing I could do was to get right back in the saddle, but I found I just couldn't do it. I only managed two more dances that night. I could no longer turn my back on a customer, and I didn't want them to see the mark on my bum. In that single moment, that Chancer had made Diamonds seem ten times bigger. Before him, Diamonds had been a safe little place where I had felt I was in control, but now I saw dangers I hadn't previously noticed and anticipated grief where I'd once expected fun. He had done something no other customer had done: he had made me feel small.

When I woke up the next day, I lay in bed and actually wondered if I could even go to work that night. He had really got to me and I didn't know what to do about it. After a couple of hours of anxious worry, I realised I couldn't let one man have such a big impact on my life, or on my earnings. Dealing with the Chancers, I told myself, is just part of the job. So I went in to work that night and I made sure I nailed it. I made about £1,500 just from treading carpet and hustling for one £20 after another. Toni still had her game.

Occasionally there were times when I thought a man was so disgusting that I could not bring myself to take his money. Objectively, this one particular customer did not do anything so bad as bite me, but he nevertheless hurt me very deeply. I'd spent most of the night with him and a couple of his clients. They were real high rollers and I'd done quite well out of them. When I saw that the guy's clients had left, I went over to him – after all, I knew how much was still in his wallet – as I thought there might be some clean-up money to be had. I sat down next to him and he turned to look me up and down. He had a sneer on his face.

'What was that look for?' I asked, only half-joking.

'Why have you come back?'

'Cos we were having a good time with your clients . . .'

'Exactly, you're a good-time girl, my clients have now gone, this is what they're into, I'm not into it. How did I give you the impression that I'd ever want you to come back and sit down?'

I was gobsmacked. The contempt on his fact was truly shocking to me: it was like he hated me, or like he had just trodden one of his snakeskin shoes into a mongrel's shit.

'Here's £20 to go away.'

Really? Can he really spend half the fucking night with me and be so fucking rude? *Really?*

'Not only am I going to give you your £20 back, but I'm going to give you a piece of advice. There was no need for what you just said. You are in an environment where when a man sits down it's my job to come round and see if he wants a dance, that's my basic job description. Seeing as we've had previous dances, I wasn't aware that you were only here because your customers were here, but I notice that they've left and you're still here. Do you know what? You're probably not the person you think you are. You are probably the person I think you are, which is an arsehole and a nasty piece of work.'

I stood up and walked away.

'By the way,' I added, 'I am about to get you kicked out and you should never come back here again. I'm a human being and there's no need to talk to someone like that when they are just doing their job.'

His contempt, his you're-no-different-from-the-shit-on-my-shoes attitude really hurt me. If I had bought food with the money he had offered me it would have tasted like poison.

The regulars

The nights I made the most money were the nights my regulars came in. Instead of earning hundreds, I would hope to take home thousands. By the time I left Diamonds, I had seven guys who would come in to see me at least once a month, and six of them always paid me more than a grand, a couple of them considerably more.

A guy decides to become a regular at a strip club because he's made to feel special. Some men spend their money on golf or football or gadgets. Maybe they have the fanciest set of clubs and the coolest gear so they look like they've made it when they play a round with the neighbours. Or maybe a guy has a season ticket and follows his team to away matches. Maybe he likes a flutter. Or maybe he has an iPhone as well as a BlackBerry and an X-Box and a Wii with all the latest games. People reckon it's women's spending that's out of control, but men know how to spend a lot of money on making themselves feel better too.

Some guys learn that the thing that gives them the most pleasure to spend their money on is visiting a club. After all, where else can he go to have several beautiful young women throw themselves at him, wrap themselves round him like boa constrictors and treat him like a god?

In just the same way that a man who tips a waiter will get the best table and the best service if he goes back to the same restaurant, a guy who tips heavily in a strip club will always get the VIP treatment. The doormen will greet him by name, he will always be shown to his favourite table and the barman will remember his tipple, even down to how many ice cubes he likes. If it's known that he likes to spend his first half an hour in the club on his own, then he will be left alone for half an hour. If it's known he only likes redheads, then the brunettes will leave him alone. For the hours that a regular is in the club he is treated like he is Tom Cruise, Hugh Hefner and David Beckham rolled into one. Whatever he wants, however he wants it, whenever he wants it. It might cost him several grand, but that's what plenty of guys spend on making themselves feel better.

I called one of my regulars The General. He was an old colonial type with Brylcreemed white hair, a silk scarf round his neck and a comb in his top pocket. A very well-to-do guy with impeccable manners. Sometimes he came in with a client, and we all knew to leave him alone while he was doing business. When the client left, he would usually ask to see Theresa and he would tell her which girl he wanted to see on that particular day. It was always one of two girls – either me or Sasha Bush Hut Woman. He had a thing about black girls from his time in Kenya.

There is a certain amount of etiquette about regulars – at least there was when I was working at Diamonds – and that meant that dancers did not try to steal another girl's regular. It's a bit like a dealer moving onto another dealer's turf – war can break out. Which is why Sasha is due a lot of respect – I had only got to meet The General because she wasn't on shift one night. But then, when a man spends five grand a time I suppose there's enough money for both of you. It was quite unusual for two dancers to share a regular the way me and Sasha did, but we understood that a man with such manners would find it unseemly for us to squabble over him, so we never approached him and waited for him to tell Theresa which of us he wanted that night.

The club grapevine meant we'd know the moment he'd walked in the club. Either one of the doormen would give us the nod, or one of the other dancers would break the news. Often we'd actually know in advance, either because he had told us he'd be in on a particular night and had requested that we work, or because he had phoned the club in advance to make sure whichever of us he preferred was rostered on.

Once Theresa had spoken to him, the bar would then send over his drink – always a gin and tonic with a little squeeze of lemon and a little squeeze of lime and two straws – and he would sit there and watch a few dances while either me or Sasha would go into the changing room and get ready for him. I really felt it was important with my regulars that they knew I had remembered how they liked me to dress, and with The General he liked long, slinky evening wear, so I'd change into something demure and put on long drop earrings, reapply my lipstick and have a little spray of perfume. I wanted to walk up to his table and make him think he was the only man I had talked to all night. I wanted to be fresh for him and I wanted him to really feel like he was on a date.

'How have you been?' I would ask. If he'd been away, I would ask about his holiday, if he had mentioned he was going to the races I would ask if he'd won, and if he said he was seeing his tailor I would ask about his new suit. I made a real effort to remember everything my regulars told me about themselves so that they knew I was interested in them, not just their money. I didn't want them to feel preyed upon, I wanted them to feel appreciated and respected.

Sometimes his client would stay with him, and when that happened The General would ask me to select another girl to come and join us. If he made a lot of money from that deal, then I would get a nice little bonus for choosing the right girl. He never gave the money to me directly, he always asked Theresa to take it because he wanted the club to know how much he was spending. And I suppose, if there was no direct exchange of money, then it maintained the illusion that we were on a date. Theresa would then put the money in an envelope and give it to me at the end of the night, which was the discreet way of hiding a windfall from everyone else – although everyone knew he only liked black girls, if everyone had known just how much money he spent they might have started pestering him, and that would have meant he wouldn't have come back. The money in the envelope was never less than £1,000, but sometimes it was as much as £5,000. I would then share that out with the other girl, perhaps £500, maybe a similar amount to Theresa and give £50s to the barman and the guys on the door. It was only because those people were doing their job correctly that I was able to earn my money, so the etiquette was always to spread the money around. Most of it, however, was just for me. In cash. The General's money bought me a lot of handbags, a lot of clothes and a whole closet full of shoes.

When a customer is paying you that kind of money, you take them very seriously. When I got home, I would make notes about the conversations we had had so that I would be able to ask him the right questions when he next came in. If he mentioned his birthday, I made a note of it. How many kids, what ages, boy or girl. His wife's name, his wife's birthday. I wanted them to know that I'd been listening because I wanted to be that perfect girl for them. I saw it as part of my job, and it was a crucial part too, because they kept coming back, and kept paying me in stacks of notes. People always think that a stripper makes her money with her body and never think that she makes a lot, lot more with her mind. At one stage I had different regulars coming in on three nights of the week, and that meant I was taking home a very healthy sum.

I very nearly missed out on one of my most lucrative regulars. It was one of those nights when there were so few punters in the club that Theresa had let some of the girls go early. And for those of us who were left it was going to be a struggle to make back our house fee and our cab ride home. There were probably about 20 girls at the bar waiting for the clock to strike 4 a.m. so they could get to bed. Every now and then, though, you'd do a little tour of the place to see if anyone wanted a dance, but because I already had a couple of hundred in my garter I wasn't too bothered if I didn't make any more.

I'd noticed two guys – middle-aged, grey, spreading around the middle – early on in the evening, but they were deep in conversation and hadn't had a single dance off anyone. They were there to talk business and so I left them to it. It was probably around 2 a.m. when one of them called out to me.

'What's wrong with me then?' He had a broad Irish accent.

'I'm sorry?'

'What's wrong with me? Do I smell?'

'I . . . no . . . er . . .'

'Well, every other girl in this place has asked me 20 times if I want a dance and you haven't even said hello. It's a form of cruelty.'

'Are you talking to me?'

'Yes, I'm talking to you with that big round arse of yours, come and sit down.'

So I did.

'So,' he said, 'why have you been ignoring me all night?'

'To be honest, I didn't think I was your cup of tea.'

'Did you now?'

'And I've made enough for the night, so I'm just taking it easy. So, are you after a dance, then?'

'No, not really.'

'You don't want a dance?'

'What are you drinking?'

'Ah, get me a gin and tonic, Paddy.'

His mate started laughing at this point.

'What? Every Irishman's called Paddy, isn't he?'

He laughed again as 'Paddy' waved a waitress over to order some drinks. The three of us sat there chatting and laughing for the next two hours, getting merrily pissed.

'Do you know,' Paddy said when he got up to leave, 'we've been talking all this time and you haven't hustled me for a dance. I don't think that's ever happened to me in a club before.'

And just for that he handed me £500.

'It's been lovely talking to you, Toni. I'm going to be in town next Tuesday. Will you be working then?'

'Well, I could.'

True to his word, he came in on Tuesday – on his own this time – and the two of us sat there with a selection of food and drinks and carried on the conversation as if we were old mates. I asked him if he wanted to go into the VIP area, but he said he didn't want to be rushed and was quite happy where he was. I felt I should just sit back and relax: he'd already proven himself and I knew I would get paid for sitting and talking to him.

Even though it felt like we were buddies, when he did want me to dance there was no embarrassment because we both knew what we were there for. Sometimes he'd give me £500 and ask me to go and find a couple of other girls who I thought he might like, and we'd either do doubles for him or sit and talk.

Doing a double with another dancer can be odd. If the customer has chosen both of you, there's a chance that you might not like each other, or might never even have spoken to one another if one of you is new to the club. If that's the case, then it's important that the customer doesn't know that: for the time the two of you are together you pretend to be the best of friends and let him indulge his fantasy for a little bit longer. And when you dance together, you might untie the other's dress or flick her hair off her face – small, intimate gestures which convey that more is going on than actually is. With Paddy, because I could pick my own doubles, it was much easier to spend time in the other girl's company, which meant at times I was being paid to hang out with my mates.

He always said he didn't mind what a girl looked like so long as she was like me, and by that he meant funny and polite and definitely not hungry. He used to love watching me run round the club finding him girls, and I loved dishing out the money. It was like being the banker in Monopoly. Sometimes there'd be a little parade in front of our table and I'd be like, 'Go and change your outfit and there might be a dance in it for you' or 'Come back after midnight and we'll see how we're doing.' I'd act like another punter and we'd sit and chat as the girls scurried away to get changed. Those nights with Paddy were my chance to pay back dancers who had helped me make money in the past or to give a newbie a confidence boost.

I never negotiated money with Paddy. He had proved himself to me and I knew he would always make it worth my while. Most of the nights I saw him, he would hand over a grand; once it was £700, but many times it was £3,500. I never asked why the amount changed so much, and he never offered an explanation. It was always enough.

Normally, I never found out how my customers made their money. It's just one of the unwritten rules of dancing that you don't ask, but with Paddy it was hard not to know. The more we talked, the more I realised just how big his empire was and how rich he was. His wife and kids lived in a mansion in Ireland, his mistress had an apartment in London and that was in addition to his own apartment in London. Plus a house in France. Him coming into a club and spending £5,000 was like most people going into a pub and buying a round of drinks.

Because Paddy knew there was no chance that I would become another mistress, it meant there was a really healthy boundary to our relationship. I might have wanted some of his wealth and a big slice of his lifestyle, but I wasn't prepared to sleep with a customer to get it. I think most dancers probably would have. Marrying a rich man, or being kept by one, is most dancers' dream. The fact that I wasn't asking him for more when he knew a lot of other girls would meant that we had a very honest friendship. After a few months, we started seeing each other outside the club. He took me to see my very first football match from his own private box and even took me shopping to buy an outfit to go to the match in.

Then, after about a year and half, Paddy never came in again. At first I thought he might be spending the summer at his place in France, but then I started wondering if he had found another club or had simply tired of me and – like Tricky – had moved on to someone new. I racked my brain to think if I had said something that had upset him, but the last time he'd been in we'd been laughing our heads off. It was a mystery that I wouldn't solve for several years.

I didn't just make money from my own regulars; sometimes another dancer's regular could be very generous. Max started off as one of TJ's regulars, but he asked for doubles so often that we all got to know him – and love him. Max was a tiny little Indian man who we would have called Min if we hadn't liked him so much. He was probably in his late 50s but could have passed for early 40s and always wore the same outfit: jeans, polo shirt, white trainers. It was his Rolex that let you know he really had money. He ran about 20 corner shops in west London and always had ready cash. He probably popped in most nights, but on Friday nights he brought in all the guys who worked for him. They all got a dance and a few drinks. It was his team-building technique.

Max was very well connected and loved to help out. If a girl needed a new phone, he would get her a phone – no charge. He would come in with gifts of jewellery and perfume for us. Once, he even arranged for my flat to be recarpeted. Again, no charge. There's a way a guy can offer you something and you know he's looking to see if he can expose a weakness, to try to find out how much you want something so he can see if he can make you beg for it later. Max just was not like that. You meet a lot of sharks in nightlife and a lot of arseholes, so when you meet a guy like Max they tend to shine in that environment.

We all liked Max because he knew why we were there. As soon as we'd sit down he'd get his wallet out. He never wanted a favour and if we ever tried to thank him for his gifts with a free dance he would always refuse. The gifts were genuinely gifts and he didn't want anything in return. If you'd had a bad experience with another customer, you'd go running to Max for half an hour to reassure yourself that not all men are shits.

Max liked the feeling of having girls cooing over him. A short little Indian guy with a Buddha belly was not going to get that attention anywhere else. So most nights he would spend a bit of time in the club. When TJ ruffled his hair and stroked his cheek he was as delighted as he was the first time she did it. TJ and Max had a real bond; it was a very odd friendship because TJ also got to know his wife Mira. She wasn't exactly happy that her husband came to Diamonds so often, but she was reassured that none of us were trying to steal her husband.

My flatmate at the time, a really lovely, honest and generous girl called Julie, also had a regular I made money from occasionally. I'd got to know Julie on doubles, and she had always sought me out at the end of the night to give me my share of her tip. Not everyone bothered to do that if they thought they could get away with keeping the cash themselves. But Julie wasn't like that. She was a real honey. Her regular was so posh he probably had a title and a seat in the House of Lords. Born in pinstripes, that kind of posh. Eton. Oxford. City. And one night me and Julie were doing some doubles for His Lordship when he mentioned that he was going to Ascot at the end of the week.

'I've never been to Ascot,' Julie said.

'And I'd love to go to Ascot,' I added.

Within ten minutes, His Lordship had formed a plan. He decided he wanted to take a group of dancers to experience Ascot for the first time. He picked six girls who, like me and Julie, were really, genuinely curious to know what going to the races was like. He didn't want to take the girls who would be on their phones all the time moaning to their boyfriends; he wanted the girls that would be wide-eyed and excited by it. He then gave us each £500 to buy an outfit for our day trip and arranged for his driver to pick us up the next day.

Just as he had promised, his driver pulled up outside our house in this massive black limo and took us to Mayfair and then on to a little Italian restaurant at the back of Harrods for a meal. The bill was, naturally, taken care of.

Then, on the Friday, the driver turned up again and took the six of us to the races. It was the first time I'd worn a proper hat and we all felt very la-di-dah about the whole adventure. And when we got there, His Lordship was waiting in his box for us with several bottles of champagne on ice. We were squealing like little piglets with excitement, and that was before he gave us £500 in betting money. Each.

Until we'd got there, there was always a chance that he wasn't who he was pretending to be and that his box would also be full of a few mates who had been told a gaggle of strippers were on their way. And when 'mates' hear 'strippers' they think 'hookers'. But His Lordship wasn't like that and he simply enjoyed having us all to himself. I think he really liked the noise girls make when they're together, and, of course, he also liked the looks he got from the people in the next box – a mix of envy and disapproval.

He clearly had loads of money and this was the kind of thing he chose to do with it. He loved us frittering away a tiny portion of his wealth on horses with ridiculous names. He loved us getting tipsy on his champagne. And he loved that he could do that. Looking back, it was one of the nicest days of my life because all any of us wanted was to have fun.

One of the reasons I enjoyed myself so much that day was because I knew that if it wasn't for dancing, if it wasn't for nightlife, I would never have come across someone like him. Our paths would never have crossed and I would never have had that experience. On another occasion, a customer couldn't believe I had never tasted oysters and insisted on taking me to Quaglino's to try some. There were customers who would buy dancers a car, or sort out a loan for you when you couldn't produce proof of earnings, or who would pay the deposit for a flat: there were just some men who liked to help damsels in distress, and we were plenty happy to be helped.

It's one of the reasons why I found dancing so addictive: I never knew who was going to come through the doors or how much they were going to pay me. I rarely knew how they made their money, but I was fascinated by the way they spent it and I was hungry for as much of it as possible to end up in my garter. By the time I turned 20, my fascination with big money was turning into a little bit of an obsession.

The danger zone

Working in clubs can make relationships with men difficult, even if they're not gangsters. For starters, you're never sure why a man wants to date you. Is it because he wants to tell everyone he's dating a stripper? Has he had all these fantasies of good girls going bad? Or is it because he wants to do filthy dirty stuff and he thinks you're the kind of girl he can experiment on? Does he think you're going to spend your entire time together teasing and titillating him? No matter who he is, no matter where you meet him, you're going to doubt his motives at some point, and that's never healthy.

Then there's the practicality of dating a stripper. Is he going to tell his family what you do for a living? Will he ever be able to take you home? Even before the first date you know you're going to have to avoid every family party, which can make it difficult to connect and even harder to commit. A lot of girls get dumped for being secretive or distant and it's all because they're trying to avoid being asked the question that everyone asks at parties: 'So, what do you do?' It's such a normal question, but it is terrifying to have to answer it if you're not sure of your ground. Which is why a lot of girls lie about what they're doing, which in turn means they then have to remember every lie they've ever told because there will always be some aunt who asks about that conference you made up or that deal you were fabricating. The stress is immense.

Even if you tell your boyfriend what you do for money, he might be put in the position of lying to keep your profession from his family. That means – at some level – a distance opens up between him and his family, and the stresses and strains that follow on from that creep into your relationship.

It took me a decade of working in clubs before I realised what the biggest danger was – it's missing out on the good guys. The problem is that, as a stripper, you think you know men. You know what makes them tick, you know how to manipulate them and, often, you pity them. There is a look a punter gives you – and none of them know they're doing it – when you are dancing in front of them that I can only describe as hunger. They look at you and they *want* you. And when you see that hunger you know you've got them. However, when you see guys in the civilian world, they get that look too – it's genetic, it's evolution – and as a stripper you make the mistake of lumping the good guys in with the guys in the club. You miss out on a lot because you think you know the signs men give, but it takes a long old time to properly interpret those signs. In the meantime, you've missed out on something good and more than likely ended up with something twisted or rotten or doomed.

That's because there are plenty of men out there who like to date strippers because they are easy to manipulate, bully and abuse. Most dancers don't want people outside of nightlife to know what they do, and when people are trying to keep a secret they are easy to blackmail. Guys will say to dancers, 'No one else would have you, you've got to stay with me because I know what you do, and I understand why. It's not ideal that you work until 4.30 in the morning, but I love you and that's why I pick you up.' And then, of course, when a girl is in a relationship, it's natural to feel a bit of guilt about undressing in front of other men, and sometimes the girl herself will make it up to her boyfriend, but other times it will be the boyfriend who demands compensation in the form of money or sexual favours or the forgiveness of bad behaviour.

Dancers don't realise they're vulnerable and I never quite understood how a girl who could feel so powerful performing and teasing the men in the club could become so afraid with men outside the club. I saw so many girls date and sometimes marry losers for the primary reason that he was still awake at 4.30 a.m. You make compromises when the pool of talent on offer is so small, and at least if someone is awake you have some company rather than being alone. Those dancers had someone to talk to but no self-respect.

No one knows how a relationship will pan out. A dancer might think she can handle a less-than-perfect man, and a man might think he can handle a dancer, but as the months go by things happen that make good people do bad things. Imagine if your partner came home at five in the morning with £10k in cash. Would you believe them if they swore blind that no one had touched them and that they hadn't had sex with a stranger for that money? And if you were the dancer, might you try to smooth things over by giving your partner some of your money?

In my experience, girls who went home with a lot of cash had to answer a lot of questions. And when men learn that by turning up the heat they can get their hands on some – or all – of their wife's earnings, a vicious and abusive cycle starts. Anyone who carries that amount of cash is vulnerable to getting mugged, but more often than not it was only when dancers got home that they were robbed.

What was really sad was that sometimes the way a girl would deal with the fact that she was being abused was to take it out on another dancer. My flatmate Julie was just about the sweetest girl you are ever going to meet in a club: a good-natured honey with decent morals. She was also, it has to be said, a target for the less scrupulous.

Most nights, we shared a cab back to south London with two other girls who lived near our house. I called them Ulrika and Cornelius because one of them looked like Ulrika Jonsson and the other like one of the monkeys from *Planet of the Apes*. If Ulrika or Cornelius had had a bad night, and they had seen Julie have a good night, you could guarantee that they would start a conversation in the back of the cab that would go something like this:

'You didn't have a very good night tonight, did you?'

'No, how about you?'

'Rubbish.'

'And we've got our rent to pay tomorrow.'

'I don't have it cos I had to pay for my highlights, didn't I?'

'Yeah. What are we going to do? The landlord said he'd chuck us out if we were late with the rent again.'

And so it would go on until good-hearted Julie said that she would lend them the money. They never paid her back and when they did have a good night they never offered to pay for the cab or buy everyone breakfast. They were just mean. Actually, no, they were total bitches, but I soon found out why – they were getting it far worse from their boyfriends when they got home. They couldn't take it out on their men, so they took it out on Julie.

Ulrika's boyfriend was a particularly awful waste of space. Mikey was the real reason she could never pay the rent because he spunked it on the bookies and dope. He was the kind of guy who said, 'Oh, it's your birthday next week, if you give me some money I'll buy you a present.' Mikey was an arsehole. By contrast, Ulrika had a regular called Richard who wanted to marry her. He bought her gifts and regularly paid for her to get her hair and nails done. He put her on a pedestal, yet she stayed with her waster boyfriend. One of the gifts Richard gave her was one of the very first Playstations. I think he'd worked for the company that imported them and it was one of only a hundred in the country at the time. As soon as Ulrika got it home, Pikey Mikey took it to the pub and sold it for a tenner. It was probably worth 50 times that.

A few months after that happened, I was out on the floor at Diamonds and saw Ulrika with Richard. They started off having a few drinks and then she stood up to dance for him. This night, though, Ulrika had a surprise in store for Richard. Tattooed on the body he knew so well and paid so much to see each week were the letters M I K E Y, right above her money-maker! Richard stood up and left, never to come back because he could no longer pretend that Ulrika was his.

I later heard that Mikey had not been able to deal with the fact that Richard could do things for Ulrika that he couldn't afford to do. He had become so paranoid about her running off with her wealthy client that he insisted on Ulrika getting the tattoo to prove that she belonged to him and no one else. The good news, if there is any in this kind of situation, is that with Richard out of the picture Ulrika's earnings nosedived and Mikey found himself with a lot less money to spunk. Some kind of justice, I guess.

Mikey was not the worst of boyfriends I heard about. I never met Angel's boyfriend, but I heard him. Every half-hour without fail. He had got Angel so completely under the thumb that she had to phone him every 30 minutes and I would hear his tinny little voice through the receiver. His manipulation was subtle: he didn't bark at Angel and she didn't come in with bruises that needed to be hidden, she didn't even have to tell him how much money she was making when she called. She would say things like, 'I'm just hanging out in the changing rooms with the girls', or 'I'm just changing my shoes', and make it sound like it was her decision to call him and see how he was doing. But as the months went on I realised he had programmed her to call and that the fear of what he would do to her if she didn't call kept her loyal. I even saw her leave a regular to go into the changing room and call him.

Every now and then, a girl would be so abused by her boyfriend that it wasn't just me who noticed. The first time you help a girl to cover her bruises you just accept the excuse she gives you. The second time, you know you need to ask if everything's all right at home. The third time, you know there's no point in asking.

The abuse isn't always violent. We all got a surprise when Cornelius – a ballsy, feisty woman who would give as good as she got – ended up in a relationship with one of her regulars who turned out to be a drug dealer. First it was free cocaine, then heroin, and once she was addicted he would get her to pay for her drugs any way he chose – her entire week's takings, making her sleep with a client, or just taking so much shit from him that she suffocated under it.

It's not surprising, then, that I often found myself having conversations with TJ and Julie about whether there were any decent men in the world, and if there were, what chance was there that they would want to marry us. It seemed nightlife and a good life could not go together. Which is why when a beautiful Colombian girl called Maria was proposed to by one of her regulars we organised the biggest hen party ever for her. Most dancers have a dream – whether they say it out loud or not – that a man in shining armour and riding a white charger will swoop through the club and carry them off into a happily-ever-after situation. Maria's regular wasn't a millionaire, but he was a decent man with a decent job who had completely fallen in love with her. They bought a house together, planned to start a family and it was as if all our dreams had come true: if it could happen to Maria, it could happen to any of us. Her hen night was one of the biggest celebrations I have ever been to.

When Maria came back to work about a month after her hen night, we knew something bad had happened. We didn't know how bad. On their honeymoon, she told us as mascara-coloured tears streaked her face, they had stayed in a beautiful new hotel. Everything was pristine because they were among the first guests. Unfortunately the hotel was not quite finished, and when her husband had leant against the rail on their balcony it had given way. He fell over 100 ft and died a few minutes after he'd hit the ground.

Her dreams had been shredded and her heart was broken, but she now had a mortgage to pay and the only way she knew to get the money together was to come back to Diamonds. We all wanted the best for Maria, but I think we all felt the same way about her after she came back: she was a painful reminder of how difficult it was to break away from nightlife.

Maybe all the lunches at Harvey Nicks or the shopping sprees on Bond Street were a form of compensation. We couldn't see a future for ourselves so we may as well spend what we had as soon as we had it. And if a customer had treated you badly, or shown contempt, the best revenge was using his money to buy something that made you feel good. And if shopping made you feel good, then you had to go back to work to earn the money to be able to shop. It was a cycle, and it was also – I can see now – a trap. Once you're in, getting out of dancing is so much harder than you think it's going to be.

I still saw Alison most months, if not most weeks. When we'd come back from Denmark, she'd made the decision not to dance and it was fascinating to me how different our lives were. If I'd had a good night, I'd text her at four in the morning saying, 'I know you're still in bed, but I'm going to meet you after work tonight and buy you dinner.' I'd get a text back from her at 7 a.m. when she got up and at 5.30 p.m. we'd meet in Soho for cocktails and dinner. At 8 p.m., I'd go to work and she'd go home.

It was bizarre how different our lives had become. She had made a different choice and was now firmly on another path, working in the civil service in a smart little Dorothy Perkins suit and earning £25k a year. I would turn up to meet her in short skirts and thigh-high boots and people must have looked at us and wondered what on earth we had in common.

The sad thing, the truly tragic thing, is that I pitied Ali. I thought her life was boring, I thought she was stupid to work so hard for so little money, and I thought anyone who shopped in Dorothy Perkins was boring and conventional. I liked shocking her with my tales from the club, and I was so sure that my life was more interesting than hers that I rarely asked her about her work. It pains me to say this, and I'm ashamed of myself, but I've got to come clean: I thought I was better than her. Despite all the pain and misery I saw inflicted on girls in clubs, I thought Ali had made the wrong decision and I had made the right one.

What a fucking idiot.

Fast money, fast times

This might sound odd, given the stories I've just told you, but a strip club is actually – well, it was back then – a surprisingly safe place to work. If a punter misbehaved, the security boys were only too happy to show him the error of his ways, and as everyone made money on the back of our looks, our talent and our presence, they all had to look out for us. We were the sweets in the sweetie shop, and the merchandise needed to be protected. When we left the club each night, we were walked to our cabs by one of Eric's boys, and as we always used the same cab company the drivers knew to treat us well or end up a) out of pocket, and b) in hospital. Without us, no one made their cut. Or to quote something Brad told me one day: 'Every day we come in here and open up and we just pray that you girls will turn up. A strip club without dancers is like a pub without beer.'

Which is why when we went through a stage where Julie and I kept getting burgled I knew it wouldn't end up well for the burglar. What was odd was that we only ever got burgled when there was money in the house, so my inner Miss Marple detected that it was someone who knew if we'd had a good night. The prime suspect was Ulrika's waster boyfriend Mikey. If she couldn't get Julie to hand over money in the cab on the way home, then perhaps she was sending him round while we were at work.

One of the doormen at Diamonds said he could set us up with a security camera so we could find out who was doing it. It was quite exciting looking at the footage, even though nothing happened for most of the tape, cos it felt like being on a TV cop show. First of all we saw Julie and me leaving, then we fast-forwarded until we saw some flyers being posted and then fast-forwarded again until we saw someone we recognised knock on the door. When there was no answer, he nipped round the back. It wasn't Mikey; it was our taxi driver.

It made perfect sense: he heard us talk about having good nights and he knew when we'd be out of the house. And once he'd got inside it wouldn't have taken him long to find the money: we hardly spent any time at home so didn't really have a lot of furniture and the kitchen cupboards were bare; looking back, the bright yellow biscuit tin was the only place in the entire house to keep the cash.

There was no point calling the police, especially because Eric's boys saw it as a point of principle to protect us. The taxi driver was dealt with in the nightlife way. I don't suppose he ever nicked anything again. There's also a pretty good chance he never drove a car again.

The shocking thing about this story is that even though the driver had taken about six grand in total, it didn't really mean anything to me. I felt sick about it for approximately two seconds. In fact, I got home that night, pulled the two grand I had made out of my boots and my bra and put it right back in the same biscuit jar. Easy come, easy go. If he hadn't taken it, I would only have spent it on shoes or bags or clothes. When you can earn money so easily, it doesn't seem to hurt when it goes.

Towards the end of my time at Diamonds I was earning £5,000 most weeks. I can't quite believe it, but I probably made around £200k a year and pretty much all of it was in cash. If I'd stayed in retail, I would have been doing well if I'd taken home 10 per cent of that. These days, I wish someone had told me that £25k would have been enough to put a deposit on a house, or £10k would have set me up with a small business, but there was no one in my life who could make those kinds of suggestions because we were all doing the same thing with our cash: spending it as quickly as we earned it.

I was definitely one of the top earners and it felt really good to be a big fish in a small pond. If they had given out degrees to strippers I would have a whole wall of certificates. I remember, every now and then, a new track would be in the charts and all the girls would want to dance to it. One of them was Montel Jordan's 'Get It On'. But because I tipped the DJ, and because everyone knew I would make money if I danced to it, and because they knew that when I made money I would spread it around the club, I was the one that got to dance to it.

I took a great deal of pride in my stage shows. I had never forgotten what Auntie Nya had told us that first night in Denmark: your stage show is your shop window. I wanted every man in the room to notice Toni, and I wanted him to think that to get my level of performance up close for just £20 was the bargain of the year. And most nights I did walk off stage and straight up to the men who had smiled at me on stage or nodded their approval.

What you won't realise if you've never been in a club is that there is a lot of hanging around. For the first few hours, there might be more dancers than punters – especially these days when clubs deliberately have up to a hundred girls working each shift – and so you are sitting waiting for your turn on the stage and your luck to change. When you finally get on stage, you are desperate for every man to look at you, to lust after you. You want to be leered at cos it is way, way better than being ignored. And the best way of dealing with men who said they weren't into black girls was to get on stage and say, 'Yeah? How about a black girl who can hang on with one hand and do the splits in mid-air? Still think I'm not your flavour?' Even when I didn't have a regular coming in, I could still take home £1,500, and about half of that was tips.

Because Mother Theresa was so good at sorting out the rota, every girl who worked was likely to make good money. Thirty of us, sometimes five hundred of them: the maths was definitely in our favour. And when everyone was making money, everyone could be generous.

'Toni. Guy at table 23 wants a black girl.'

'Cheers. Some guys over in the corner said they wanted some double trouble later, so come and join me.'

Then Theresa would come up and say that a gentleman near the door had requested the pleasure of my company, plus I'd have at least five guys who I'd made eye contact with from the stage to approach. It was constant mental arithmetic: £20 here, can't stop to talk cos there's a guaranteed ton in the corner, a double at 11 o'clock . . . and so on. Honestly, a stripper's mental arithmetic is better than a barman's, and our constant juggling of opportunities and promises means our brains are earning us as much money as our bodies. Even the drunk girls could do it. Seriously, the person who realises the skills dancers acquire in clubs and hires them when they leave would have a very able, and very loyal, workforce.

On the good nights, I was able to negotiate fat fees for VIPs because customers knew that if they took me off the floor they would have to compensate me. And knowing that I was in demand made certain men want to have me to themselves even more. After every dance, I would still say, 'So are you going to tip me, then?' And they always did. When getting money is as easy as asking for it, you really don't learn how to value it.

It doesn't matter how you make fast money, whether it's selling drugs and guns like Tricky or having your horse come in on the 3.30 at Ascot, you don't just get addicted to the money, you get addicted to the way you make money.

If I learnt that one of Jackie and Terry's outfits always made me tips, I wore it again and again. If I learnt that doing a certain move on the pole always led to table dances, I did that move. Certain behaviours became linked to the money they made, and the money then became linked to the way I felt about myself. Sexy, cocky Toni equalled monied, happy Sam. My self-worth, my self-image, was tied up with how much money I earned. If I didn't earn, I felt fat, ugly, useless. If the money came in, I felt like a movie star.

Money was a real turn-on for me. People don't realise that being in a club isn't just a turn-on for the customers: there were nights when I had to wear a tampon I got so turned on. Knowing I could control a man's emotions and his wallet, knowing that I looked so good that I could make a man catch his breath, and knowing that I was so good at what I did that I was worth tipping £1,000 – I felt desired, I felt powerful, I felt in control and, believe me, I felt very sexy.

Even the night I had an accident on stage couldn't dent my earning potential. It was one of those nights when it was like a carnival atmosphere, money was being tossed in the air like confetti and champagne was flowing like it was free. I was wearing an elegant dress Jackie and Terry had made me with slits all the way up the thigh. When I spun round on the pole, the dress helicoptered around me. Very flamboyant, very showtime: I felt like I was in Vegas, baby. Up on the pole, I did the splits and came very slowly and seductively down the pole, keeping my legs open as I slid down.

I could hear a lot of noise and thought it was because I was putting on a very good show. All eyes were on me so I really went for it, and the noise level in the club went up a few decibels. I had it all locked down.

Then I realised that it wasn't the men who were making the noise, it was the girls: their hand gestures told me to look at my crotch. Not only was my tampon string poking out of my G-string, but it was glowing under the UV lights! Everyone started laughing. I turned my back to the audience and tucked it in, but when I went back to the pole, I could hear laughter again. I looked down: there it was.

What could I do? Laugh my head off is what. I shrugged my shoulders and went into the changing room to a huge round of applause. When I came back out on the floor, I got a lot of sympathy money that night and a lot of tips for being so entertaining.

The tampon thing will happen to most dancers at some point. As I say, we used them even when we didn't have our periods because the punters weren't the only ones enjoying the dancing or, indeed, the dancers. You've got to remember, it wasn't just the gangsters I found attractive – some of the women in Diamonds were unbelievably beautiful.

When it comes to girls, I'm what you call a dabbler. After the Karina situation in Denmark, I could chat up girls just fine. And the way dancers talk in changing rooms, you get pretty relaxed about talking about every sexual experience you can think of.

'Oh, I had hardcore anal last night.'

'I can't walk cos he fucked me so much.'

This was normal conversation, as was having a hug or a nuzzle of a boob. When you cuddle, when you stroke each other's hair, when you rub a twisted ankle, I guess things just happen when you're allowed to be who you want to be. There was one memorable night when things really happened.

It was Max, the little Indian guy with the Buddha belly, who suggested we go with him to a new club that had opened up near Heathrow. (Looking back, that was a big clue that things were about to change, but I'm getting ahead of myself.) As it always makes good business sense to check out the competition, one night Ulrika and I met him at Golden Eye. Typically, we turned up late (it takes a long time for a stripper to get ready – there's a lot of hair and make-up to coordinate) and by the time we got there Max and his friend were already talking about leaving.

That night in Golden Eye was such a laugh because Ulrika and I were in the position of being punters. You get female customers more often than you think – men come in with wives and girlfriends, the occasional lesbian couple, as well as girls who come in wanting to see if they could work in a club – and we both knew that when you dance for a woman you go a little bit further. You will always, for example, give a woman a kiss or run your hand up the inside of her thigh. You just go further than you would ever do with a man, and the girls at Golden Eye were doing exactly what we would have done if we had been dancing for them.

'We're going to head off,' Max announced. 'But here's £500 each to spend on dances. And here's something else for you.'

He put a plastic hotel key on the table.

'I've booked a suite at the Landmark, but I won't be using it. If you want it, it's waiting for you.'

So we ordered a couple of bottles of champagne and all the girls in the club started hanging round our table. They'd seen us with a big spender (that was another clue about what was about to happen) and so they all knew we had money. We were a bit tipsy, they were a bit sniffed up, and pretty soon we started dancing together and the temperature definitely started to rise. With every dance, their hands were moving a little bit further up.

We were ecstatic to be giving other girls money because we know how it feels to be tipped. And of course it wasn't our money, so we were being very generous with the girls who really moved. They were sexy, we felt sexy – it was clear there was something going on.

One girl was dancing for Ulrika. She was leaning in real close and then pushed Ulrika's legs apart and didn't stop leaning. So I tapped one of my dancers on the shoulder and said, 'Can I get a bit of that, then?'

Later, one of the dancers came and sat between us. 'Listen, we really fancy you.'

'Do you now? It just so happens that we've got a suite at the Landmark. What are you girls doing when you finish here?'

There were five of them and they all went off into a huddle. Ulrika and I knew exactly the conversation they were having, cos it was the same conversation we'd have been having if it had been them making the invite: who had we come in with, how genuine were we, how far could they trust us?

About an hour later, a convoy of our cars pulled up outside the Landmark. Even though it's a hotel known for all sorts, we split up and made our way to the room in ones and twos, just in case any of the security people decided to spoil our fun.

Max had booked a beautiful suite, and as soon as we got in there we ordered some champagne from room service and the girls did a couple of lines. I dragged Ulrika by the hand and pulled her into the bathroom.

'I can't believe we're doing this!'

'Me neither!'

'So which ones do you like?'

'I have to choose?'

In the end, there was no choosing to be done cos it was a case of share and share alike. You hear about daisy chains. You see 'em in porn films. You never think you'll take part in one of them. If there had been a camera on that ceiling it would have got some amazing footage of the seven of us in a circle just getting down to it.

I have rarely been so drunk. My memories of everything after that are patchy and blurry. I remember one of them coming in to see me in the bathroom and saying something along the lines of 'My mate really fancies you' and a couple of minutes later me and her mate were taking a bath together. And we did more than wash each other's hair. In fact, this girl who had never been with a woman before turned out to be a very smooth operator. We had an amazing time and evidently a very noisy time because when we came out of the bathroom we got a little round of applause! Then the seven of us got into this huge bed and concertina'd up together before drifting off to sleep.

God knows what the chambermaids thought.

STRINGFELLOWS

Stepping up a league

The fact that Max was well known at Golden Eye should have told me something. He clearly wasn't happy with the service he was getting at Diamonds. One night he came in and he took me, TJ and Julie to one side.

'Look,' he said, 'I don't want to go into it but I won't be coming here any more.'

Now at this point, we were all making a grand a week from Max, so him not coming to Diamonds was devastating news. What he said next surprised us: he wasn't going to be visiting Golden Eye either because he'd found somewhere he preferred to both places.

'I still want to be your regular, you know I do, but I'm going to be at Stringfellows on a Thursday from now on. I've arranged for you all to have an audition there next week, and if you want to work there then I'd love to still see you.'

Well, there was no way I wasn't going to audition for Stringfellows, even if I was still very happy at Diamonds. Working at Stringfellows for a dancer is the equivalent of an actress transferring from some little theatre to the West End. Stringfellows was the big time. Everyone's heard of it. It's right in the middle of Covent Garden and it's always in the papers. Celebrities go there. Peter Stringfellow is always on telly. Even the name is glamorous. Sure, it was a strip club, but it was also old-school burlesque: it was practically show business. Every busboy and concierge in London knows to send gentlemen who ask to Stringfellows. An opportunity to work there was a chance to change your life. You hear stories about Strings – a customer bought a dancer a Cartier watch, or a Porsche, or gave her the keys to his Caribbean villa. If you want to earn big money, you want to work at Strings. By this stage, I *really* wanted big money.

TJ, however, said she didn't want to leave.

'Whaddyamean? It's Strings! Are you some kind of crazy?'

It turned out that TJ had been cooking a plan to do something new. She'd been thinking about starting her own business and she knew if she stayed at Diamonds she could get together the money she needed, even without Max. Moving to Strings was a risk she didn't need to take. Of course she would miss seeing Max, but the chances were that she wasn't going to be dancing for that much longer anyway. Julie, however, was just as excited at the prospect of a move to the West End as I was.

As it got closer to our audition, I got more excited and more nervous. I reasoned with myself that I came with a recommendation from Max and that they would know my presence would guarantee a high-spending regular. I also knew I was good, probably one of the best pole dancers in London at the time, but to work at Strings required something special. Page Three girls worked at Strings. Models. I really wasn't sure how I would measure up.

Seven dancers turned up at the audition and three were turned away before they even got into their outfits. Mark, the club manager at Strings, decided they did not have 'the look'. I'd made it over the first hurdle, but this was the top club and you really had to bring it. I got dressed in a pink boob-tube dress and put my hair in bunches. I thought I'd go with cute and be soft, because some people still have fixed ideas about black girls and I didn't want to go in there looking hard or ghetto. I wanted to show that I could fit into the Stringfellows format nicely.

When my name was called, I got on that stage and gave them some really nice slow moves, made some nice shapes and then I climbed the pole so I could show off all my tricks. My favourite move was crossing my legs at the top of the pole and leaning all the way back to make a beautiful crescent shape. Then I moved my hand under my bum for support and did the splits while sliding down very slowly, very seductively.

The first song was clothed, but the second song involved a striptease down to my knickers. I rolled my way up and down the pole, stopping on the beat to do freezes, making beautiful shapes out of my body. Before I had put my clothes back on, Mark had said yes. Julie got the thumbs-up too. We were over the moon: we were Stringfellows girls.

Before we left that night, we got a bit of an induction and the money side of things was explained to us. The house fee was £85, so when you added in a cab fare there and back, you were looking at having to earn £120/130 just to break even. The first six dances were effectively for nothing. Still, with Max as a regular I knew I could cover my costs. The rota system was also explained and if you didn't show up when your name was on the list, it was pointed out that you would be fined £100. There was no having a quick word with the House Mother because you'd made your money that week and wanted a night off. If you were on the rota, you were in the club. No messing.

Another difference was that instead of being paid in cash, customers would pay us in Stringfellows' own currency, Heavenly Money. The club added 20 per cent to whatever the customer converted into Heavenly Money and the club also deducted 20 per cent commission from the dancers when they changed their Heavenly Money back into cash. You might earn £5k in Heavenly Money, but you'd only take home £4k. Still, the good news was that at Stringfellows, I was pretty much guaranteed to earn more than I had at Diamonds. At least that's what I thought.

We were also told that we wouldn't be paid in cash. Our Heavenly Money would go into an account and we would be paid at the end of each week. I didn't know how I felt about being paid weekly. I had got very used, and quite addicted, to the cash machine called Diamonds sending me home with notes every night. I wasn't sure I wanted to switch to earning wages. It seemed so, well, conventional. But if you wanted to work at Strings, you had to play by Strings' rules.

That wasn't the only thing that unsettled me slightly at the audition. By the time we were getting back into our civilian clothes, the other dancers had started to arrive and were getting into their costumes. They were all absolutely stunning. I mean so beautiful that they made me stare. And their outfits were like something from the window display at Harrods – beautifully made, exquisite garments. It was a repeat of my first time at Diamonds when I compared the outfits there to the ones I had worn in Denmark. I suddenly felt massively intimidated, which is why I told Mark a little white lie that I had a holiday booked and wouldn't be able to start for a couple of weeks. The truth was I wasn't sure if I could work there, nor was I sure I could leave Diamonds.

It was odd: as soon as I got back to Diamonds the next day I had this really strong sensation that it was home. Brad and Sandy were like having a big brother and a fabulous sister-in-law, Theresa was like an aunt, Jackie and Terry were like a second mum and dad. It was home and they were my family. What was odder was that, almost as soon as I had realised how much all these people meant to me, things started to change.

For starters, Brad and Sandy took off for a while and with them out of the picture it meant Warren, one of the owners, took over as General Manager. Although I knew Warren well enough to say hello to, I'd never really had that much to do with him because he had a thing for Oriental girls – his nickname was Yellow Fever – and so he'd always left me alone. However, one of Warren's associates did have a thing for black skin and Warren approached me – literally the day after my Stringfellows audition – and told me to get friendly with his mate.

'Whatever he wants, give it to him,' were his exact words.

He expected me to sleep with him and when I refused his attitude towards me changed from indifference to intolerance. Then Theresa made an announcement that really sealed my fate: she was leaving. Having been told for the past 20 years that she couldn't have kids, she had just learnt that the diagnosis was wrong. She was already into her forties and if she was to stand any chance of getting pregnant she had to lead a healthier life than working seven days a week in a strip club would allow. I was ecstatic for her, but I knew it would change everything at Diamonds. Even when Brad got back from Down Under, he couldn't protect me and the other girls from Warren like Theresa had done. It was really pretty simple: no Theresa, no Diamonds.

I had done four years at Diamonds. Four fabulous years. But it really felt like the timing was right for me to leave and join the big league. 'You're ready, Sam,' Theresa said to me on my last night, 'I think you're ready for the big time and the big money.'

You bet I was.

Showgirls

When you've been the top dog, starting over somewhere new is always going to be tough. I was prepared for that but took confidence from the fact that a) I had passed the audition and therefore they thought I was good enough, and b) the fact that Max guaranteed me at least a grand a week. Plus, working with Julie again would mean there would be a friendly face around. *Give me a couple of weeks*, I told myself, *and I'll have Stringfellows licked*. Oh boy, was I wrong.

Stringfellows has three sections to it, a bar and restaurant on the ground floor with a club downstairs. It attracts a different kind of customer from Diamonds – bankers, brokers, international businessmen, government types, ambassadors and celebrities. Savile Row suits and handmade shoes. It's the kind of place where a man can say to his wife that he went for a meal to impress clients. She knows there are naked girls there, of course, but it's so high class that there's no suggestion of any hanky panky going on. Peter Stringfellow somehow made his club both sexy and respectable.

When I turned up for my shift and walked down the stairs to the club, I really felt like I had made it, but as soon as I walked into the changing room I felt like it was my first day at school. I was told that – no matter where you've worked and how long you've worked there – you are expected to pay £15 to one of the resident make-up artists, because Stringfellows girls have to be flawless girls. That meant it wasn't six dances for nothing, it was seven.

There was no equivalent of Mother Theresa, no buffer between the girls and management, and no referee for the petty squabbles dancers will always have about shoes and hairspray and fake tan. I instantly realised just how important Theresa had been to Diamonds: the girls needed that nurturing figure, that source of strength and comfort, and without her the dressing room at Strings felt tense and stiff.

I'd told Jackie and Terry that I was moving up to Strings and I'd asked them to make me a new outfit, a very sleek dusky-pink dress with a ribbon trim. I thought it was the right kind of dress for Stringfellows, but as soon as I had wriggled into it and saw what the other girls were wearing I felt like I was in a potato sack.

The clothes these women were wearing were just stunning. Properly tailored, real silk, expensive jewellery. Suddenly Jackie and Terry's dress felt like something my mum had made for me to wear to the school disco. I didn't know it then, but I found out that the top earners at Strings made monthly shopping trips to Las Vegas – spiritual and financial home of the showgirl – where they stocked up on high-quality outfits. I was spending £50 a dress; they were putting a zero on the end of that.

I thought things would get better when I walked out onto the floor of the club, but it turned out that it wasn't just the other dancers who looked down their noses at me: the punters had a mean streak running through them too. At Diamonds, I was used to pretty average guys coming in. They might have earned more than the average, but they were regular blokes from regular backgrounds. The Stringfellows customer was like another species: these were men with a sense of entitlement, who were used to feeling superior to the people whose wages they paid, and they really expected a subservient, dutiful act from the dancers. Cocky Toni was in trouble.

Right, I said to myself, *this is what you wanted, now you have to make it work for yourself.* I told myself that I knew how to read a room, I knew how to be seductive, so I started asking guys if they wanted a dance. But all I got was 'No'. No. We're having a conversation. No. Come back later. No. We're just leaving. No. I'm waiting for Rose. No. No. No.

I tell you, it doesn't matter who you are or what your game is, if you keep getting rejected like that it crumples you and squashes you till you feel so small you could fit inside your own pocket. And when your confidence goes, you can't hustle. You just can't bring it. It didn't help that there were so many black girls – there were eight of us that first night – and not enough of those brash, flash City types have a thing for black skin. You can't make someone want you when their prejudices are so deeply ingrained. And you can't make money when you're a black girl in a blondes' club. I made £50 on my first night. And that was in Heavenly Money. After the house fee and cabs, I was seriously out of pocket. As soon as I got through my front door I burst into tears. *What had I done? What the hell had I done?*

Julie was still up – she wasn't due to start at Strings for a couple of days – and she went to the kitchen and came back with a bottle of wine. I was in bits. Utterly distraught. I questioned whether I wanted to dance any more, whether I *could* dance any more, or if I was ugly or fat or old – all the insecurities just came flooding out of me.

'We've heard the rumours about Strings for years,' Julie said. 'We know it's going to be tough to start over. We know it's going to be competitive. Look, we'll go back in a couple of nights, I'll be with you and we'll give it our best-ever shot. All right?'

I nodded, but I didn't really think it was going to get better because I had seen the competition. I knew who we were up against. The top earner was a girl called Rose. She was pretty plain to look at, certainly not a supermodel, but the way she carried herself meant you couldn't help but take notice. She had poise, etiquette, presence. If you found out she was a minor royal you wouldn't have been surprised as she was incredibly well spoken. And those jewels she was wearing weren't Swarovski crystals, they were real, sparkling, fabulous diamonds that had probably been bought for her by one of her many regulars. Rich Chinese guys, rich Middle Eastern guys, rich Indian guys – they all went potty for her. She was the archetypal English rose who always dressed like she was going to an evening wedding: her hair was always up and her dress was always classically understated. Rose had class. Rose never wore a stripper dress, but then she never stripped. In all the time I worked there, I never once saw Rose dance.

She could make so much money on the floor that she didn't need to dance, and if she had got up on the stage she wouldn't have been able to maintain the English rose exterior if she'd started bumping and grinding. Nor did I ever see her give a dance at a table. Rose – who was in her late 20s – had got her week locked down and only ever saw regulars. It would always start with dinner in the restaurant, primarily so they were paying for an hour when all she had to do was push some salad round her plate, and then she would either sit in a booth with her client or disappear into a VIP room.

The more I observed Rose, and the more I heard about her, the more I realised why so many girls want to work at Stringfellows. For starters, she probably made in a night what I earned in a week at Diamonds. She owned three properties; probably one was a gift from a client, but she had paid for the other two. She drove a vintage sports car and took very expensive holidays, and I even overheard her talking about her stocks and shares portfolio.

I am pretty sure she did extras. I think some of her bigger clients offered her too much money to turn down, and if she did sleep with them for £10,000, then it meant she kept them as a regular and they didn't look for someone else. If you've got a couple of well-heeled, well-groomed guys giving you £10,000 a week, you probably don't need to do anything else.

It used to puzzle me why a man would pay so much for sex when he could go to a massage parlour and get tugged off for £30. It was only working at Stringfellows that made me realise why a man would pay to be with a woman like Rose – it was because he can. Paying that kind of money for that kind of woman validated every choice he made to earn the money he was spending. Paying £10k for sex felt a lot better than paying £100 for it.

Although Rose stood out as the number-one earner, there were another seven or eight girls who never made less than £2,000 a night. They looked like the kind of girl you could take to a

Buckingham Palace garden party, or to your boss's house for dinner, and she would be the perfect, gracious escort. They were – in so many ways – most men's picture of the perfect woman.

It wasn't just the styling and the grooming that intimidated me, it was also the performances. Some of the girls had been in major ballet companies and they could do things that defied gravity. One girl, Laura, was ripped like a racehorse. If you found out she had won an Olympic medal for gymnastics you wouldn't have been surprised because she was that strong and that supple and so damn *good*. Whenever she got on the stage, the entire club stopped what it was doing to watch her.

Laura had boobs that were flatter than pancakes. I've never yet met a man who doesn't like a nice pair of boobs – for most men tits like sand bags are an instant turn-on – but Laura still raked in the cash because she was sexy. She made eye contact with punters like I've never seen anyone else do, and she would hold their gaze for a long time, making them think she wanted them, making them uncomfortable, making them reach into their wallets just for a reason to look away. But when they looked back up, she was still staring at them. She made her customers feel desired and if she picked on you from the stage you didn't stand a chance. It was like a praying mantis and a fly.

Toni had a lot of catching up to do.

Hey big spender!

My first big night at Stringfellows did not get off to a good start. The place was dead. I don't know whether there was a football match on somewhere, or if a bar round the corner had a 2-for-1 offer, but there were the odd nights when – for no reason that any of us knew – the punters just didn't materialise. Then around 11.30 p.m., the place started to fill up. You heard the sound of ties being loosened, of wallets opening up and Grey Goose being glugged. The night was about to change and I decided I was going to seize the moment by giving my best-ever stage performance. I was going to make love to that pole and I was going to give every man in there the thrill of his life.

I started my routine on the floor, then snaked my way up the pole. Under the stage lights, you can't see the audience, but I could hear that the front row was filling up. *Right, Sam, time for your signature move.* I wrapped my legs around the pole, leant backwards to make a beautiful S shape, then put one hand under my bum for support and slowly opened out my legs before sliding gently down towards the floor. By this stage in the routine, all I was wearing was an eye-patch thong, so when I got down to the bottom, the customers' eye line was level with that eye-patch. Basically, I was naked apart from something the size of postage stamp. It's usually at this point that I will look up and make seductive eye contact with a salivating punter in the front row.

I could not believe what I saw: the entire front row – about 15 seats – was filled with boys from my year at school! They looked at me. I looked at them. Frozen. Solid. I could tell from the shock on their faces that they had had no idea I worked there.

Right, Samantha, what are your options? I reasoned that I could either curl up and cry, or I could make some money. *Fifteen of them. Twenty quid each. Three hundred quid for me. Show time!* If they were going to talk about me to people back home, they were at least going to say that it was the best fucking show they had ever seen in their lives. So I went for it. Super slinky, super slow, super sexy. And as soon as I came off stage, I put my clothes back on, magicked up the most out-there version of Toni I could muster and strutted right up to them. Sam couldn't have done it, but Toni was up for anything.

'Well, well, well,' I said to their dumbstruck, open-mouthed, embarrassed little faces. 'Shall I call the news desk on the *Romford Recorder* and tell them 15 escapees have been spotted in a strip club?'

Right away I had made them feel more embarrassed for being there than I was. I had decided that they were on my territory and that meant I was in control.

'I think a bit of bribery is in order, otherwise someone's parents are going to get a phone call. How many of you have been to a strip club before?'

To my surprise, not many had.

'Right. That means you need my help, because if you're not wise to the tricks you will be leaving here in debt. Let me take care of you, and then we can all pretend this never happened.'

Once they knew that I wouldn't tell their parents if they didn't tell mine, we could have some fun and I could make my money.

'Do you all fancy a dance together?'

They didn't really have a choice but to say yes.

'Right then, £20 each and I will show you to the VIP area.'

For young lads from Essex on a budget, the VIP area of Stringfellows would normally be off limits, but I had a word with the VIP manager and explained that – although not strictly a VIP – I was making a good wedge out of the transaction and I wanted a VIP room for the next half-hour.

I told the boys to come with me. I knew what kind of scene I was creating: the entire front row of Stringfellows just got up and followed me to VIP. I could hear every other dancer in the place thinking, *What fucking wand has she just waved?* It felt brilliant. Toni was loving it, and when we got into that VIP room I gave them a dance to remember. It was fully nude in VIP, and half of them could not bring themselves to look. The other half gawped. Then the drinks were brought in and we started to have a riot.

'Do you remember,' one of them said to me, 'that when we left school and we were all talking about what we would go on to do, half the class thought you'd end up on TV, and the other half . . .'

I finished his sentence for him: '. . . thought I'd be on Page Three.'

'Even the teachers thought you'd be on Page Three!'

The noise of us laughing could be heard throughout the club, so when my time with the boys came to an end, there were plenty of curious customers in the club wanting to know what Toni's special secret was. The night that had started out slowly ended very well indeed.

I didn't have many nights like that to start with for the simple reason that there weren't many customers like that in Stringfellows. Julie found her groove much more easily – she had very fair skin, masses of red hair and a very nice pair of boobs – so if a man had a thing for redheads, he probably had a thing for Julie. I got a lot of dances out of her in those early months because she would always try to bring me into the money if her customers asked for a double. Thanks in large part to Julie, I averaged around £300 a night after I'd paid my house fee and my fares. It wasn't nearly as much as I'd been making at Diamonds, but I got the feeling that with all that money in the club, at some point it had to start rolling my way. The trouble was that cocky, cheeky Toni didn't really fit the Stringfellows mould, and I knew that if I was going to make money from all those wanker bankers, then Toni had to make some changes.

I had enjoyed being Toni. She was like an unleashed version of me – cheekier, bolder, louder. Being Toni was like me on cocaine, and playing the part had always been some kind of release because

Toni could get away with anything. But Toni did not fit into Stringfellows. I had to transform Toni into an elegant, sophisticated seductress.

It started with the clothes. Jackie and Terry's outfits were too cheap-looking to cut it at Strings, so I went to West End boutiques and found outfits that were more grown-up, more sophisticated, while the hot-pant cowgirl number was deleted from my wardrobe. Then I upped my grooming. I found a different hairdresser and must have been her most intimidating new client ever: how good are you, what references have you got, can I watch you cut someone else's hair, what guarantees do you give? I impressed on her that if I had bad hair, I wouldn't earn. She let me watch her style a couple of other women, and only when I was satisfied she was up to the job were her scissors unleashed on my hair. She was amazing. A real artist, and she introduced me to a whole new level of weaves and hairpieces. She also suggested that I start buying the hair for my weaves from Brazil.

'It's jet black and luscious, and you can style it so many ways.'

It sounded great. The only problem was that Brazilian hair cost £90 a gram, and it took ten grams to make my weave. If I wanted to save money, I could go for Persian hair at £70 a gram, but I could always tell the difference.

I had always got my nails done once or twice a week, but now if I so much as scratched the polish I went right back to my nail technician for a manicure and maybe a new set of acrylics. Every aspect of my appearance was enhanced – without surgery, I should add – until I looked like I belonged at Stringfellows.

Lots of other girls did go in for surgery. You often read that Hollywood actresses feel the pressure to look good and that if they don't have something lifted or tucked then they'll never work again. It's the same for dancers: the paranoia that the girl with the new breasts or the tucked tummy will earn more than you compels lots of dancers to go under the knife. Girls would go on holiday and come back looking slightly different. The question you asked wasn't 'Did you go anywhere nice?' it was 'Did you have much done?'

Normally the girls would be ecstatic with their new figures and would be showing them off in the changing room.

'Here, have a feel.'

'You can't even see the scars.'

'I know, it's brilliant, isn't it?'

So when I found one of the girls who had just had her boobs done in floods of tears, I was really stunned: only a couple of hours earlier she had been giggling away and letting us all have a little grope.

'Becca, what is it? What's up?'

Something was seriously wrong. I didn't know her very well, but as the only other girl in the room I couldn't ignore her.

'Are you in pain? Is it the scars? Talk to me.'

'Toni, I . . . I . . . I . . .' She was sobbing too much to speak.

'Come on, you can tell me, what's wrong?'

After a couple of minutes, she calmed down and was able to get her words out.

'I've just been with this customer.'

'Yeah?'

'While I was on stage, I could hear him making all these oohs and ahhs and so I went over to him.'

'Your new tits are getting a lot of attention.'

She shook her head. 'That wasn't it. He kept saying to me that I was really brave.'

'I don't understand.'

'Neither did I, but he kept on about it and said that I must be really committed to get it tattooed.'

I hadn't realised until that point, but when Becca had been on her surgery retreat she had also got a tattoo done between her shoulders. It looked like a poem.

'He said he had been through the same thing and that it was great I wasn't ashamed.'

'What on earth was he going on about?'

'Oh, Toni.' She started crying again and it was another few minutes before she was able to get any more words out. The poem, she blubbed, was actually a prayer, and not just any prayer: it was

154

the prayer said at every Alcoholics Anonymous meeting!

'I had no idea,' she sobbed. 'I just thought it was a really pretty prayer.'

It is wrong to laugh in a situation like that, isn't it? I was so good because somehow I managed to keep a straight face. I felt so sorry for her, but, boy, could I see the funny side. I said all the encouraging things I could think of. I got the boys on the door to call her a cab. I told her everything would be all right. But when she had gone, I absolutely pissed myself.

I walked back out on the floor with a massive smile on my face when a familiar figure walked up to me.

'Hello, I'm Peter.'

'Hi, I'm Toni.'

Like most people who had seen Peter Stringfellow on the telly, I thought he was a bit of a prat with a ridiculous haircut that wasn't even trendy in the '80s. We'd often see him in the club and it was really noticeable that the girls never sniggered behind his back. The kind of comments you'd expect about dodgy hair, perma-tans and age-inappropriate clothing were never made. And that's because all the other girls already knew what I was about to find out: Peter Stringfellow is a genuinely lovely man. There's something really nice about working in a business where the guy who started it – and the guy who loves it so much he puts his name above the door – is often walking around. When Peter was in, there was always a much warmer atmosphere.

'Listen,' he said, 'I've got some very wealthy friends over there, one of whom thinks you are gorgeous.' Peter then pressed a handful of Heavenly Money into my palm. 'Go and sit with them for me, will you?'

Whenever you would sit with Peter's friends, you knew that Peter would ask them what they thought of us. Which girls had been friendly? Which had been good dancers? Which had been sexy? I obviously got good feedback because there were some girls that Peter never asked again. When I saw Peter later that night, I thanked him and told him that his friends had been charming.

'Have a drink with me,' he said.

He ordered champagne and some food and the two of us spent the rest of the night talking. He was just so friendly and so easy to talk to. I started to understand why girls in the club got angry on his behalf when cruel things were written about him in the papers. He loved his business and he loved being surrounded by beautiful girls – he is one of the most contented men you will ever meet. Everyone always thinks that he preys on young women but I can tell you – for sure – that it is the women who throw themselves at him. In the entire time I worked there, I never saw him hit on a dancer and I never heard stories of him doing it. He did date dancers, don't get me wrong, but they were the ones driving it. They wanted to be with him. For me, it was interesting to see that he was never with the easy girls or the pushy girls. The only dancers who got to date Peter were the nice ones, the genuine ones.

Peter's friends tended to be either rich or famous, or both. There were lots of faces I recognised from the telly, but if they were sportsmen or politicians there was no way I would know their name or what they did. I think that probably helped me to talk to them – I wasn't in awe of them and I didn't behave like a groupie. One night, though, I absolutely did recognise one of Peter's friends and I was really, really hoping that Peter would ask me to sit with him.

It wasn't because I was a big Tom Jones fan. It certainly wasn't because I fancied him. It was because I was hoping he could settle a long-standing family argument. So when Peter gave me the money to dance for him I was thrilled.

Tom Jones had a really nice aura about him. He wasn't there to perv or sleaze over girls, he was just enjoying the entertainment and the company. Which is probably why I felt able to be cheeky with him.

'Hello, Tom.'

'Hello, lovely.'

'I would like to give you a dance.'

'Well, that would be very nice.'

'I've already been paid for it, but I'd like to give you another dance for free if you answer one little question for me.'

'All right, then.'

'Who in your family is black?'

Thankfully, he roared with laughter.

For years my mum and dad have insisted that no one can have that voice, or that hair for that matter, and not have a bit of black blood in his veins, and sure enough some aunt or great uncle or someone was indeed black.

'I knew it! As soon as I finish these dances I have to call my mum and tell her!'

Between the celebrities and the wanker bankers, there was a lot of money flowing through Stringfellows. In fact, it was pretty much standard for the girls at Strings to live in a flat that a regular was paying for. Maybe he had bought it for her, maybe he was renting it for her or maybe he already owned it, but if you found your Mr Big and you were his fantasy girl, you were set up for life.

Despite the amount of money some men were prepared to shower them with, some dancers were surprisingly moralistic and wouldn't go near a married man. Others actively wanted a married man, as it ensured that they could have his money and his lifestyle without having to spend every night with him. Of course, sometimes the apartment was some kind of tax dodge, or an accountancy offset, or some other angle we didn't know about or care about.

I never assumed that if a customer bought a girl a flat that meant she was sleeping with him. The customer/stripper relationship is often more complex than you'd expect. These men would typically be married and have a long-term mistress. They would probably also see a third woman for sex. That woman might be a call girl, or he might be the type of guy who gets his thrills persuading women to sleep with him rather than making risky bets at the blackjack table. And then, often, he'd also have a dancer he saw regularly. That dancer might be like a daughter to him, or she might be his substitute for a therapist. Sometimes it was as simple as the fact that he liked a dancer to be in his flat so that he knew where she was, and he knew that she would be beholden to him. I know it's odd, but these relationships weren't necessarily about sex. Which is why

I was desperate to find myself a rich regular. Working at Stringfellows made my craving for money even stronger. The punters had it, the other dancers had it, and I wanted it. Very, very badly.

I had been there six months when a buzz started going round the club. You could see news being passed round from dancer to dancer like a line of dominoes falling over. When the news reached me, I felt dizzy with excitement . . . and a little weak with envy.

Upstairs, outside the club, a beautiful Mercedes convertible sports car had just been delivered wrapped in a bow. It was a gift to a Venezuelan dancer from a man she had been dancing for just the night before. The guys on the door told us that it was – easily – a £50k car.

Spirits in the club went into orbit. We were all on such a massive high that something like that could happen to someone like us. Now, every man in the club was a potential source of a new kind of lifestyle. We shook our booties with skill and passion that night; all of us were hustling that bit harder, had that bit more hope.

When there's that much money flying through the air, there are always people around to help you spend it. Almost every night it seemed that someone knew about a sample fashion sale or limited-edition Louis Vuitton bag on special offer, a new business venture to invest in or an off-plan property to snap up before it went on the market. At one point, several of the girls were making money from a pyramid scheme. You paid in £2,000, but once you'd moved up the pyramid you stood to make £20k. Given that others were bragging about their windfall, I decided I would 'invest'. Of course, with all these pyramid schemes and chain-letter scams, it's the people who get in first who make the money. By the time I joined, there just weren't enough dancers left in the club who hadn't already put money in. I just about got my £2,000 back, but no windfall.

My financial situation wasn't terrible, but I was spending everything I made on costumes, grooming, house fees and cabs. There was nothing spare after rent and bills. This meant I was very reliant on Max's appearances – if he went on holiday, I went into the red.

I always knew when he had come in. I'd be on stage and a dancer would come up and put a £50 note in my garter and let me know that my regular was here. I'd had a soft spot for Max for years, and seeing his round, happy face in that competitive Stringfellows environment made me relax. The fact that he would be emptying his wallet all over me undoubtedly also made a difference. What really mattered, though, was that the other girls saw me make money, that they saw me with a customer who had come in just to see me. Max was good for my bank balance, but he was essential for my self-esteem.

The reason I say he was coming in just to see me was because Julie had left. The pair of us had been working the same shift when I realised I hadn't seen her for over an hour. I asked around: she wasn't in a VIP. I checked the restaurant and the bar: she wasn't there either. The guys on the door told me she hadn't left the building. There was only one place left: the toilets.

I checked all the cubicles. Only one door was locked.

'Jools. It's Sam. What's up?'

I heard her unbolt the door and I pushed it open.

Her face was as red as her hair. She had been crying so much her eyes were red too, and I have never seen anyone look so fucking sad.

'What's happened?'

She gestured that I should look in the toilet. I peered over her shoulder and down into the water beneath her: she was having a miscarriage.

'Oh, baby. I am going to get you out of here.'

To give all due credit to the meat heads on the door, when I told them what had happened there was no 'You can't leave till you've finished your shift' routine that we would otherwise have got if we'd tried to leave early. And by the time Julie was able to get dressed and climb up the stairs, there was a cab waiting for her that was already paid for. I took Julie home and put her to bed. She had only just guessed she was pregnant. She hadn't been sure how she felt about it so she'd kept schtum. It was only in the past day that she had decided she was going to keep it and try to make a life with her boyfriend. She just howled and howled that night, and all I could do was hold her. It was such a shitty thing to happen to such a sweet girl. Unsurprisingly, after something like that she felt she couldn't face going back into Strings.

Julie's departure meant I had more of Max's money for myself, but I really missed having a friend in the club. After a couple of months of hustling much harder than I had ever worked at Diamonds – in fact, it had never even felt like work at Diamonds – I realised I needed to see more of my mates. I called TJ.

'Take me away from all of this, will ya?'

'Your timing is perfect – there's a group of us going away this weekend if you want to come.'

'Where are you going?'

'Ibiza.'

'Why would you go there? That's just like going to Ilford-on-Sea.'

TJ explained to me that Ibiza wasn't just full English breakfasts and shrimp-pink Brits chucking up on the beach. There were old villages to explore, a spiritual side of the island to get to know and beautiful chilled-out bars on secluded beaches.

'Oh, and a friend of mine has a villa out there and says we can all stay.'

I asked if I could take my little sister Amanda with me. She had just turned 18 and at her birthday party I realised just how much of her childhood I had missed out on. She had only just started secondary school when I'd left for Denmark and all of a sudden she had grown up and I realised I had missed out on so much. I felt really guilty for not being there for all the big-sister pep talks and I thought a holiday would be a good way to start making things up to her. There was just one problem: there was no way I could take her on holiday with a bunch of strippers and not tell her how I made my money. The problem I didn't foresee was actually more problematic: when Amanda saw what a stripper lifestyle was all about she wanted to start dancing herself.

I completely understood why Amanda thought our life was

fabulous. We were staying in an amazing villa belonging to a husband-and-wife team from Birmingham who owned a handful of clubs in the Midlands. Kerry and Bez's working week consisted of logging on to their bank account to see how much money had been deposited. Very nice. What Amanda didn't see, though, was that Kerry and Bez were putting cocaine and vodka on their cornflakes rather than sugar and milk. She was just like me in the early days, only seeing what she wanted to see.

Kerry and Bez's villa wasn't the only thing that impressed Amanda. There were clubs you could only get into in Ibiza if you paid £5k for a table. Unless, of course, you happened to look like us. We wore the skimpiest, boobiest, shiniest outfits we had. Our hair was massive, our nails were like talons and we looked like we knew how to have a good time. You could fill your club with Page Three rejects in white stilettos, or you could invite in the professionals who really knew how to turn up the fun factor. There was a whole line of people outside Amnesia just hoping for a look at the people who were ushered into its legendary interior. When the bouncers saw me, TJ, Amanda and a couple of other girls approach, the rope was unhooked and we were shown the last remaining table before two bottles of complimentary champagne were brought for us. At the next table was a billionaire who took a shine to TJ. For the rest of our time in Ibiza he treated us all to day trips and rides in his vintage sports cars. Amanda was amazed that just by looking like party girls we could get treated like VIPs.

'Mum would never forgive me. It'll be bad enough if she ever finds out that I work in clubs. But if she found out I had got you a job too she would never speak to me again. Dad would kill me. No.'

'But Sam . . .'

'No! You're a smart girl. You've got options I never had.'

'But . . .'

'No!'

I had persuaded her, but I sensed it would only be a matter of time before she brought it up again.

That week in Ibiza also got me thinking about my future because I found Kerry to be really inspirational. If I looked beyond the fact that she was a functioning alcoholic with a £5k-a-week drug habit, she was actually a woman I could really admire. I was obsessed with how the people around me were making their money and I was always trying to work out how I could get a piece of it for myself. *Why were they different? What were they doing? How could I copy them?* She had made her fortune out of running clubs, and it really hit home that it wasn't just the dancers who made money – the club owners made a whole lot more. She encouraged me to see working in clubs as more of a career and less of a job. She suggested things like getting approved to be a licensee or looking at ways to get management experience. The only woman I had ever seen in a management capacity in a club was Theresa, and it was in Ibiza that I realised what Stringfellows really needed was a House Mother. *Hmmm. Interesting thought. Let's park that idea for a bit and see what happens.*

The unicorn

At Stringfellows it was often feast or famine. I'd been in the game long enough to know that you can have a zero-pound night followed by a five-grand night, but when those Big Fat Zero nights came along it was still hard to take. Same moves, same lines, but no one wants you. It's only the thought that the next man down the stairs will be your sugar daddy that keeps you there.

On this particular night, it was getting towards the end of my shift, about 3 a.m., and I hadn't even made my cab fare home. My sugar daddy wasn't coming. I felt ugly. Undesirable. I'd been up to every guy in the club and asked him if he wanted a dance, but it was no, no and no. It doesn't matter who you are or what game you've got, when you hear 'No' a hundred times, it crushes you.

So I went upstairs to the restaurant, where I saw a guy in his 50s sitting alone in a corner booth. He had a big bottle of rosé champagne on the table and he hadn't even opened it. I went over to him and said, 'Are you going to open that? Because I need a drink.'

He barely looked up at me.

'You look like you need a drink too. Whatever's going on with you, let's just drink it out together. OK?' I wanted to get drunk as quickly as possible. This was one bottle of fizz that was not going to get wasted on the pot plants.

'I don't want any dances.'

'Did you hear me ask you for a dance?' I was pissed off and the tone of my voice didn't hide it. 'Crack open that bottle and let's just drink, yeah?'

So he did, we drank it and then he ordered another one. I was so

163

distraught that I was not being the dutiful hostess with the mostest.

'You're quite . . . you're quite assertive, aren't you?' For a posh guy he was surprisingly softly spoken.

'What if I am?' By this time I wasn't about to apologise to anyone.

'Um, er . . . are you . . . are you a dominatrix?'

Let me tell you, I have never sobered up so quickly in my life! You hear about these submissive guys, but when you never meet one you start to think they're a myth. Straight away, I knew I was onto something.

'Yes, I am.' My voice instinctively got harsher. 'What of it? Why are you asking?'

'Well . . . well, I wondered, mistress . . .'

The minute I heard the word mistress I knew I was about to make some money. Dear. God. Thank you.

'Don't ask me any questions until I tell you that you can.'

He immediately put his head down and just sat there, not touching his glass, not making eye contact. He wasn't going to say or do anything unless I said so. Oh boy. Oh boy, oh boy, oh boy.

Girls talk. Girls in clubs talk more than most, so I'd heard all about submissives, but in seven years in nightlife I'd never come across an actual live one. They were like unicorns or imps, some kind of fairytale creature that you were never quite sure existed. Certainly the tales you heard about them were fabulous. I knew of girls who had their submissives come to their flats and do their cleaning and ironing wearing a maid's outfit. They have a reputation as the easiest people to do business with because all you have to do is shout at them and tie them up and they pay you. When you hear stories like that you think, *When am I going to get someone that easy?* And there he was. Just there. Right in front of me. Fantastic.

'Permission to speak, mistress.'

'Make it quick.' I was getting the hang of it.

'I've been really, really bad, mistress.'

As he spoke, I wondered if someone was stitching me up. I decided I would play along.

'So you deserve some punishment?'

'I do, mistress. But I've forgotten my shin pads.'

He started telling me some story about playing football. The details didn't matter: I knew he wanted me to kick him. So under the table, the points of my shoes found their way onto his shins. Repeatedly. For the first time that night I saw something like a smile on his face.

'Permission to speak, mistress.'

'If you're quick.'

'May I be excused?'

The second bottle was practically empty. He needed to go to the toilet. I granted his wish and sat there draining my glass. *Well, well, well,* I said to myself. *Samantha Anne Bailey, congratulations! You've finally found yourself a unicorn. The hours are ticking down, you've made no money and you've got a submissive. Really? Really! This. Is. Brilliant.*

I looked at him as he came back from the toilet. Grey hair. Well dressed. I could tell from his voice he was well off. For all I knew he could have been an MP.

'Do you have any more requests for me, mistress?'

You bet I do!

'Get your arse up right now, go to that booth over there and you get me £2,000 of Heavenly Money. Now!'

I honestly did not expect him to get out of his seat but he did, and as he walked over to the Heavenly booth I held on to my breath as well as my chair. When guys cash up more than £1,000, the girl in the booth always puts the money on a silver tray, so when he turned round with the tray I knew he had done as he was told. I was pretty sure this was no longer a wind-up. He put the tray on the table and I stared at the money.

'Mistress?'

'You may talk.'

'Mistress, I think there is a reason why I found you tonight. I have been really bad.'

He explained that he had just returned from a trip abroad but hadn't told his wife he was back in the country. He was spending a couple of days at his flat in London while she was safely looking after the kids at their house in the country. 'You see, I have been very bad.'

'And you must be punished.' I started kicking him again.

'Will you punish me properly? All my equipment is at my flat.'

Now, I know what you're thinking. You're thinking: *Sam, are you some kind of crazy? You don't know this guy. You don't know anything about him. Do not, whatever you do, go home with this guy.* What you've got to remember, though, is that I had drunk a bottle of champagne and it seemed that the £2,000 was now staring back at me and it was daring me to do it. And you should know by now that I like a challenge. Besides, the one thing I knew about submissives is that they are never, ever going to hurt you.

I couldn't leave with a customer, so I told him to hail a taxi and pick me up round the corner. It took me about ten minutes to get changed and out the back door where the cab was waiting. Just in case he really was a nutter, I had devised a little test for him. I got into the taxi and when the driver pulled away I told the unicorn to get on his knees.

'You don't deserve to sit on the seats, do you?'

'No, mistress.'

If he was going to be trouble, I figured he wouldn't do it. But he did, and so I knew I was in control. I caught the cabbie's eye in the rear view mirror and raised a finger to my lips to tell him not to say a word. I don't know how we stopped ourselves from laughing. The cab pulled up outside the unicorn's building in Kensington High Street and we took the lift all the way up to the penthouse. It was a classic bachelor pad: all glass and polished stainless steel. I wondered if his wife even knew it existed. I went straight into the bathroom and I locked the door.

I caught myself in the mirror. I couldn't quite tell if I was scared or excited. I got out my phone and called my brother.

'Alan, listen,' I whispered.

'Sam? What time is it?'

'Probably about 4 a.m. Alan, you've got to listen. I'm at this guy's place . . .'

I gave Alan the address and told him that if he hadn't heard from me in an hour he had to come and get me. Then I checked my hair in the mirror and gave myself a pep talk. *Right, Sam, you don't know anything about being a dominatrix. You don't know what to whip him with, how to whip him, or how long for. Somehow, Sam, you're going to have to follow his lead but still make it seem to him that you know what you're doing. How hard can that be?* I unbolted the door.

The unicorn had disappeared. It seemed the entire flat was empty, and it was then that I noticed all the hunting gear about the place. *Oh, great. He's got guns.* Then I spotted a spiral staircase in a corner of the living room. I could hear him upstairs. *Well, you're here now, Sam.*

I found him sitting on the bed, completely naked, with his hands in his lap and his head bowed like a naughty schoolboy. On a window seat he had laid out all these different paddles and whips. I told him to get on his knees and as I looked at his slightly saggy, slightly crinkly white arse, I asked myself if I was really going to do this. *Yeah. Fuck it.*

I turned round and looked at all the implements and wondered if it was like the first time I went to a fancy restaurant and I hadn't known which knives and forks to use. Had he laid them out in a particular order? I seriously didn't know what was expected of me. The only thing I knew was that I was meant to ask him for a safety word in case I hurt him too much. And I only knew that from watching *Band of Gold*.

'Now, I'm going to let you decide on just one thing.'

'Yes, mistress.'

'You can choose which tool I use first.'

'Mistress, I think I would like the studded paddle.'

I took a look at the window seat. There was only one paddle with studs on it. Phew. I picked it up and tried a little tap on his arse. He made a little moaning noise so I tried it a little bit harder, then a little bit harder still.

'Now, because you've been such a naughty boy I'm going to go down the line of all the different things that you've laid out, and you're going to feel every single one of them.'

'Oh yes, mistress, that would be perfect, mistress.'

His arse started to get a bit red, but he didn't seem to want to be hit anywhere else. Although he moaned a bit, he didn't cry out in pain, and as far as I could tell he wasn't getting an erection. The closer I got to the end of the line of implements, the more I started worrying about what I would do with the last one. It wasn't a whip or a paddle. It was a collar and lead. Was I supposed to take him for a walk in Kensington Gardens?

I kept whipping him and he kept saying 'Thank you, mistress', and it really was the easiest money I'd ever earned in my life, but the collar and the lead were starting to trouble me. What the hell was I going to do with them?

'Right. Get your head off that bed.'

He knelt up and I put the collar on him.

'Even though you've been a very, very naughty boy, I'm going to give you one more choice, one thing that I will let you do. Tell me where you want me to take you.'

He said he wanted to go out on his balcony, so I took him out there and chained him to the railing before going back inside. I didn't know how long I was supposed to leave him there for. Ten minutes? Two hours? All day?

The sun was starting to come up, so I thought I'd better text Alan and tell him I was OK. I had a bit of a snoop round the flat. A family coat of arms. Nice. Some trophies for hunting. The question I couldn't stop asking myself was why does a man like *that* want to do something like *this*?

I probably should have snooped a bit more because when I went back on the balcony he was having a little wank. Six storeys down, early-morning shift workers were getting off night buses and he was on his balcony tugging away. I stepped back inside and gave him another couple of minutes.

The fascinating thing was that as soon as he'd come, he turned into a completely different person. I took the collar off him and he went and had a shower. When he came back wearing a robe, he was a proper English gent again.

'Thank you very much,' he said, handing over those Heavenly pounds. 'I hope to see you again next time I'm in town.'

I took the money, got in the lift, hailed a cab and gave the driver Alan's address. This, I *had* to tell someone about.

I saw the unicorn maybe four or five times after that, and each time he paid me £2,000, and each time all I had to do was whip him. After a couple of sessions, I started to understand why he did it. He was a very high-powered guy who had a lot of responsibility and a lot of people looking to him for answers. What he needed was a release from that, the exact polar opposite of his regular life. But with his status, he couldn't ever be seen as anything less than the guy in charge. Any fall from grace, any drop in status and people would stop calling him. In his world, if you don't own this pony, or go to this polo match, or know people called Tarquin, then you're not going to be invited to certain places, and you're not going to get the work. I think that's a lot of pressure. I can see how someone else making the decisions for an hour or two can be an enormous relief. He wasn't a sleazy guy in a raincoat who had cut holes in his pockets. He was actually just a really lovely guy.

Money, money, money

With Max, the unicorn and a couple of other regulars, I eventually found my groove at Stringfellows. I even found myself a customer with an apartment he wasn't using in Earls Court, so I moved in, rent free. For a little while, I thought I might know what it felt like to be a proper Stringfellows girl, and it felt good.

Let me tell you, when you've had a good night and you push open those double doors onto the throbbing streets of London with several thousand in cash in your handbag, you feel amazing. *Amazing.* You feel sexy and powerful because all night long you've had men wanting you. You feel good because you know that you are at the top of your game and you're an expert at what you do. The city is still throbbing, you are bursting with energy, and that money in your bag is screaming 'Let me out!' This is the most dangerous time of the day. Instead of going home to count your money, you go to a club and spend it. And when you come out of the club, you go for breakfast. And when you've finished breakfast, the shops are open. So you shop. But then there's not enough time to sleep before you start work again, so you take up one of the constant offers of a little bit of sniff. And then, there you are, back in your G-string and shimmying up that pole.

I had seen enough dancers in Diamonds and Denmark with drug dependencies to know the horses on that particular merry-go-round have a habit of throwing you off. Drugs weren't my thing, but that doesn't mean my addictions weren't serious. My shopping might have been done without chemical help, but I was still spending every penny I earnt – £400 handbags, £100 perfume, an £800 pair of boots. I loved walking into shops where the assistants were forced to treat me like the wife of a Russian billionaire because I had the cash. Was it the shoes I was addicted to? Or was it the respect?

It wasn't long after I'd found my groove that things changed at Stringfellows. Permanently. We'd always had the odd night when no one made their house fee back, but we never had that situation more than once in a blue moon. But then we had two nights in a row where the club was completely dead, and some of the girls started to get worried – they had rent to pay or debts to clear. The place was so empty it was like a sign had been placed outside the front door that said 'Chemical hazard. Do not enter.' The place was as empty at midnight as it had been at midday. Something was wrong.

The following night, a handful of punters came in and I finally found out what had happened.

'Good evening, gents. Can I interest you in a dance?'

'Depends how much it costs.'

'Well, a topless dance is £10 and if you want to see all of me it's £20.'

'You've got to be kidding.'

My face let them know I wasn't.

'Why would I give you £10 to see a pair of tits when I can see them for free up the road?'

'What's up the road?'

'You must have heard?'

I hadn't.

Theirs weren't the only complaints I heard that night about the cash:nudity ratio. Other customers wanted to know why we weren't wearing see-through underwear. Peter was in the club that night and every time I saw him he was shaking his head. The whispers started circulating that even the busboys and concierges weren't sending their guests to Stringfellows any more. The place wasn't just empty: it was dying. We all knew we were in trouble.

That night, after making precisely £40, I got changed, got my stuff out of my locker and walked outside to get a taxi. As the doormen ushered me into my regular cab, I checked my phone for messages. A little flashing icon told me I had several, one of which was a complete blast from the past: Brad had called. I hadn't spoken to Brad for well over a year and I had no idea why he would be calling me. Had something happened to Sandy? Or one of the girls? I listened to his message. It was so good to hear his Scottish accent again that it took me a while to work out what he was actually saying.

'Hey there, Sam, long time no speak. They tell me you're a Stringfellows girl now. Congratulations. Listen, darling, I was just wondering if you're happy there, because if you're not I've got a job for you. I've just opened up this new club off Oxford Street and I think you'd fit in great here. Give me a call – we've got a special night coming up, invite-only, and we know all the customers will be monied. No house fee.'

So that was why Strings was empty: Brad had opened a new club. On the one hand I felt threatened – my earning capacity had been obliterated at Strings – but on the other hand Brad was giving me a lifeline to still make money. What harm could it do to go to Brad's invite-only night and check it out?

When I saw Brad's new club, I could not believe the size of it. If Diamonds had been a cruise ship, this was the size of an oil tanker. Or maybe even a small oil-producing nation. It was *enormous*. It was on a side road off Oxford Street and on the ground floor it took up the space of one shop but on the lower ground floor it felt like it extended beneath both the shops next door, and the shops after that. It was probably big enough to take the entire population of London in the event of a nuclear attack. It was massive. And it was packed.

Strip clubs had stopped naming themselves after Bond films and each new club had a sillier and sillier name. Spearmint Rhino. Platinum Lace. Pink Vegas. This one was called Liberty Steel and its promise to customers was that the girl of their dreams was working there. That meant that there were at least 100 girls on every shift, so that whenever a man came down the zebra-print stairs and through the double doors he would see the blonde/brunette/Oriental/skinny/milf/virgin of his dreams. I could understand why Liberty Steel was taking customers away from Stringfellows, but it wasn't until I did a shift there that I understood just how bad things were going to get at Strings. There were girls in Liberty's who would do anything for £20.

They were sitting on customers' laps, wriggling around and letting men touch them. They were getting their nipples out and letting customers suck them – and this is before the customer has paid £20 for a dance. *How on earth,* I thought, *are you expected to get £20 from a customer for a dance when he can grope you for free?* Yet, because there were so many girls on shift, you had to compete. If you won't let a punter touch you then maybe the next girl will. Chills rippled across my skin: I was horrified.

The stage shows weren't seductive, they were practically pornographic. There was so much more talent on the stage at Stringfellows, but the sleek moves and supple muscles weren't what these men were looking for. I went into the VIP area to check it out and a customer grabbed me.

'Oh no, no, no, no. You naughty boy.' I thought I could get away with being cute, but he was clearly shocked that I was pulling away from him. 'You touch the merchandise, you pay for the merchandise. Capisce?'

He practically pushed me away in disgust.

I had been in the club for about two hours when I saw something that really, truly shocked me. And it takes a lot to shock someone who's worked in a strip club since she was 17. Actually, I wasn't shocked; I was appalled. Right in front of me was an Oriental girl and a customer, and right there, in the VIP lounge – so not in a private room, just the lobby area for the VIP rooms – she did a handstand, spread-eagled her legs and let her customer DP her. Double Penetration. Thumb in her arse, finger in her pussy.

I went straight to the changing room, collected my stuff and left. In the cab on the way home, I left a message for Brad. 'You know me better than that. You know I don't do that. So thanks for the offer, but I won't be working at your new club.'

The problem was that I didn't think I could earn money at Stringfellows either: Peter's place felt doomed. I wasn't the only one who felt it. The managers knew it, the customers knew it, most of the dancers knew it and, finally, Peter acknowledged it too. We all got a text asking us to come in early at 6 p.m. for a special meeting. Things were so bad we feared what he was going to say: he certainly wasn't going to be handing out pay rises.

At this point, it was less than a week since Liberty Steel had opened. Its impact on Stringfellows had been instant and after sending spies to check it out Peter felt sure the opposition wasn't just experiencing beginner's luck.

'You all know me,' Peter said, 'you know that I think you are all the best dancers in the world, the best girls in the world, but things are going to have to change here or else none of us is going to have a job. I want you to know I've got a heavy heart about all of this.'

He was a broken man. His voice was quiet and he wasn't in the mood to make jokes. I thought: this is what it looks like when a man is fighting for his livelihood. He informed us that from the following week, dancers had to wear knickers with the gusset taken out. A rush of air was audible as we all gulped in unison. *Really*? At Stringfellows? The establishment was known for not even allowing sheer knickers as the place was all about etiquette. Now they wanted us to go crotchless?

Before he could say anything else, Rose stood up. 'If that's the case, Peter, then I can't work here.'

He nodded. He completely understood why. Rose made her money precisely because she was classy and demure. You can't get away with wearing pearls *and* crotchless knickers.

'If anyone else feels that way, I completely understand,' Peter said.

About ten girls stood up and said their goodbyes. Those of us that were left were dumbstruck – the club's biggest earners had just walked out, never to return. I reckoned that Rose and the others probably all had regulars that they would continue to see. They would still earn good money from them for a couple of years: the truth was that they didn't need Stringfellows as much as it needed them. You could see the pain in Peter's face as they collected their belongings and walked up the stairs.

Then Peter announced that he was abolishing the £10 topless dances. There was another gasp from everyone and another five girls stood up to leave. If you had big tits and knew how to work them, you could make quite a nice living keeping your knickers on. These girls weren't just leaving the club, we all knew they were leaving the industry: if you were only prepared to do topless, then you didn't have a job any more.

Peter knew he had to try to stop any more girls from leaving, so he said that anyone who wanted to go to Liberty Steel was free to do so but that they wouldn't be able to come back. 'I understand if you need to chase the money, but you can't work there as well as here, you've got to make your choice.'

We had already heard how much girls at Liberty's were making, so those that needed the money for their bills or their habits got up to leave.

The atmosphere was awful. Peter was devastated. We were all scared and in shock. Yet somehow we had a show to put on. If it hadn't been for the fact that Max was due in and I was likely to pocket a grand, I would have probably left there and then. But I stayed for one last night, snaked my way around that pole one last time and made sure I cleared my locker when I left. At the end of the night, Mark the manager approached and handed me an envelope. It had all my earnings in it from the previous week: without me saying anything, he had realised I probably wasn't coming back.

As I sat in the cab on the way back to Earls Court, I realised there was no 'probably' about it. I had left. The thing was, I knew I hadn't just left Stringfellows, I had left dancing. I couldn't help it, but I started to cry. Not full-on sobbing, just uncontrollable water streaming from my eyes and there was nothing I could do to stop it.

I knew I couldn't go back to Diamonds. I knew I could never work at Liberty Steel. And Stringfellows wouldn't be the only club that would suffer. Dancing had changed. Burlesque was gone. Teasing was out the window. We were in the era of bump and grind, and it wasn't for me.

I had no idea what I would do next. I knew that TJ had left Diamonds to start her own business. Maybe she could help me out. Then I remembered that the customer whose flat I was living in was also starting a new business. Maybe I could work for him. I knew I was going to have to find something because the only money I had in the world was in the envelope in my hand. A couple of grand wasn't going to last me very long.

Civvy Street

Some people leave dancing because they burn out. Some people leave because they get injured. Some just get too old to get the work (there are only so many milfs a club can accommodate). Some marry money. Some were only ever dancing to put themselves through college. Those women all get to look back on their dancing days knowing that they couldn't have given it any more. Not me. I wasn't done with dancing. Leaving nightlife felt premature, as though I'd been pushed out against my will.

One of the things I had always, always loved about dancing was that I crossed paths with the kinds of people I would otherwise never meet. It just so happened that some of those people were in the process of opening a new health club in central London and I begged and pleaded with them to give me a job.

'Well, we need someone to hand out flyers.'

'Bugger that, I want a proper job.'

So they gave me one: on reception. It was regular hours and regular money. I thought I would die of boredom, swiping members in and out all day. But I found ways to make things more interesting – I started a nail bar concession that did very nicely for a while, and I was also highly entertained whenever a customer from Strings came in to use the gym. Sometimes they recognised me, but more often than not they didn't. I knew they had never seen Sam, but I thought they might have at least recognised Toni. I realised that in Stringfellows they had only seen a stripper – and possibly just a pair of tits – and in the health club all they saw was a receptionist. I felt invisible.

I also felt incredibly poor. Getting paid monthly was very, very difficult for me. I would look at my diary and imagine one of those sequences from a movie where the pages of a calendar flip over to indicate that time has passed, but my diary didn't have a fast-forward function and I had to wait with all the other salary slaves. And when my pay cheque did arrive, it was missing something – tax and National Insurance contributions. It was all very different from flattening out the endless supply of crumpled £20 notes I used to find in my bra.

I couldn't live on my salary. My monthly wage was less than I used to earn a week. And now that I was no longer a Stringfellows girl, I couldn't expect to hold on to my sweet rent deal in Earls Court. I needed more cash and the only way I could get it was if I went back out there and danced. The London clubs were all out of the question – Liberty Steel meant guys could now touch you in every club in the capital – so I found a place in Watford where I could do the occasional shift. An extra £1,500 a week would do nicely. I had left Strings with a physical craving for money, and I spent hours daydreaming about meeting a rich man who would marry me and pay for everything I wanted.

People don't realise that it's not just the buzz of dancing that you walk away from, and it's not just the glamour and the fun, it's also the cash. And when you live in a penthouse and have lunch at Harvey Nicks several times a week, it's psychologically very hard to go back into living in a flatshare and doing your weekly shop at Asda. Dancing once or twice a week gave me the money I needed, but it also gave me an identity. I was finding that if I didn't dance, I didn't know who I was.

Of course, dancing all night and then starting work at the health club at 6 a.m. wasn't always easy, and at times I felt like I was back at Next, because managers were always asking to have a quiet word about my time-keeping. I knew I couldn't do a regular job for long. There was too much of Toni in me desperate to leak out.

Talking of leaks, a very funny thing happened one morning . . . I was opening up the club and as soon as I pushed the doors open I was practically floored by this appalling smell. It was like a cross between the gunge at the back of your boyfriend's fridge and the gunge at the bottom of his belly button. I felt physically sick.

I called the owner.

'Steve, I'm so sorry to call you so early in the morning.'

'Hey, Sam, I'm just pleased to hear you're at work on time.'

'Don't be funny.'

'Sorry, what do you need?'

'I'm not sure, but it stinks in here. I mean *stinks*. Like a sewer. I can't let people in there.'

Steve explained that the swimming pool had been treated overnight and his best guess was that a chemical had been spilt.

'Don't let anyone in until the pool guy gets there.'

Two hours and over a hundred pissed-off members later, the pool guy's van pulled up. Within a few seconds of sticking his nose inside the door he had identified the mistake – too much of one chemical, not enough of another. He could fix it.

Another two hours later, the problem had been rectified, the air conditioning had been put into overdrive and I found myself talking to the pool guy.

'That was just about the worst thing I have ever smelt in my life,' I told him.

'That was nothing. A few years back I got the chemicals wrong for a hotel out in west London. They reported it to the police, who decided it smelt like mustard gas, so they closed off the entire area. The whole of the Hanger Lane gyratory system was shut off because I'd got my measurements wrong.'

'Where did you say?'

'Hanger Lane. You know, the big roundabout?'

I started giggling.

'What's so funny?'

How could I possibly tell him? His story had taken me right back to that hotel room, a rucksack full of money and Tricky going bananas because he thought the police were about to cart him away. My giggles turned into belly laughs. If only this pool guy had known the impact he had had: Tricky wouldn't have been less scared if another gangster had put a gun to his head. I couldn't stop laughing and the poor pool guy never found out why I thought his was the funniest story ever. I mean, what were the chances that I would meet the man responsible? Still makes me laugh.

Thinking about Tricky again might have made me nostalgic for nightlife if hadn't been for the fact that I had started dating another bad boy. Although this one was trying very hard to be good . . .

I should explain that there is an unwritten rule about how to behave when you see someone from the clubs during civilian hours. I've lost count of the number of times I've seen another dancer out shopping with her mum and the two of us have glided past each other like total strangers. It was the same with punters. You never wanted to expose anyone else to the difficult question, 'So how did you two meet?' Unless you're completely sure of your ground, you just smile and walk on by. So when I was on reception at the health club and someone said 'Toni, is that you?', I looked up warily from my computer screen.

'It is you!'

'*Johnny?*'

Johnny the Hat, the biggest gangster I had ever met, had – incredibly – just got a job as a fitness instructor at the club.

'What time do you finish your shift?'

'Two p.m.'

'Right, I'm taking you to lunch.'

Well, I was so excited I couldn't stay sitting down. What the hell was Johnny the Hat doing teaching kick boxing? What rabbit hole had I just fallen down? What parallel universe was I living in? All was revealed when we went to lunch.

He took me to a little Korean restaurant he wanted to try out down a tiny backstreet. Gangster + backstreet = alarm bells.

'Where on earth are you taking me?'

He gave me the loveliest smile: he'd known exactly what I was thinking. 'Don't worry, I've heard they do fantastic food.'

We took a table and started talking. There was so much to catch up on that I never got round to looking at the menu. When the waitress came to take our order, I was about to ask her for more time when I got the surprise of my life: Johnny started ordering in fluent Korean! I wasn't the only one who was amazed. The waitress stared at us in astonishment. She had never heard a black man speak her language before. Two minutes later, every member of staff from the manager to the bottle washer was standing at our table, listening open-mouthed as Johnny explained to them that he'd studied martial arts in Seoul for four years. When it turned out that he had studied with an instructor who happened to be a relative of one of the waitresses, their respect for Johnny soared. We had the most amazing food – and so much of it. All on the house.

'You are a dark horse,' I said, 'with some serious explaining to do.'

To cut a long story short, over the next few weeks Johnny and I never stopped talking. When it became clear I couldn't stay in the flat in Earls Court, he arranged for me to rent the flat above his friend's shop in Finchley, but I actually spent most of my time round at his house, a very nice detached place with a double garage in suburbia. It wasn't the kind of place you'd expect a gangster to live, but then this house hadn't been bought with illicit money. Johnny now ran several martial-arts schools throughout Europe, and they provided him with a very nice level of income. Nothing compared to his nightlife days, but nice enough and honest enough.

The more we talked, the more I came to understand how an ordinary boy from north London can become one of the most feared men in the country. It had started when he was 15, when he'd been beaten up so badly that his head looked like a football. I winced when he told me it had been so touch-and-go that he'd spent a month in hospital. It had been a racist attack and when he recovered he vowed never to be a victim again, which is why he started studying martial arts. He'd got into a few fights, won them, and then been recruited into nightlife as an enforcer. His martial-arts training allowed him to harness his anger at the attack, and nightlife gave him the opportunity to unleash it.

Johnny did bad things. I don't know how bad, and I don't want to know, but he probably let go when he dangled people off balconies. He earned his stripes and gradually made his way to the top of London's biggest protection racket. But then, just as dancing had changed, nightlife changed too. The codes of honour he had put his faith in were no longer adhered to. He realised that not only did he need to get out but also that he was in search of something that could help him make sense of the things he had done. He found the forgiveness he needed in Islam. Johnny knew his new faith and his occupation were incompatible and so he left nightlife and decided to better himself, to become respectable.

Is there anything more attractive than a beautiful man winning the battle against his demons? Johnny was a good man who had lived a bad life, and his repentance gave him a beautiful soul to match his muscled, lean, hard body. He came into my room one morning and asked if he could get me something for breakfast.

'Right now, Johnny, all I want is you inside me.'

Getting together with Johnny felt so easy. When it turned out that our mothers had a mutual friend and that we had probably actually met as kids, it all started to feel meant. The universe wanted us to be together.

We both knew what we had done in the past; we didn't have to lie to one another about anything, and he was offering me the lifestyle I couldn't afford on my own. Before we'd got together, he'd found me crying at work and he asked what was wrong. He was one of the very few people who would understand: I had been crying because I had walked past a shop and hadn't been able to afford to buy anything. It sounds so ridiculously, so stupidly shallow to me now, but at the time I was in mourning for the lifestyle that had been taken from me. He got his wallet out and handed me a sheaf of notes. He was the knight in shining armour I had been waiting for.

I still kept my flat in Finchley, but in reality I moved in with him. With my nice little reception job and my rich, handsome boyfriend to pay for the luxuries in life, it seemed on the surface that I had everything sorted, but the truth was I was missing something. And that something was dancing. Even after a year in Civvy Street, I still felt like a stranger in daylife and that I was never quite sure of where I stood or what the rules were. I didn't like being on the streets with the commuters and the faceless hordes of shoppers. I didn't like the petty squabbles and double-talking of daylife politics. I wanted the straightforward, know-where-you-stand transactions of the clubs. Plus, I was bored. I mean really, truly, dying of the stuff. A day felt like a week. A month felt like a year. I could practically feel the life draining out of my soul.

Just when I was about to drown in nostalgia for the life I had left behind, I bumped into a girl I had known at Diamonds while I was on my lunch break. Angel was the dancer who had been programmed to call her boyfriend every half-hour. A bit of a mouse, but once she got on that stage she came alive, a real showstopper.

She had lost so much weight that I didn't recognise her at first, but as I got closer her phone rang and when she put it to her ear I was taken straight back to the changing room at Diamonds. She had a very definite phone face.

Angel was standing in a doorway at the back of one of the theatres on Shaftesbury Avenue. My first thought was that she must have got a job in the chorus line, but when she hung up and I went over to say hello, a very different story emerged.

'Angel!'

She looked at me blankly.

'Angel, it's me, Sam. Um, I mean Toni.'

'Toni?'

'From Diamonds?'

'Diamonds?'

The girl was as stoned as it is possible to be while still actually breathing. Her pupils were swimming in the middle of her eyeballs. Her make-up was smeared across her face. Her hands were trembling.

'Oh, Angel, honey. What's happened to you?'

She couldn't maintain eye contact long enough to recognise me. She had no idea who I was, just like she didn't know who any of the men who came to visit her were.

'Honey, is there somewhere I can take you? Can I buy you some lunch?'

I reached out to take her hand, but she recoiled from me like I had been about to hit her. She started to freak out and panic. I couldn't leave her like that. I had to at least get some proper food inside her, but before I had a chance to persuade her she could trust me a door opened on the other side of the street and a man came out to collect her. He pushed me to one side and practically picked her up and carried her back inside. Was he the guy she had always called so faithfully?

I went and got myself a sandwich and while I was eating it I was forced to admit that nightlife wasn't as glamorous as I had been choosing to remember it. I also wondered why I had been able to cope with clublife when other girls hadn't. Was I in the minority or were they? Was Johnny the Hat the exception or the rule? Why could some of us handle it while others got sucked under?

In Islam, it is expected that a man will marry and produce children, and when Johnny was made an elder at his mosque he started to feel the pressure to conform – to grow a beard, to fulfil his vows and settle down like a good Muslim. In the weeks leading up to Valentine's Day, I sensed a marriage proposal was on the cards. I thought long and hard about what Johnny could offer me – cars, holidays, clothes, shoes . . . a double garage in suburbia, security, a daily routine of chores and childcare. I started to panic. That wasn't me, that wasn't my life. I called TJ for advice.

'Right, we need to talk. Come over to my mum's house. It's a beautiful day and they've got a pool in the garden. Let's meet there.'

I was amazed when I saw the house TJ had grown up in, somewhere off the far reaches of the Piccadilly line in Southgate. A leafy, tree-lined street. Detached houses with BMWs in the drive. Hers wasn't the only house with a pool. You make assumptions about who ends up working in nightlife, but those assumptions are almost always wrong. TJ came from one of the nicest streets in London, but she had still made her money in sweaty £20 notes.

Her mum and dad were in the kitchen making a pitcher of

sangria, her younger brother Pete was in the living room watching a black-and-white film on the telly, and TJ and I sat in our bikinis by the pool. The discussion about Johnny the Hat took about five minutes. He wasn't the guy for me, I wasn't the girl for his suburban dream, and the sooner I told him the better: it was three days till Valentine's and the chances were he had already bought a ring.

The bigger problem, I discovered as we lay there talking, was that I also wanted to end my relationship with daylife. The people were boring, the hours were relentless and the money was shit.

'I'm not doing anything with my life, Teej. I feel like I'm just wasting away.'

I told her about Angel, and although it was pretty obvious how she had fallen through the cracks, I also felt like I was disappearing too. I felt invisible. I felt *useless*.

'I dunno,' I said, as I took a sip of sangria, 'I feel like I have all this knowledge, all these skills about clubs, and what am I doing? Sodding reception work. If I had ten years' experience in any other profession I'd be moving up the ladder, getting paid for my expertise.'

'Then why don't you go back?' TJ asked.

'You know my rules. I'm not prepared to do that for money.'

'I don't mean as a dancer.'

'What do you mean, then?'

Since leaving Diamonds, TJ had set up her own business providing tequila girls for clubs and pubs. She paid them a fee to trade on their premises and made her money every time a girl sold a shot. The first place she got a contract was at Liberty Steel because of her friendship with Brad.

'He was saying the other day that things just aren't right at the club, the atmosphere is all wrong and the girls are a mess. He was trying to get Theresa to come back from the Emirates or wherever she is, but she's not interested. But you, Samantha, you could be the new Theresa. In fact, you'd be brilliant at it. You would make a fantastic House Mother. You know what, that is such a brilliant idea that I am going to call him right now.'

TJ put her glass down and tottered inside to get her phone. She was gone an awfully long time and I lay there thinking that she was absolutely right: I was completely and utterly born to be a House Mother. It was perfect: I could take a little bit of Auntie Nya, a dollop of Theresa and a whole slice of Toni, and I could really make a difference. I lay there thinking about Angel and the other vulnerable girls I had worked with: without a House Mother, those girls had no one in their corner. I could help them. I could be of use to someone. I wanted the job really, really badly.

When TJ didn't come back out into the garden, I wandered into the house to see what had happened. The only noise was coming from the TV, so I went into the living room. Pete was lying on a sofa.

'What are you watching?'

'I don't know what it's called.'

'Mind if I join you?'

He patted the cushion in front of him and – as if it was the most natural thing in the world – I curled on the sofa beside him like a cat nestling into its favourite spot. He propped his head up on one hand and stroked my arm with the other.

His touch was *electric*. Nothing has ever sent shivers down my spine like that touch and I knew – I absolutely knew – from that very moment that I was going to spend the rest of my life with this 17-year-old boy. It was the weirdest and most wonderful moment of my life. Eternity in an instant.

We must have been watching the TV for about 20 minutes when TJ came in. The sight of her little brother with his arm round her stripper friend in a bikini took her by surprise.

'Er, right, um. Listen, sorry about the delay, I had to sort out rosters . . . Are you two . . . OK?'

Pete and I nodded in unison.

'Well, I spoke to Brad. He said it was fantastic timing – he's just advertised the House Mother's position. If you want an interview, go in and see him on Tuesday.'

On that day, in that room, on that sofa, my life utterly, totally changed.

I fell so fast and so completely for Pete that it took my breath away. The contrast between Johnny and Pete was almost total. Where one drove a Mercedes *and* a BMW, Pete took the bus. Where one was older and ready to settle down, the other had barely left school. TJ wasn't the only one who found it weird that I was with her little brother: I did too. How could I go from wanting all the material possessions Johnny could offer to wanting to just spend time talking with Pete? It was like he had cured me of my money addiction.

Pete didn't just make me re-evaluate my relationship with money, he also made me work out what I really wanted in a man. I didn't want someone who could buy me things any more. I didn't want to be someone's wife, or someone's lifestyle accessory. He might have only been 17, but Pete was the most mature person I had met in a long time. He didn't know the price of anything, but he sure knew the value of the things that mattered. I called him Manboy. It's a nickname that stuck.

LIBERTY STEEL

Mama's home

On my way to my interview at Liberty Steel, I passed the branch of Next I used to work in. I peered in: there were about 20 shop assistants riding the slow train to boredom while listening to mind-numbing pop. It reminded me how deeply, how desperately, I wanted the job at Liberty's. I got my strut on and swept into the club. The lone security boy was expecting me and let me through those fabulous double doors.

As soon as my stiletto left an indent on the carpet I knew I was home. Breathing in that stripper air! The aroma of feet, of alcohol, of *money*: it was such a sweet smell to me that the broadest of smiles split my face in two. And then, waiting for me at the bottom of the stairs was Brad. We beamed at each other, then he picked me up and spun me round.

'It is so good to see you.'

'You have no idea how happy I am to see you,' I said, 'how happy I am to see this place.'

The interview was little more than a formality. We both knew I could look after dancers, but Brad and his sidekick Barry wanted to be sure that I could cash-up and prepare the rosters. I'm dyslexic. These things aren't easy for me, but I told them that if they showed me how to do it a few times I'd quickly get the hang of it.

Brad explained that they wanted to bring back a bit of the old days. There were nights when the dancers' behaviour meant they could be in breach of the licensing laws and they thought a House Mother would be the right person to keep the dancers in check.

'We also need to shift the level of showmanship up a gear. I

190

remember some of the moves you used to do,' Brad said, blushing, 'and, frankly, half the girls here don't seem to know what the pole is for.'

Yup. I can do all of that.

'When do I start?'

Brad said that they had one other candidate to see, but if I took a seat in the lobby he'd let me know shortly. I saw my rival come in and was pretty sure the job was mine. When I saw her leave, I was certain: I had spent over an hour with Brad; she was back out again in ten minutes.

So, just two days after I had broken up with Johnny, I wrote my letter of resignation to the health club. I kept it formal, but what I really wanted to say was your job is boring and poorly paid, there is a more exciting world out there and I'm going to live in it. Bye-bye early mornings, farewell having to book annual leave months in advance, adios petty bureaucracy.

Hello nightlife!

I was so excited about getting out of daylife that I even told my parents about my new job. I was round at theirs for Sunday lunch and they asked what I was up to.

'Well, I just got a new job.'

'Well, that's a lovely piece of news. Another health club?'

'No, actually, I'm going to be House Mother at Liberty Steel.'

'What's that?' my dad asked.

'I'm glad you said that because I would have had problems if you'd known.'

I explained what the club was and what the role of House Mother entailed.

'Now what qualifies you to do that?' my mum asked.

'Well . . .'

I had a choice: I could lie; I could tell the truth; or I could kinda fudge and wriggle and combine the two. Option 3 it was.

' . . . well, you know when I went travelling when I was younger? Well, I did a bit of dancing to pay for things.'

My mum giggled just a teeny, tiny bit. My dad said nothing.

'You know TJ? Well, she supplies tequila girls to the club and she made the introductions. There are some really nice people working there.'

The conversation moved on. Neither of them wanted to ask any questions just in case they heard something that made them choke on their Yorkshires. I was just happy that I could tell them where I worked and why I never answered the phone before 4 p.m. I still had to protect them from the truth – they would have thought they had raised me wrong if they knew everything – but I no longer had to live a lie.

For my first couple of nights I had to shadow Barry, Brad's second-in-command, and learn the cashing-up procedures and get my head round the rosters. I had my own desk set up inside the changing room where I had a big red cash box to put the house fees in. Each dancer had to pay £85 a shift: £60 at the start of the night and the remainder by midnight.

Oh my God! Being back in a changing room again was just wonderful. I felt like getting to my knees and kissing the ground. A random glass shoe under the lockers – how does someone lose one glass shoe unless her name is Cinderella? – or a G-string caught in the grille of the extractor fan. A slight discolouring on the counter where foundation and concealer had been spilt and probably fought over. Every item, however random, told me a story and I loved, loved, *loved* it.

Barry introduced me to the girls as we went round the club. There were so many of them I knew it would take me weeks to remember everyone's name. It didn't help that every girl had a stage name as well as her real one. I made a decision to call them by their stage names because a) they were easier to remember, and b) they were kind of fabulous:

Alexis
Aura
Bambi
Brianna

Chanel
Demi
Faith
Harmony
Honey
Kyla
Mercedes
Nikita
Pixie
Rhiannon
Roxy
Sapphire
Summer
Sydney
Talulah
Temptress
Trinity
Venus
Zizi

I loved their names, but I got very confused when I met a girl called Destiny and found out it was her real name. There was also a dancer whose parents – in their peculiar wisdom – had called her Kaluha! Some dancers were very suspicious of a new member of management, while others were all hugs and kisses in a blatant attempt to befriend me so they could ask for a favour at some point in the future. It had been three years since I'd left Stringfellows, and in that time the dancers had changed. There had always been women from all over the world working in London clubs, but the majority of dancers had always been Brits. Now it was noticeable how few British accents I heard in the dressing room. About 20 per cent were from Eastern Europe, 20 per cent from South America and 10 per cent from Asia. Brits made up about 10 per cent, Londoners even less. After Vegas and New York, London was the place where every dancer wanted to work. It was known as a place where a girl could earn money, and it was a honey pot that brought dancers buzzing in from all over the world.

At the end of my first night, Brad invited me to join him for a drink.

'How's it going?'

'Honestly? Fucking fantastic. I knew I'd missed it, I just didn't know how much.'

'Want a drink?'

'You bet.'

He waved over one of TJ's tequila girls. So as not to take earning potential away from the dancers, TJ's girls wore catsuits. Completely covered up and *completely* sexy. Miaow.

'This is Joni.'

'Hi, Joni.'

'Hi. You're Sam, right?'

'How did you know?'

'TJ's talked a lot about you. Reckons you're going to get everything sorted.'

Joni teed up the shots, and Brad and I knocked them back in celebration.

'One more?'

'You bet!'

As Joni walked away to serve other customers, I told Brad we should try to get her to dance. 'No, she's like Sandy, she's absolutely happy working in the bar and would never get near the stage or the G-strings.'

'So, how is Sandy?'

You know how sometimes you ask a question and before you've heard the answer you've wished that you could instantly invent a time machine and just wind things back a minute? This was one of those moments. Brad didn't actually have to say anything.

'I am so sorry. I thought you guys were set for life.'

'Me too,' he waved to another waitress to bring him more booze. 'Me too.'

I tried to change the subject. 'What did Joni mean about getting everything sorted?'

'Oh, you know, things have been getting a bit out of hand lately. You'll see.'

'What do you mean?'

'You'll see.'

And I did. On my first proper night on the job without shadowing Barry, I walked down the stairs and slap bang into an almighty row.

'Who has nicked my Ugg boots?' It was the whiniest Essex accent I had heard in a long time. 'Who has nicked my fucking Ugg boots!'

The cheese-grater voice belonged to a dancer called Rhiannon. She was so angry it was like someone had stolen her first-born. Clearly, this was not about the boots – she could earn the money back in 15 minutes – it was respect. So I followed her into the changing room, where she continued her tirade. She spotted me and then launched both barrels in my direction.

'Are you the new House Mother?'

There wasn't a chance for me to answer.

'What are you going to fucking do? Some mug's stolen my boots, some tramp who can't afford her own damn boots.'

Other girls arrived on the scene.

'What's up, Rhiannon? What's happened?' The way the girls were swarming round her in mock concern and fake sympathy told me Rhiannon was one of the queen bees of Liberty's. *Get her on side, Sam, and you'll be making things easy for yourself.*

'Yes, I am the new House Mother, and I will sort this out. When did your boots go missing?'

I radioed – all the management carried walkie-talkies – Barry and asked him to look at the CCTV footage. When he radioed me back, I asked Rhiannon if she wanted to come and look at the footage with me.

Over the next couple of years, I would spend a lot of time in the security room monitoring misdeeds and bad behaviour on the bank of TV screens, but on my first visit in there I was struck by just how much it felt like being in an episode of *Prime Suspect*.

'She's not allowed in here.'

'I asked her to join us, Barry.'

'Dancers aren't allowed in here. Management only.'

'Well, if security was being run properly, things wouldn't get stolen, would they? As the victim of the crime . . .' – I was in complete Helen Mirren mode – 'I think Rhiannon here should be able to see who stole her property.'

Barry was not happy.

'Just this once?'

He grunted something and then pressed play. Sure enough, the grainy, grey footage showed another dancer coming into the changing room, sitting down and looking around. Sometimes you've got to be careful with new girls because there are some who only come in for the audition so they can get access to the changing room. One little nicking spree gives them all the outfits and accessories they need to earn money at their regular club.

It was pretty clear this girl was eyeing up Rhiannon's Ugg boots. She looked over one shoulder, then the other, then she leant to one side and kicked off the most decrepit, mangled Ugg boot you have ever seen, then leant the other way and kicked off the other one. She then put her boots on top of Rhiannon's locker and pulled on the new pair. Case solved. Easy.

'You wait till she comes in. I am going to fucking murder her!'

'No, you won't, Rhiannon, you are going to let your new House Mother handle it. OK?'

As the two of us left Barry alone in the security room, he piped up, 'Never bring another dancer in here. OK?'

'Never talk to me like that in front of a dancer again. OK?'

Clearly Barry and I were going to have issues. It helped that I had worked out who he reminded me of. He had a massive chin and lopsided mouth: he was the spitting image of Popeye! I was not about to be pushed around by a cartoon.

About an hour later, the boot-stealer walked down the stairs and she was actually wearing the boots! Rhiannon and her posse were all sitting in a row at the bar, staring at me, waiting for me to get the bloody boots back.

'Hello, babe, we haven't met yet. I'm the new House Mum.'

'I'm Cindy.'

'Do you want to come with me for a minute, Cindy?'

Cindy looked like someone from Studio 54. She was kinda weird-looking but hip with it, and her walk was this kind of lolloping lope like she was stoned. In a very strange way she reminded me of Pokol, the DJ from Denmark. Cindy was just too damn cool for school. As we walked off towards the CCTV room, all the heads at the bar followed us round the room as if they'd been choreographed. Then the security boys all came down the stairs in unison, craning to get a better look at the villain. It looked like a scene from *Guys and Dolls* or something. The entire club was buzzing with The Ugg Boots Bust-Up.

'Where are we going?' Cindy asked.

I showed her into the security room.

'What are we doing in here?'

'I wanted to talk to you.'

'What about?'

'Your boots.'

'What about them?'

'Well, they're not yours, are they?'

'Yes, they are.'

'Listen, before you get yourself into any more trouble, do you want to watch this?'

I asked Popeye to replay the footage, and as we watched it Cindy turned redder and redder. When he pressed stop, I turned to her and saw that she was grinning.

'What have you got to say?'

'What can I say? You caught me, didn't you?'

'You know you can't work here now, don't you? Not today, not any day. You are going to take those boots off, and Barry here is going to take you to lost property, give you your old boots and you are going to leave by the back door. Unfortunately for you, the girls know you've stolen these boots and if they see you in the club we can't promise we'll be able to protect you. So you will leave, and you will not come back. Is that understood?'

I couldn't quite believe how grown-up I was being and how serious the theft of a pair of bloody shoes was turning out to be, but Cindy clearly didn't care. I reckon she was probably a kleptomaniac and she just couldn't stop herself from nicking anything she could reach. She was probably just pleased we weren't calling the cops. Anyway, Barry took her out the back way, and I took the boots to Rhiannon, who was still at the bar with her cronies.

'Oh, House Mum, you are the best! Look, I got my boots back. No one fucking messes with me. Best. Ever. House. Mother.'

A group of them gathered round the boots like someone had just brought their newborn in for a show-and-tell and I stood there thinking, *It's just a pair of bloody boots*. But of course it wasn't. It was all a little power play in which Rhiannon was the leading lady and by getting her on-side I had already started to make my job at Liberty's much easier. She convinced all the British girls to trust me; now I just had to work on the Eastern Europeans, the South Americans, the Asians and the rest of the United Nations.

In my second week, Liberty Steel had its third birthday party, when we closed to the public and just had a laugh. All the busboys, the waitresses, the tequila girls and the kitchen staff hung out with the dancers and bouncers and make-up artists: everyone was there and a couple of things happened that night that helped me win over some of the others. For starters, I got up on the pole a couple of times. I was rusty – I was bloody sore the next day – but the girls could see that I used to dance, and that I had been very good at it. That helped them see me as an ally.

They also got to see me and Brad together, and word got round that we went back a long way, longer than Brad and Barry had known each other. In the pecking order, that put me somewhere near the top. Then, just to seal the deal, an old friend walked down the stairs: Ashley. The one-time foot soldier had become a general.

At first I couldn't see who had arrived; I just heard that cooing, giggling sound dancers make around a very good-looking man. I also saw a parting of the throng as this figure and his entourage made their way across the floor to where I was sitting with Brad. As the group approached, Ash and I made eye contact. He ran over to me, picked me up and twirled me around. I could almost hear the dancers saying, '*She knows Ashley too?*'

It turned out that – after taking the rap for a couple of things and keeping his head down – Ashley had become one of the Higher Ups in protection and it was his posse who were responsible for keeping trouble out of Liberty's. It was clear we still fancied each other a bit, and the attention he showed me made the other girls just a teensy bit jealous.

'You knew him before he was even a courier?'

'Wow.'

Sometimes, the way those dancers spoke to me made me feel like an old-timer reminiscing about the war! I had to remember not to start every sentence with 'In my day . . .' in case I sounded like their mothers.

Knowing that I had experience, and that I had contacts, helped most of the dancers accept that what I said was to be respected. There were just two more people I had to win over: Popeye and a dancer called Brianna.

Troubleshooter

The thing was, though, that I really did want to keep saying that 'It wasn't like that in my day' because I was so shocked at the way things were at Liberty Steel. If I could sum up the difference between the dynamic at Diamonds and the atmosphere at Liberty's it would be this: at Diamonds, everyone went out of their way to maximise the chances dancers had to make money; at Liberty's, everyone went out of their way to maximise the money they could make out of dancers.

Instead of a dancer tipping one of the door guys for a good bit of information or for treating a regular respectfully, the door guys were now bullying the dancers to get their cut. 'You wouldn't have made that money if I hadn't let him in.' 'You didn't hear me say it, but I recommended you to that guy.' The security boys had had enough of dancers making thousands of pounds a night and they had this attitude that – just because they had seen you earn it – they were entitled to their piece of it. Dancers were no longer the sweeties in the sweetie shop or the beer in the pub, and everyone was feasting and feeding off the girls. Mercilessly, without any shame.

I'd been there about two or three weeks and was starting to feel that maybe the changes that needed to be made were beyond me. I was just getting a little bit demoralised when I walked into the changing room and saw something that made my heart soar: Jackie and Terry.

'Toni?'

'What are you doing here?'

'Whaddaya think, you dopey mare? Come here and give your uncle Terry a hug!'

The three of us hugged for ages and I could not hold back the tears. It was so good to see them. They really had been my surrogate family at Diamonds and I felt really emotional seeing them again.

'You back dancing, then?' Jackie asked.

'No. Didn't Brad tell you? I'm House Mum.'

'That is fantastic. Good for you. Our Toni: House Mum. Can you believe it, Terry?'

They had this lovely little banter with each other, and it just felt so homely being around them. Somehow, in the middle of all those pussies, boobs and sequins, Jackie and Terry made everything normal.

'Why didn't Brad tell me you were here?' I said.

Later, I asked Brad himself and he told me exactly why: he had gone to the CCTV room to watch our reunion. He wanted to see the looks on our faces when we saw each other for the first time. That told me a lot about what he was looking for: by bringing in TJ, me and Jackie and Terry, Brad was trying to sprinkle a bit of Diamonds dust over the joint.

I started looking through all the clothes Jackie and Terry had brought in. I got really nostalgic looking at all their little Velcro catches and it took me right back to being on stage and making their clothes pop open. No one made a stripper dress quite like Jackie and Terry.

'So, you can have 20 per cent on that one,' Jackie said.

'And those were straightforward, so 25 per cent is fine on those hot pants,' Terry added.

'What on earth are you talking about?'

'Well, you've got to earn your commission.'

'And I'll say again – what on earth are you talking about?'

They explained that the previous House Mother had sold their clothes for them and taken a commission.

'Well, that ain't happening on my watch. So long as I'm House Mum, you can come in here any time you like and sell your clothes. I would never take a commission off you guys. Never.'

They were welling up.

'Remember that pink cowboy outfit you made me? I made two and a half grand in that outfit one night, and I never properly thanked you. You already paid me my commission, all right?'

'Oh, Toni,' Jackie sighed. 'It's so good to see you again, but I gotta warn you. Things ain't like they used to be.'

'Why do people keep saying that?'

'Don't get disheartened, love,' Terry said.

I made them both a cup of tea and they told me just how much things had changed.

'It's not like it used to be.'

'That's why Brad's brought me in. To bring a bit of magic back.'

'Well, good luck, love, I think you're going to need it.'

Obviously I already knew that standards had dropped, but I had been so excited to be back in a club that I hadn't noticed just how bad things were getting. Jackie and Terry wanted to open my eyes to exactly what was going on. We couldn't understand why Brad didn't seem to be doing anything about it, and we couldn't work out how I could make changes. After seeing the pair of them, I decided that the best thing I could do was lie low, observe what was really going on and not show my cards too soon.

I had won over the Brits with Rhiannon's help, but I was really struggling with the South Americans, in part because they already had their own unofficial House Mother and that was Brianna.

I have no idea how old Brianna was. She could have been 22, she could have been 42. She had had so much surgery done it was hard to tell, especially as her surgeon's work was maintained with regular fillers, collagen injections and botox. Although she looked fake, she did look amazing – 5 ft 10 in., long blonde hair, long legs extended with eight-inch heels. I watched as men went into shock around her. It was as if she was more woman than they could handle. The word I am looking for is *intimidating*. Brianna intimidated as surely as she enticed. A dangerous combination.

She was definitely the top dog among the other Brazilians. The Venezuelan and Colombian girls weren't quite so tightly bound by what Brianna said, but the Brazilian girls were like followers in

Brianna's cult. Whatever she said was the law, because they all felt indebted to her. She had been the first to come to London, and as soon as she had made the money she bought flights for the others to come out and join her.

The money they could make in London in a year was more than they could make in a decade back home, and most of them had the attitude that they were going to make as much as possible as quickly as possible. Two of them – a lesbian couple called Luisa and Ana – had plans to make enough money to build their own club in Brazil. They reminded me of the Jamaicans I had met in Denmark: they were prepared to do anything for two years so long as it meant they never had to do it again.

If I could use one word to describe the Brazilians as a group it would be *hungry*. The exchange rate meant the British pound was more valuable to them if they took it back home, and every night they arrived at the club starving for cash and willing to do anything to get it. As soon as a man started walking down the stairs, you could hear the clattering of 20 pairs of stilettos as the Brazilians crossed the club and got ready to pounce on him as soon as he reached the bottom.

'Hello, darlink.'

'Hello, sexy.'

'You want sexy, yes?'

'You think I sexy, yes?'

They were so determined to get every punter before anyone else did that they were like vultures feasting on a carcass. The poor guys didn't stand a chance. One of the first things I did as House Mother was to instigate a new rule where the girls couldn't approach a man at the bar immediately at the bottom of the stairs. I thought it was important that there was one area of the club where a man could relax. I insisted that he be allowed to come into the club, be served a drink, have a chance to take a look around and see who he wanted to spend time with. I then made it my job to introduce myself and ask him if there was anyone or anything in particular he was looking for.

I would then bring girls into the bar, or the customer would move on to the main floor of the club, where there was nothing I could do to save him from the Brazilians. They wrapped themselves round customers like boa constrictors, squeezing them until their wallets emptied.

For several nights, I watched as they all breached the terms of the club's licence. It's really pretty simple, even if English isn't your first language – the punters can't touch you, and you can't touch them below the waist. Yet I saw their hands wander into all sorts of crevices and I couldn't work out why the management weren't doing anything about it. If one of those men getting groped was an undercover guy from the licensing committee on the council, the entire club could be shut down within hours.

So I watched a bit more, gathered a bit more intelligence, and waited.

It became clear that there were two reasons why management weren't intervening: Brianna was a big tipper, so that meant the entire security team wouldn't touch her; and Brad was not the manager he used to be. His split with Sandy had hit him hard, and he was there in body but not in spirit; in reality, the person in charge was Popeye, who had slowly taken responsibilities away from Brad one at a time.

It was really sad to realise what had happened to Brad. He had always been the exception that proved the rule, who showed the world that nice guys could work in strip clubs. But there was no getting round the fact that some very bad things were happening on his watch, and I had to make him see. I had to find a way of making him take back some control.

I started spending quite a lot of time in the CCTV room watching the cameras, waiting for the right fight to pick. When I'd been in the job about a month, I finally saw what I needed to see. In grainy black and white, I saw Brianna take a customer into one of the corners where the booths were arranged in such a way that there was a blind spot for the cameras. There was just one seat in the entire club where your every move would not be recorded. I watched as she placed him very carefully, then she glanced up at both the cameras pointing in her direction just to be completely sure what she was about to do would be invisible. However, her positioning wasn't quite right. She had placed her punter in the wrong seat, and I watched her every move.

First of all, she did a normal dance and took off her clothes as he watched. Then, as she was putting her clothes back on, they had a little conversation and instead of getting out a £20, he handed over a £50. *OK*, I think, *she's doing a rollover*. But on the second dance, she didn't just take her clothes off, she leant over and unbuttoned his shirt. She then checked the cameras again to make sure she was still out of shot. The dance ended, she sat down, she put her clothes on, and he handed over another £50. *This is not rollover money. She's got a hustle on*. During the next dance, she leant over again and this time unzipped his trousers, and I saw him adjust his position so that it was quite clear his junk was no longer in his pants, and for the rest of the dance she was grinding into his lap. For £50, she was rubbing her bare pussy on his bare cock. I was so angry, I felt sick. He buckled up, another £50 was handed over, then they went through the whole routine again.

I stormed out of the CCTV room and – knowing that I didn't want to make a scene because I didn't want to take on all the Brazilians – I asked the DJ to call Brianna to go to the changing room. A few minutes later, she came in with a massive smile on her face. After all, she'd just made £200 in the space of 15 minutes.

'Brianna, can you come with me, please?'

'Why?'

'I want to talk to you about the customer you've just been with.'

'Talk to Barry about it.'

'I've already radioed him.'

I took her up to the security room where I had asked Barry to meet us, but I had also radioed Brad and one of the doormen who I sensed could be a decent man if he could only break free from Barry's shadow. His name was Dennis. All four of them were very surprised to see the others in the meeting: they had no idea what I was about to do.

'Dennis, would you press play, please?'

I had cued up the footage at just the right point, and, just as I expected, Brianna's face didn't flinch, Barry didn't say a word and Brad looked totally fucking lost. Dennis, on the other hand, was gobsmacked. He couldn't believe what was going on and instantly knew that what Brianna had done could see the club closed down and him out of a job. He had a wife. He had kids. A mortgage. Bills. In his eyes, Brianna's actions were putting his family in danger, and he was so angry he was fit to tear her a new arsehole. His anger meant Brad was going to have to do something. His anger meant this couldn't be ignored.

'Do you realise, Brianna, that your actions could have seen us all out of a job?' I asked.

She looked at Barry, who looked at his shoes.

'But I've seen him in here before,' was her explanation. 'And he's a friend of Barry's, so I knew he wouldn't say anything.'

What? *What!* I realised then that Barry was taking tips from customers as they came through the door for directing them towards girls who did extras. Together, they had a very nice little sideline going that meant they were going to defend each other.

'Put that to one side for a moment, can you tell me, woman to woman, dancer to dancer, why you think it's OK for you to do that? Why is it OK for you to put your naked pussy against his naked cock? Why? For fifty measly quid. Why?'

She didn't say anything.

'Have you got a certificate saying he doesn't have any diseases? Do you know if he's even washed today? What do you suppose he thinks of you? He thinks you're dirty, that you'll do anything. What if he's waiting for you outside because he thinks he can do what he likes with you?'

It's fair to say that everyone in the room was now as shocked by my lecture as they were by Brianna's behaviour.

'As House Mum, imagine I'm taking a new girl round on her

induction and she sees you do that. What am I supposed to tell her? That we're a fucking knocking shop? That that's the only way she can compete and earn money? Who the hell do you think you are?'

What she said next almost impressed me.

'Well, I'm top dog, aren't I?'

I couldn't believe she had actually said it, and in her Brazilian accent it sounded very funny. I realised in an instant that her behaviour wasn't just about earning as much money as she could, it was about power. She got her kicks doing things other people wouldn't dare to do – it's an industry that obviously attracts a lot of thrill seekers – and knowing she was getting away with behaviour no one else in the club would be allowed to was the biggest thrill she could get.

'Well, you won't be top dog anywhere if we get closed down. This is so unacceptable it's not true.'

She turned and looked at Barry, but he looked away. In Brad's presence, there was nothing he could do to defend her. She was on her own. She knew it. So she turned on the waterworks.

'I'm not falling for it, Brianna. Ten minutes ago you were swinging your bollocks out on the floor of the club for everyone to see. One minute ago you're telling me you're top dog, and now you're doing the lost puppy act. I don't buy it. I am here to tell you that your reign here as top dog is over. Finished. Kaput. Now go and get your things, cash out your money and go home.'

Neither Barry nor Brad attempted to contradict or overrule me.

'Dennis, perhaps you can make sure Brianna leaves quickly?'

He escorted her off the premises and I was left alone with Brad and Barry. For several minutes, the three of us sat in silence. I felt I had said enough. I desperately wanted Brad to be the one to speak next, but his mouth was still wide open in shock. Barry knew I had his number and wasn't about to say anything that might incriminate himself. So we waited and waited for someone else to speak.

'Can't happen again, all right?' was what Brad eventually said.

'Never,' Barry agreed, reluctantly.

'All right, then, let's get back to work.'

For me, this was a big, big moment. Barry knew I wouldn't take his shit, and he also knew that Brad would back me up. Obviously, lots of the girls had known what Brianna was doing, and they were ecstatic that someone had put a stop to it. Girls who had never said a word to me finally said hello, or felt that I was on their side and confided things they would have otherwise kept hidden. Brianna was suspended for a month – which for her meant she was losing maybe as much as £10k – and when she came back she never did it again, not on our premises at any rate.

Dennis told the other security boys about it and they even gave me a little round of applause when I walked past them later that night. Word went round the entire club that someone was finally doing what needed to be done.

The really big difference, however, wasn't how people treated me but how I felt about myself. I had Brad's backing and Barry's number, and I had proved that I knew what I was doing. After that night, I felt able to take a girl to one side and tell her that her grooming could be better. 'Here's the number of a skin therapist, she can help you find products that are right for you.' 'Your tan is streaky on the back of your legs, here's a really good tan shop to visit.' 'Your roots are showing, forget the house fee tonight and get that sorted tomorrow, then you can pay me double.'

I just felt able to take charge, and I made other changes too. For instance, at 2 a.m., the only options for a girl to get a meal were McDonald's or Subway, both of which are bad for your skin and leave you bloated. So, when I met a mate of Pete's who had just qualified as a chef, I asked him if he'd be interested in setting up his own business. Every night he made 70 healthy meals for the dancers and sat in the changing room and sold them. It was instantly apparent that the dancers had more energy at the end of the night when they were eating better.

It might not sound like a big change, but the message was clear: someone is looking out for you; someone here sees you as more than your £85 house fee. The dancers responded to that level of care, and when you enjoy work, you shake your booty with a bit more enthusiasm, you earn a little more, you get a little happier. It was all good.

Girls! Girls! Girls!

My working day usually started at about 6 p.m., and the first thing I would do was check my email. Every day, I got between five and twenty-five requests from women wanting to audition. Unless they had teeth missing, grey hair or were obese, I would let most of the women who wanted to come in for an audition. One thing working in a strip club teaches you is that you can't judge a dancer on looks alone: some of the most ordinary-looking women take home the most extraordinary amount of money.

Very occasionally, it was obvious when the girl turned up that she had sent someone else's photo, and if there were punters in the club I just couldn't let a really ugly woman take to the stage. A couple of times a week, a woman came in who we both knew had no intention of becoming a dancer, but I realised that her audition was ticking a box she just had to get ticked. Maybe it was a dare, or a fantasy, or some act of affirmation after weight loss, but there are quite a few women who need to get up on a stage and get naked in front of strangers just once in their life.

Occasionally, a DJ would call out a girl's name and she was nowhere to be seen. I would usually find her under a pile of coats in the changing room rocking backward and forward with fear. It always reminded me of that first night in Denmark and Ali's palpable, knee-knocking terror. But knowing how much fun Ali had had in that year, I would take these girls by the hand, lead them out onto the stage, get them to the pole, wiggle with them a little bit and then back away.

I made sure I took the time to talk to the girls who came in. For them to make money in a strip club they had to be able to talk to people, because if you haven't got the gift of the gab, it doesn't matter how fit you are or how good your moves are, you won't make money. I also wanted to be sure that they could actually speak English. 'Where are you from?' 'Did it take you long to get here?' I wasn't looking for an in-depth conversation about Victoria Beckham's hemlines; I just wanted to see if she could pronounce the place she lived in. I couldn't have slept if I'd put a girl on the floor whose only option was to let someone touch her because she couldn't speak the language.

Every now and then, a dancer would come in who would blow me away. One girl came in who would not have been out of place in Cirque du Soleil. She was stunning to look at and mesmerising to watch, but I made the decision not to give her a job. She wanted to dance for a living, not strip, and I think she thought a year at Liberty's might lead to opportunities on cruise ships or Vegas, but I knew she would more likely to close off those opportunities if she worked with us. She was desperate for money and begged me to let her work, but I knew she just wasn't strong enough, mentally, to deal with some of our customers.

At another audition, a black girl called Donna asked for the stage to be put in darkness while she danced with just a single spotlight. It was immediately obvious why: she was wearing an outfit with luminous material in it, so in the darkness, with her dark skin, all you could see were these geometric shapes moving up and down the pole. She climbed all the way to the top and then dropped down, freezing midway like something from *Mission Impossible*. It was stunning showmanship and I knew that having a few girls on the rota who could get the house talking was good for atmosphere, so when I signed Donna up I gave her half-price house fees. And once the DJ got to know her moves, whenever he felt the place flagging he would call her to the stage and it raised the temperature throughout the club.

Probably only half of the girls I auditioned got to work at Liberty's. Brad wanted me to exercise a bit of quality control, but I couldn't just say to a girl 'By the way, love, you're too darn ugly for us, so, thanks but no thanks'. Some people don't recover from that kind of insult, but if I thought a girl didn't look the part, I had to tell her why she wasn't getting the job. I would say that I felt her grooming needed to be improved but always offered suggestions of salons she could visit and shops where she would find the right kind of outfits. If her dancing wasn't up to it, I suggested she take lessons, because loads of gyms had started to offer them. I was always really impressed when a girl took on board my feedback and came back a few weeks later with a proper game on her. At least I could be sure she was tough enough to handle the customers. If I got any sense that a dancer couldn't brush off a negative comment, there was no way I could let her work. She just would not have survived in that environment.

One of the things I was always looking out for at an audition was a Roamer. Some of them I recognised from my days at Diamonds and Strings, but mostly they were hard to spot. A Roamer looks like a dancer, moves like a dancer but works like a hooker. Basically, they roam from club to club doing a week at a time until they have picked up enough clients that they then see privately. You then see them again a few years later doing the same rounds to pick up new clients.

Not only did Roamers waste my time, but if a girl was found soliciting on the premises then we could get shut down. The chances of that happening were fairly slim, so the real trouble they caused was for the girls who stick to the rules and have to deal with customers who say, 'Well, I was in here last week and a girl slept with me.'

If a girl passed the audition, she could start work that night if she had brought the right paperwork with her – passport, proof of address, utility bill. I explained that, at Liberty's, we had our own version of Heavenly Money and that when a punter cashed up he was given chips, a bit like in a casino. When they cashed them out, the club would charge the dancers 20 per cent (of course, the club had also added 20 per cent to the punter's bill when he had bought the chips).

I'm sure most of the dancers from Australia, South America and Asia needed some kind of work permit, but I was never asked to check for one. I would then instruct her on the requirements of our licence, let her know what the council allowed and what the club expected from her, and if she agreed to all of that I'd get her to sign a contract.

The house fee was discounted for your first three nights to £20. To encourage girls to work, if they did five shifts in a row their fifth night was charged at £30, and to get dancers to start earlier on a Saturday, when you would sometimes get groups coming in after a match, I would charge them £65 if they started at 6 p.m. instead of 8 p.m.

I had about 300 names in my book of dancers, 200 of whom worked in the club at least once a month, and it was my job to make sure there were between 100 and 120 girls on every shift. When I started at Liberty's, there was just one shift a day, but by the time I left, the club had started opening at midday, and that meant there were some girls who chose to do 12 till 8, but most went after the money and worked 8 till 4. Of the 120 girls who would work the night shift, about 80 of them would work most nights of the month. Their money addiction meant they only took a night off if they were ill or on holiday.

There was a day, when I'd been there about six months, when I had arranged for about twelve girls to audition at the same time. I remember sitting there with a Diet Coke and realising that all 12 of them had had boob jobs. I tried to think how many dancers in Denmark had had surgery, and it wasn't nearly as many as the women who dance these days. Some augmentations were really obvious, like jelly moulds stuck on with plasticine, but some you would have to be an expert to spot. And let me tell you, I was becoming an expert on breasts. PhD. Masters. MBA. Got 'em all. I am a boob master. I reckon a House Mother in a strip club knows more about breasts than most surgeons.

Tear drop, hemispheres, over the muscle, under the muscle (which most people say looks better, but it depends on your stature and how much weight you're carrying), scar at the nipple, sliced under the breast, through the belly button or in from under the armpit. Every night before the girls went on the floor you'd see them lift each breast and dot on a bit of concealer over their scars.

Whenever a girl has new boobs, she goes round the changing room saying, 'Touch them, touch them.' I must've touched thousands of boobs and some of them, unless you were told, you would not know.

Of course, every now and then you hear – and see – a horror story. One boob up here, the other one down there. Sometimes it just looks like someone has shoved a tennis ball in there and stapled the skin back. Get the wrong surgeon and you are in for a world of pain. I had one girl come in three days after her operation because she was desperate for the money. I watched as she took off her training bra in agony.

'Honey, really. You ain't working tonight.'

She started to cry.

'Here is your house fee back, now go home. I do not want to see you here for another three and a half weeks, OK? Go.'

For some girls, they felt so confident with their new breasts that the confidence alone earned them more money, but they were so sure it was the surgery that had done it that some of them even gave each one a name! And of course, when one girl gets her boobs done and starts earning more, another three visit her surgeon. It got to the stage where I could tell which surgeon had performed the operation just by looking at a girl from the other side of the club.

Most dancers these days have had their boobs done. I think there is this little nagging fear that if you don't, you might not earn the best money. And at around £6k a go, it was only a week's money for most girls anyway. I still go through cycles of thinking I should get mine done, but I always come back to the point that I made good money with the boobs I was born with, so I never have gone under the knife.

And, of course, it's not just boobs girls get done – buttock implants, tummy tucks, facelifts, and more than a few go in for a bit of 'vaguvination'. I reckon I could probably write a book just on pussies alone – big lips, little lips, uneven lips, big clits, invisible clits, the full bush, the landing strip, the Hollywood. Some days you'd be sitting in the changing room trying to have a serious conversation with a dancer about her time-keeping or her house fee and you'd have to laugh because over her shoulder would be a bum hole or a pussy or someone tucking a tampon string inside. You just didn't know where to look, so you might as well stare.

People assume that working in a strip club must be bad for your self-esteem because you are surrounded by pert, beautiful, naked women. What you realise – within an hour of being in a club – is that it is actually a very good place for someone with low self-esteem to give themselves a boost. Whatever insecurity you have about your own body quickly dissolves when you see other women's stretch marks or love handles or cellulite and you see that they still earn money. If there's one thing I would like women to know about strip clubs, it is that men do not pay to see perfect dancers. We do not all look like models. Sure, we make the best of what we've got, but concealer and good lighting can only cover so much. In fact, more often than not, the girl-next-door types with the wobbly belly and the crooked smile earn more than the vixens and glamour pusses.

There was one girl at Liberty's whose dancer name was Princess. When my sister Amanda came into work one night – ever since the trip to Ibiza she had wanted to see what dancing was really like – she saw Princess and came up to me.

'Sam, I think someone has, like, snuck in here. Someone who shouldn't be here.'

'Ah. You've seen Princess, then.'

'You've made a mistake, Sam. You can't give her a job.'

I smiled, in part at my sister's cheek for telling me how to do my job when it was her first ever visit to a club, and in part because I knew by the end of the night Amanda would be amazed.

'She was already working here when I started and I thought the same as you, but believe me, this girl can earn.'

'Really?'

'Truly.'

It wasn't that Princess was plain, she was actually bona fide, 100 per cent, totally ugly. Buck teeth, acne scars and a nose you could more accurately call a snout. There really wasn't anything make-up and grooming could do for her. Even the Look Good Lighting didn't make a difference. Body-wise she was all right, but there was no muscle tone, no hourglass figure, no amazing rack. And, oh my God, when she opened her gob the voice she had on her was like a smoking chimney. I was very familiar with the Girl Next Doors making the money because customers are too intimidated to speak to the spectacular-looking women, but Princess was about five leagues below the Girl Next Doors. Yet her level of self-belief and confidence was unreal. If anyone wants to test the theory that what you believe is what you project, then they should study Princess.

When I had first met her in the changing room, I actually went to see Brad to ask him if there had been some mistake. His reply was, 'Wait and see. She makes money for herself, and she makes a lot of money for this place.' By the time I got back to the changing room, she was in a little red outfit and ready to get to work. That was the last I saw of her all night until – six hours later – I heard this crashing noise as she emptied out her purse. She had spent all night in the VIP area and her purse was distended with chips. She counted them out – £5,500. I was amazed.

'I've only got £2,000 in cash. I'm going to have to get Brad to write you a cheque for the rest.'

'All right, House Mum.'

Clearly, getting paid by cheque was something that happened frequently.

Mostly, the girls liked it when their customers paid them in cash, as that meant they didn't lose 20 per cent when they cashed out their chips at the end of the shift. Princess was different. She liked to get paid in chips because it meant she couldn't spend it. So she hoarded them and one day she came in with £35k's worth of chips. Three days after that, she turned up in a beautiful sports car.

Princess had a very nice life. She had a place in London, somewhere in the country where she kept a couple of horses and, if the rumours were true, a nasty little cocaine habit. She probably earned £250k a year, maybe more, and yet she looked like a girl who worked on the till at Lidl.

I got more complaints about Princess from other dancers than I did about anyone else, and that was because Princess was the Olympic champion of stealing customers. A dancer could have spent ten or fifteen minutes with a customer, but as soon as Princess sat down that customer would ditch the first girl and follow Princess into a VIP room. I got so many complaints about this that I started to watch Princess very carefully – how on earth was a girl who looked like the horses she owned getting away with it? In an odd way, Princess actually restored my faith in men because she proved, beyond any shadow of a doubt, that men are not just interested in how a woman looks.

Her brazenness stunned me. If a dancer was sitting on the left-hand side of a customer, Princess would sidle up and sit on his right-hand side. Within a few minutes, the original girl was out of the picture and Princess started negotiations. Often she would bring in other girls to her VIP sessions, charging the customer £100 for each girl while paying them £50. The guy who would have happily paid the first girl £150 for a VIP was now shelling out £500 to Princess.

I had to find out what on earth she was saying to these guys to make them switch. Literally, three or four words in their ear and the first girl was history. *Is he blind? Can he not see? She is inches from his face, he must know that she is ugly.* Eventually I managed to position myself in the booth next to one where she was making her move. I couldn't work out everything she was whispering, but I did catch a handful of tell-tale words . . . 'treat me like the dirty little slut you've always wanted . . .'

I realised that Princess had no boundaries. Because she didn't look like any man's ideal woman, she didn't have to play a certain role. If you think about Rose, the big earner from Stringfellows, she could only earn money in a certain way, by projecting a certain image, because her customers bought into her look and her demeanour. Princess was not bound by any preconceptions and she could say anything to a guy, *absolutely anything*, and not risk disappointing him.

When Princess or one of the other dancers cashed out several thousand pounds at the end of the night, I'd be lying if I said there wasn't a part of me that wished I could still earn that kind of money. Some of the dancers could see that I was changing the environment so that they could make more money, and if they had a good night they would tip me. Occasionally a customer might want to thank me for bringing him the right girl for his mood, or to suit his client's taste, and he would also tip me. Most nights, I'd make a couple of hundred quid in tips on top of my salary, and very occasionally I'd have a four-figure night. I enjoyed the extra money – it felt good to be rewarded for doing my job well – but I was actually pretty happy with my salary. It was less than a dancer's income, for sure, but way more than a receptionist's.

Having Pete in my life made money seem so insignificant, especially when you consider what a hold it had had over me for all those years. I had gone from desperately wanting the kind of man who could buy me a flat, to falling head over heels in love with a teenager who couldn't even buy me a bus fare let alone a burger. My Manboy was teaching me what really mattered.

I still found it odd that I was in a relationship a) with TJ's little brother, b) with a teenager and c) with a guy who was absolutely broke. For money, Pete did a bit of DJing, or a bit of acting (he'd been in a couple of commercials), or a bit of labouring. So long as he had a roof over his head and food in the fridge, he didn't care about earning any more. And the madder it got at the club, the crazier the antics of Brianna or Princess, or the meaner and more manipulative the security guys got, the more I needed Pete. He became my sanctuary. He kept me sane.

Mama Sam's School of Etiquette

In the month that Brianna was suspended, I took the opportunity to weed out the other rule-breakers and troublemakers. I identified around 25 girls who no longer met the club's standards and requirements, either because I was pretty sure they were soliciting, or they were allowing themselves to be touched, or because their alcohol and drug problems meant their time-keeping was terrible, or their attitude was, or they just looked ravaged beyond repair by nightlife. I took a list of names to Brad and told him we should let them go.

'There's something else I want to do too. I want to start an etiquette school.'

'A what?'

'I want to show the girls how they can make money without letting themselves be touched. It is possible, you know. I did it for years.'

'You think you can do that?'

'Just watch me.'

Mama Sam's School of Etiquette held lessons twice a week. I charged the dancers £25 for two hours of tuition, and I usually had four to six dancers at each class. When I'd started, I'd been told not to spend more than 15 minutes on inductions – the clear instruction was to get their house fee off them and get them on the floor as quickly as possible. For girls who were new to nightlife, this wasn't enough. Letting a girl go on the floor with 15 minutes of induction – which, if I'm honest, didn't include a lot more than 'Here's your locker' and 'There are the loos' and 'Sign this' – was the equivalent of letting a soldier onto the battlefield after saying, 'This is a gun, that's the enemy, walk in that direction.' I actually felt it was negligent, especially in a club that size, where it was easy to feel lost, so I told every new girl, even if they had danced at another club beforehand, that I expected them to attend my etiquette class at least once. And as soon as other dancers saw that my students were earning more money, even the old hands wanted to come and see what Mama Sam could teach them.

I based my lessons on the questions I regularly got from dancers and on what I thought I would want someone to tell me if I was just starting out. Most girls' big fear was getting into a conversation with a customer who wanted more than they were prepared to give. So we did quite a lot of role-playing where I was the lecherous git and they could rehearse the lines that would get them out of trouble. I really tried in those situations to be as mean and disgusting as possible so that whatever a girl heard from a customer wouldn't be the worst thing that had ever been said to her.

I gave girls ways to close off an encounter if she wanted to get away from a customer, but mostly I gave her ways to get another dance out of the same guy. I told them to always look in his wallet when he pays for the first dance – how many notes are in there, what colour are they, is there a photo of his kids, what kinds of credit cards does he have? All those tricks I had learnt over the years, all that wisdom, got handed down in the space of a couple of lessons.

I got the girls to write down five facts about themselves.

'Why, House Mum?'

Well, because in a profession where you are talking to hundreds of men every week, how on earth could you keep track of everything you had said if you made everything up? If, on the other hand, you base all your conversational repertoire around five memorable facts about yourself you will never let your customer down. Whether it was the fact you once went skydiving in Tenerife or have always wanted a Mercedes sports car, if you stick to the same topics you can a) invent things on the spot about those subjects without worrying they will come back to bite you, and b) when a customer returns and says 'How was the skydiving lesson?' you can answer him and he feels like you've remembered him. That means you must like him. He now feels special, he feels memorable and you have made him believe that you liked him enough to remember your entire conversation with him. Guess what: he's now going to spend even more money with you.

I encouraged girls to make notes and keep files on their customers. If you remember a guy's name and the business he says he works in, then he's going to feel wanted and is more likely to come back in and ask for you by name. If you create familiarity with a customer, you make it much easier for him to decide to come back and see you.

I took girls up onto the stage and got them to tell me what they could see. Then I told them what I saw: I blocked the club out into zones – the champagne tables, the spirits tables, the beer tables where the first-timers often sat, and Death Row, the name I gave to the bar area where men who had run out of money would sit and nurse their last inch of beer until it was chucking-out time.

'Focus on the areas of the club where the money is,' I told them. 'Make eye contact, get a guy to wink at you. You might not open your gob, but you can start a conversation with a guy when you're on stage.'

Newbies always hated it when it was their turn to dance on stage, but I encouraged them the way Auntie Nya encouraged me, to see it as their sole opportunity to make every man in the club empty his wallet all over you. The effort you put in on the stage is rewarded on the floor. I showed them some pole techniques and told them to watch other dancers and pick up ideas. I talked to them about the importance of striking poses: it gives the guys a chance to look at you, but it also lets you scan the room. I taught them how to take money off a customer while they were on stage using every bit of their body from their toes to their teeth. I had observed over the years that as soon as one guy starts waving £20 notes at the girl who is on the stage, about ten other customers will copy him. If you can take a note from guys in increasingly unusual ways, other customers are going to keep thrusting their hands up to see what you do with their £20.

When girls were dancing at tables, I again impressed on them how important eye contact is. It's something that most dancers – even experienced dancers – find very difficult to do when a complete stranger is watching them undress. But if you practise, it becomes second nature, and if a guy believes you like him enough to look him in the eye, guess what, he is going to want to get to know you. If you can make him feel that for the two or three minutes you are dancing for him he is the only man in the club, you are making it very easy to get rollovers.

At these lessons, we discussed all the ways a girl could make more money. I encouraged them to look at the big earners and try to work out what those dancers were doing and how they could replicate it. 'If you see a girl walk away from a table with a bag full of chips, be cheeky, go up to her customer and ask him what she said or did to earn the money. Every shift you work here is a chance to learn more and earn more.'

My sole objective with the etiquette school was to give dancers as many ways as possible to earn money without having to be touched. If you learn how to read a customer, if you know how to tease and seduce him, then you will never need to be touched. 'The day you start getting touched is the last day you will be able to do a seductive dance, because you will never feel sexy again and you'll have to get touched for the rest of your career. Ask yourself this: is there enough soap and water in the world for that to happen?'

I saw it as my job to bring back the standards of yesteryear, an essence of the good old days. So I told the girls to use the waitresses and the bar staff as spies and to tip them if they got good information. 'The security guys are going to look after your interests if they know you will look after theirs.' I made it my mission to bring back the tipping culture that had kept things in balance at Diamonds.

The etiquette classes were also an opportunity to warn girls about some of the tricks guys would play to get out of paying, or to tip them off about some of the regulars they should try their hardest to avoid. One of those was a guy we called Blue Shirt.

He was an Indian man in his mid forties who came into the club four or five times a week. When someone visits anywhere that regularly, the staff become very familiar with their face. And when you're familiar with someone, it's very hard not to nod hello, or shake hands with them when they step through the doors and put a £20 in your palm. He even came up to me once and gave me a hug, and it was only later that I found out why. You could easily understand why a new girl would think that Blue Shirt was friends with the management. And that's exactly what he wanted.

He would tell girls that it was all right to do things with him that they couldn't do with other customers. He could touch them, he promised, they could grind on him – it was all OK with the boss. He also tried telling some girls that he could have dances for £10 instead of £20. It turned out that the time he had come up to hug me was all part of him showing a new girl that the House Mum knew him and that what he was saying was acceptable.

I heard stories from dancers who had let him touch them that he got a little bit of an erection. Girls felt used and dirty if they spent any time with him or got taken in by his spiel.

'The good news,' I told my students, 'is that this guy is easy to spot because he always wears exactly the same blue shirt. He must have one in his wardrobe for every day of the week. The bad news is that he's not the only one. You've got to realise that there will always be guys who want to test you, who will ask for the dirtiest things, who won't care if you say no because he gets his kicks just asking and seeing you squirm. No matter what a man says to you, the rules are that there is no circumstance where we will allow you to touch guys or be touched by them.'

I asked Brad on more than one occasion why the club didn't simply ban Blue Shirt.

'Show the girls you care about them.'

'I can't,' he said.

'Why not? He's just one guy.'

224

'Yeah, but he spends money, Sam. His bar bill is maybe £1,000 a week. I can't turn him away.'

'That bar takes tens of thousands of pounds a night. Lose him, Brad. The club would be better off without him.'

Brad looked sad. He knew I was right. 'I just can't.'

'Why not?'

'I'm not allowed. The owners . . . I just can't.'

I had never really thought about who owned Liberty Steel before. I suppose I had assumed that Brad had enticed some of the investors in Diamonds but that he was pretty much running the show. I was wrong. He was their monkey, employed because of his experience not for his current appetite for the work, and it was his job to keep the money coming through the tills while they looked for a buyer for the business.

'I think they want to sell it to an American company, one of those big operators, and every extra £1,000 on the weekly takings increases how much they can sell the business for.'

Oh. I was gobsmacked. All this time I had thought that Brad would back me up if I wanted to make changes, but now I realised that I would only have his backing if my suggestions didn't impact on the bottom line. It was a different game – the business was no longer about finding ways for the girls to make money in the hope and expectation that the money would get moved around the club, it was now – pure and simple – about the club making as much money as possible.

So instead of having 100 girls on the floor, I was encouraged to put closer to 130 on the floor because that was an extra 30 house fees. At £85 per girl, that was £2,500 a night. Or an extra £75k a month. It was obvious what it meant to the profit margin; it was also bloody obvious what it meant to the dancers: more competition.

On an average weekday night, 300 to 400 guys would come in (on Fridays and Saturdays it would almost double with stag parties) and at any one time you might expect to have 60 to 100 guys in the club. At the beginning of the night you might only have 20 customers. If there are 130 dancers on shift who have already paid their house fee and their cab fare, you have 130 women who are desperate to get their money out of those men. The more girls you have, the more steals go on, the more aggression you get between dancers about perceived and actual insults, and the harder it is for the House Mother to make a difference. I could have held etiquette classes every day of the week and I still wouldn't have been able to fight against those kinds of statistics.

I know some people in civilian life think it's wrong that women should be put in such a competitive environment where they have to fight for every customer. But I've got friends who work in sales and they've told me stories of a colleague who's picked up their phone, said that they're not in the office and poached their client! The truth is, most jobs involve some element of competition with your co-workers; it's just very apparent in a club environment.

I reckon that of the 300 or so girls I had on my books, maybe a quarter would let themselves be touched. For an extra £20, they would let a man grope their breast; £50 and he could run his hand up the inside of their thigh. Another 10 per cent were opportunists: if they liked the guy and they liked the amount of money he was offering, they would take the chance that he wasn't an inspector from the council. Most girls, however, had the same morals I did and no amount of competition – even if there had been 200 dancers on each shift – would have meant they would allow themselves to be touched. Most girls really benefited from the etiquette school, but I was increasingly worried about the minority who would do anything for the money.

I started to do laps of the VIP area. The security team who normally oversaw the VIP rooms thought I was a mug and were only too happy to let me do their job, but I was determined to find out what was going on in the VIP rooms, as the security cameras could only show you things from certain angles.

Mostly, it was just as I would have hoped – rubbish-looking blokes being treated like princes by knock-out stunners whose company they could never hope to have on the outside. Often they were just talking, trying to recreate the romantic atmosphere of a date, or sometimes the girls would be dancing for the customer, but by and large whenever I popped my head through the curtains, I didn't see the kind of behaviour that would get the club closed down. One time, I laughed my head off when I saw a girl – in a bikini and 8 in. heels and nothing else – waltzing around with a guy in his 80s who was about 2 ft shorter than her. She had no idea what the steps were, but he had no idea how else he could get some female company in his life. It was very sweet, but equally it was laugh-out-loud, roll-on-the-floor funny.

Occasionally, however, I would see the kind of behaviour I suspected was still going on. There was one instance where I peered in through a gap in the curtains and saw a dancer pull a bottle of beer out from her vagina and then hand it to the customer. Technically, he hadn't touched her. Technically, she hadn't touched him. Fuck the technicalities.

'I'm really sorry, sir, I'm the House Mother and I just need to speak to this girl for one moment. She'll be right back with you.'

I stood with this girl right outside the booth in the hope that her customer would hear what I was about to say.

'Woman to woman, do you want to tell me what you've been doing in there?'

She didn't say anything.

'It's not nice, is it, putting your pussy all over a bottle and letting him lick it, is it?'

Again, silence.

'You're embarrassing yourself and you're embarrassing me. I don't want Brad thinking I let this kind of thing go on.'

She just stood there looking at the floor.

'Do you really want to make your money opening your pussy lips for a stranger? And for how much? £20? It's just not nice, it's just not on. Do you get it?'

'Yes, House Mum.'

'I expect to see you at my etiquette class one day next week. Understood?'

'Yes, House Mum.'

'You are the last girl I would expect this from.'

Some girls would respond well to a firm hand. They would come to the classes, think about the different ways they could make money and change the way they interacted with customers. But there would always be some – usually those with debts or addictions – who would say yes to pretty much anything so long as the guy was willing to pay. And that meant that girls got so used to men treating them badly that some of them could no longer tell wrong from right. Unfortunately, some of the men who were abusing them weren't customers – they were staff.

It made me angry, but it also made me very sad. It used to be that the door staff and security team looked out for dancers. They protected us, worshipped us and wanted to date us. Now they just saw dancers as victims and mugs, as walking ATMs.

What made a bad situation worse was that, in the pecking order inside the club, the security boys were at the top. That meant that the bar staff, the busboys, the maintenance guys and every other man in the club took his cue from how the security boys behaved.

I found Joni – TJ's cute tequila girl – washing out her shot glasses in the loos one night.

'Why aren't you doing that in the kitchen?'

'I can't go in there any more.'

Joni was one of those petite women whose small stature seemed to be a reflection of her self-esteem. Some short women make up for their lack of height with a big personality, but Joni seemed to know her place in the world was a couple of paces behind the bigger personalities. When she had a couple of drinks, she transformed into a monster party girl, slamming sambucas and tequilas down people's throats till they shook like shitting dogs, but when she was sober she often seemed a little bit quiet. But the customers loved the shy-girl routine as much as they loved the party girl, and Joni always made good money for TJ no matter what state she was in. I couldn't tell from her answer if she had been told that she couldn't go into the kitchen any more or if she had chosen not to go in there.

'Why can't you use the kitchen?'

Tears filled her eyes and she shook her head. She carried on cleaning her glasses.

'Joni, if something's wrong I want to know.'

She wouldn't answer, so I walked up to her, took the glass from her hand and put it down and then held her face in my hands.

'Is it a man? Has someone in here said something to you?'

The tears spilled out of her eyes and down her cheeks.

'Or done something to you?'

The tiniest of nods told me my hunch was right.

It turned out that one of the bar backs – the guys who make sure the fridges are always full and the pumps don't run dry – was coming up to her every time she went in the kitchen. He would stand behind her as she washed the glasses and put his hands on her waist. At least that was how it started. Those predatory guys judge your reaction, and if you don't give them the right signals they will escalate their behaviour. If it had been me, he'd have had an elbow in the ribs followed by a knee in the groin. Maybe he'd have even got that treatment from Joni if he'd got her in one of her party-girl moods, but he knew to push it when she was in one of her mousy phases. And when someone shrinks from your touch, you know you can carry on without resistance.

He started touching her belly and her breasts, and his hands started wandering all over the place. When she had finally tried to break free from him, he had held her firmly from behind, trapping her against the sink, and told her not to be so silly because he was only mucking around.

'You are only going to have to do that one more time. If you go back in that kitchen, and we see him do it, he will be out on his fucking arse with a couple of broken fingers for good measure. Do you think you could go back in there?'

Joni took a bit of persuading, but in the end I got her to agree. I went off to find Brad – I wanted him to be the one to witness the assault. And to his credit he said, 'We can't put her in that situation. Let's just get him out of here.'

Joni was just one of those girls you believed. She wasn't the sort to make it up and Brad knew it. It was situations like this where the security stooges had their uses: tell them to beat someone up and they're only too happy to oblige.

'Thank you, Sam.'

'You don't have to thank me, Joni. It's my job. I'm House Mum. Looking after my girls is what I do.'

Like father, like son

You know there are just some nights when everything seems to happen at once? Like the planets have aligned. Or a prophecy is coming true. Or there's some atmospheric phenomenon going on. Well, I was having one of those nights.

It started as it always did, going through the applications of girls who wanted to audition, when an email pinged into my inbox with the subject line 'WHAT R THE RULES?'

I opened it up. Someone wanted to check that dancers aren't allowed to touch customers. I emailed straight back and said that that was the case.

'What about if they meet a customer outside work?' came the anonymous reply.

I wrote back that girls were not allowed to see customers outside work. It could be seen as soliciting, and this could see us shut down.

'So what would happen if I had proof that one of your dancers had been seeing a customer?'

I wasn't quite sure if I should carry on with this correspondence, but just in case it was some kind of mystery shopper from the council I typed that she would no longer be able to work for us.

There was a delay of a couple of minutes before the next email appeared with the subject line 'LISTEN 2 THIS'.

I opened the attachment, which was an audio recording of a man confronting a woman.

'Did you get my text messages?'

'What text messages?'

'The ones I sent you. Get your phone.'

What the hell am I listening to and why on earth is someone sending it to me? It felt intrusive to be eavesdropping on a private conversation, but there was something compelling about the recording. It was like listening to your neighbours having a row on the other side of the fence. I had to find out what was going to happen.

'You sent me a text at 3.28 a.m. saying "Leaving now. xxx".'

'Yeah.'

'Well, you didn't come home until 8 a.m. So where were you?'

I was intrigued; what the hell was going on?

The woman began to tell him that she had gone for a drink with some of the other girls from the club. *Right*, I thought, *she's a dancer then*. But I didn't recognise her voice and I was pretty sure she didn't work at Liberty's. I carried on listening.

The man's voice was very aggressive, but her voice stayed calm. He wasn't at all convinced she'd just gone for a drink, because earlier in the night she had texted him about a celebrity who had come into the club. The man was clearly jealous and was convinced that she must have gone for a drink with the celebrity.

I tell you, it was like listening to an episode of *EastEnders*. The calmer she stayed, the angrier he got. At one point I thought I was going to have to hand the recording over to the police, as I was pretty sure he was going to beat her up. You just don't experience rage like this guy was exuding very often. One wrong move, one word out of place, and I feared how he would react. I still didn't have a clue who these two people were, but I was getting to know the inside workings of their relationship very intimately.

Their row simmered on for about half an hour, with him asking for every single detail of her night: who had she done doubles with, who had walked her to her car, which door she had left the club by, where the car had been parked – he had a compelling need to work out, inch by inch, the route his wife had taken the night before. It was like retrospective stalking: if he needed to control her actions that much, why didn't he wait outside the club for her?

It was a real insight for me into the lives of dancers. I didn't know this woman, but I knew that her marriage wasn't that different from the marriages and relationships of the girls who worked at Liberty's. Boyfriends and husbands might say they're OK with you working in a club, sometimes they even encourage it as it's a way of weakening a girl – 'No one else would have you, not with what you do for a living' – and keeping control. But this recording was proof that even men who support their wife's career can be invaded and taken over by the jealousy virus. This guy was burning up with the virus. I could picture him: red face, bulging eyes and fists clenched so tightly that his fingernails were drawing blood. The thought that this celebrity had seen his wife's pussy was destroying him. It reminded me that when girls are working in the club, their men aren't asleep; they are tossing and turning and raging and burning.

Eventually, the wife confessed to having gone back to the celebrity's house for a few drinks. There were a handful of girls from the club with her.

'Which girls?'

She was vague about the names.

'You were alone with him, weren't you? Weren't you?'

'Yes, but we just talked.'

'You slept with him, didn't you?'

'No.'

'Which room did you sleep with him in?'

'I didn't sleep with him.'

'Yes, you fucking did. Don't fucking lie to me. You slept with him, didn't you?'

'Yes.'

There was a long pause on the recording.

'What was his cock like?'

I burst out laughing. After 30 minutes of rage, all this guy wanted to know was if his cock was bigger than the guy off the telly's cock. The recording had gone from tragedy to comedy, and I was still chuckling away as the first dancers came in to get ready for their shift. I then got another email. The subject line this time was 'DID U LISTEN 2 IT?'

I typed back that I had.

He replied with the name of the woman in the recording and said I should check the names of the women who had asked for an audition. 'If what U say is true, then she can't work 4 U, can she? U know she sleeps with customers, so if U give her a job I will shut U down. OK?'

I checked the names on application forms and, sure enough, there was this woman's name. She'd probably been asked to leave her last club and now her husband was checking her emails and making sure she would never work as a stripper again. I felt sorry for both of them, to be honest, because her choice of profession was making their marriage impossible. Many of the girls at Liberty's must have been going home to something similar each night.

I'd got in early that night because I had come straight from the shops. I'd popped down Oxford Street to buy every pair of pink shorts and all the pink vests that Primark had. It was all part of my preparations for a charity night we'd been planning to raise money for an organisation that helps people with a skin disorder that means they can't be touched. The son of a former dancer had just been diagnosed with the condition, and we all wanted to do something to help. And the best way a stripper can raise money is by telling punters they can have a flash of her tits if they put a tenner in the bucket.

As the girls came in to start their shift, I gave them all shorts and vests, and within ten minutes each girl had found a way of customising her outfit. You would be amazed what a stripper can do with a pair of scissors and a couple of safety pins. Several of the girls had a stud machine and they added diamanté studs, while others slit the neck of the vest to make it more revealing, or cut a hole to reveal their belly button, or tied it in a knot at the waist. Honestly, the creativity and invention in that changing room was incredible.

'Right, ladies,' I said to them all, 'I want you all to put £50 each in the bucket to get things started, because that way I know you are all going to work that little bit harder to earn it back.'

I have to give them credit, because they were all very happy to make a donation.

'We're going to be having a paddling pool on stage tonight, so please be careful you don't slip and please don't get in it wearing stilettos!'

'We're not stupid, House Mum.'

'Also, there's a young lad who suffers from this disease coming in tonight with his carer, so I want you all to make a special effort with him, but please, please remember that you cannot touch him.'

'Yes, House Mum.'

'This lad has probably never spoken to a girl in his whole life because of his disease. I've been told he's very shy but very lovely and he's come to a strip club to meet girls, so will you all please go and talk to him?'

'Of course we will, House Mum.'

'As well as getting guys to pay you for wet T-shirt activities in the paddling pool, I want you to collect sponsorship from them for doing ten minutes on the exercise bike up at the bar. Tell them you'll lean right over the handle bars and they can watch your boobies jiggle as you pedal.'

'Yes, House Mum.'

'By the way, before you go out on the floor I have to tell you that you all look sensational. Nice work with the outfits.'

'Thanks, House Mum.'

I felt like a police sergeant taking roll call on a US cop show. Once the girls knew what they had to do, they went out on that floor and they worked their arses off. The atmosphere in the club that night was just sensational, and the guys who had come in didn't really know what had hit them: 130 girls were running round in the same pink outfit asking them for tenners and twenties for a flash of some flesh or a little playful doubles action with another girl. And then there was this ridiculous sight of these gorgeous women climbing onto an exercise bike in glass heels and trying not to perspire their make-up off. We raised thousands and thousands that night, and in the middle of all that pink, sweaty madness was a 19-year-old lad called Charlie with a crippling skin condition and in a wheelchair. He was having a great time, but I knew a way of making things even better.

'Hello, Charlie,' I said, crouching down beside him. 'I'm House Mum and I know you're really shy, but you can be honest with me. What do you like? Big bum? Big boobs?'

His poor little face! He didn't have a clue how to answer, cos no one had ever asked him before what sorts of things might turn him on.

'I don't know.'

'Well, you stay there for a bit, have a good look round and when I come back you can tell me what you like the most.'

I went off and did my rounds, and when I came back he said, 'Excuse me, but I think I like big boobs.'

'Leave it with me.'

I then went round the club and asked all the girls with the biggest boobs to follow me, and I got Dennis, the nice security guy, to help Charlie's carer escort him into a VIP room.

'Right, girls. You've all spoken to Charlie by now, you know he's lovely, but what you don't know is that he loves big boobs. I want one of you to go into VIP and give him a dance he'll remember. There won't be any money in it, but you will be making a young man very happy.'

I was stunned: all seven of them said they wanted to do it, and so Charlie and his very lucky carer got a private cabaret performance of boobs, bosoms, breasts and busts, and when he came out of the VIP room later that night I could see Charlie had been crying. His carer was red-eyed too. Later, when the two of them were leaving, his carer came over to thank me.

'You know, no one's ever made a fuss of Charlie like that before. I am, we both are, so grateful. Your girls are just amazing.'

'I know they are, but thank you so much for saying so.'

As I said, it was one of those nights where everything seemed to be going on. At one point I even saw Brad in one of the dancers' pink shorts and vests having his turn on the bike! The punters were loving it, the dancers were having their best night of the year and the buckets were filling up with donations.

Then I got radioed by the front door.

'Can you greet a group who have just come in, Sam? Reckon they're going to be big spenders.'

The message from the front door was that these gentlemen worked for a very big company, and as soon as I heard the name of the company I felt chills running up my spine, down my legs and across my entire body: it was the name of Paddy's company.

I hadn't seen Paddy for four or five years since he'd stopped coming in to see me at Diamonds. I had always had a huge soft spot for Paddy: he'd been my sugar daddy for a couple of years and we had got on really well, getting dancers to perform for us or going off to watch the football.

My heart started pounding inside my chest. I didn't know how it would feel to see him again. I didn't know how he'd react to seeing me again because I'd always harboured the worry that I must have upset him in some way. I watched as a group of seven men walked down the stairs and my heart was in my mouth. Although the pink madness of the charity night carried on around me, it seemed the sounds had become muffled, the lights had got dimmer, and all I could focus on was seeing Paddy again.

I scanned the faces of the men walking down the stairs. Paddy wasn't one of them, but there was still one face that was oddly familiar.

'Good evening, gentlemen,' I said. 'Welcome to Liberty Steel. My name is Sam, I'm the House Mother here and you just need to let me know what you're after and I'll make sure you get it. Now, is it a champagne table you're after?'

I led them to the best table in the club and waved over a waitress who cashed up a few grand's worth of chips for them. These men were clearly out to celebrate something and were looking forward to a long – and expensive – evening.

'Excuse me,' I said to the face I recognised, 'but is your name Danny?'

He looked very surprised.

'Um, yes, it is. How on earth did you know that?'

'Well, I used to know your dad.'

'How?'

'Let's take a walk to the bar and I'll tell you.'

He left his colleagues and walked with me.

'How on earth did you know my dad?'

'Well.' I wasn't quite sure what the etiquette was. He might have been in a strip club himself, but did that mean he was OK about knowing his dad had been in one? 'Well, you're not the first person in your family to come into a strip club.'

'Ah.'

'So how is Paddy?'

'I'm afraid he passed away a few years back.'

As soon as I'd seen Danny I had guessed as much because Paddy had always told me his son would inherit the business, but, nevertheless, hearing him say it made me catch my breath.

'I'm so sorry to hear that.'

'I can tell. Are you all right?'

'Yeah, it's just that me and your dad were quite close at one point.'

'Really?'

'Oh God, not like that, I promise, but he used to come and see me at a club I worked in in west London, and the two of us used to talk for hours.'

'God knows he could talk.'

'Couldn't he! He told me all about you. I remember when you went into hospital, it was appendicitis, wasn't it?'

'Blimey, you've got a good memory.'

'He was with me that night and he felt terrible for not being with his family.'

'Really?'

The two of us ordered drinks, delivered them to the table and then carried on talking for at least half an hour. Danny explained that his dad had been sick for a long time but had kept it from everyone and in the end he had passed away quickly, with his kids and grandkids at his side. It was a really touching conversation for both of us. It was like I knew him and the affection I had for Paddy was instantly transferred to his son. Danny was quite pleased to find out his dad had been 'seeing' a dancer, because it was much better than finding out his father had had a mistress. For me, knowing that I hadn't said anything to upset him was really comforting, but I still wish Paddy had come in to Diamonds to say goodbye.

'I haven't spoken about my dad for ages. Not many people I see really knew him.'

'I did. I really did. And I can tell you, he was a lovely, lovely man.'

And then Danny just put his arms round me and the two of us stood there hugging for several minutes. It was the most touching moment I have ever experienced in a strip club. Something spontaneous, something genuine, and for those few minutes Danny and I were caught up in an emotional mix of grief and nostalgia. He was a lovely guy and was so like his father it was weird.

I told the girls in the club to make sure that Danny's table got exemplary service, and I kept an eye on them throughout the night. They made a huge donation to the charity and several of the dancers ended up with garters stuffed with money. One dancer, Jasmine, got the tip of her life.

'Sam, Sam.'

'What is it?'

She pulled me over to one side.

'Sam, I have to ask you something.' Her voice was almost an octave higher than normal: she was so excited it was like she'd taken some sniff, but she wasn't a druggie.

'What is it, Jas? What's happened?'

'Do I have to give you notice if I want to stop working?'

'Why are you asking?'

'Well, you're not going to believe this but I just got offered a job.'

'By who?'

'That table in front of the stage. There's a guy there that wants me to be his PA.'

I looked over and made eye contact with Danny. He knew the

conversation I was having with Jasmine because it was one of his managers who had made the offer. And because the offer was coming from Danny's table, from Paddy's company, I knew that Jasmine wasn't being jerked around. I was absolutely confident she was being offered a proper job.

'That is absolutely fantastic,' I said to her. 'I'll have a look at the roster and see what I can do with your shifts. When does he want you to start?'

'As soon as possible, I guess. You know what he said to me? He said, "Half an hour ago I had £700 in my pocket and now it's in your purse and I have no idea how it got there." He said, "I don't even fancy you and you've got me to spend money. I don't know how you've done it, but if you can use your charm on my clients, if you can use those skills, then I want you to come and work for me."'

I almost felt myself welling up as she told me this. All these years I'd heard dancers say how they wanted a man to take them away from working in clubs, and they had always meant a husband or a sugar daddy. But here was a man who recognised that a dancer's talent isn't what you can do with a pair of tassels, it's about how you read your customer and handle yourself. I was so thrilled for Jasmine. I just wished more customers would appreciate a dancer's repertoire of skills.

It had been such an emotional night, and as I was leaving I bumped into Brad.

'Wasn't that the best night you've ever had in a strip club?' I said to him.

'It was fantastic, wasn't it? We should do more charity things. The girls love it. The punters love it.'

'Nowhere else in the world I would have rather been tonight.'

'I know what you mean.'

We had reached the front door, and I could see Pete in his old banger waiting for me across the road.

'Night then, Sam.'

'Night, Brad. See you tomorrow.'

'Oh, Sam?'

'Yeah?'

'Did you see Joni tonight, the little tequila girl?'

'No, I don't think she was on shift. Why?'

'Her flatmates called a couple of times tonight. They've not been able to get hold of her.'

'Well, I'll be seeing TJ in the morning. I'll ask her to get Joni to call them.'

'Thanks, Sam.'

I got in the car, gave Pete a massive hug and said, 'Take me out dancing. I don't want this night to end.'

We went to a couple of after-hours clubs and finally got back to Pete's parents' place about 9 a.m. TJ was sitting in the living room staring into space.

'What's up, Teej?' I asked.

She looked up at me, locked eyes and shook her head.

'Joni's dead.'

Billionaire's plaything

Joni's flatmates had been looking for her for two days. They all worked crazy hours, so it was possible she'd been missing for longer, but after two days of worrying they decided they should have a look round her room to see if there might be a clue to where she was. They found Joni's body inside her wardrobe: she had hung herself on the clothes rail with a belt.

I think the first thing everyone does when they find out that someone they know has committed suicide is to agonise over whether there was something they could have done, some sign they should have picked up on. There had been a night about a month previously when Joni had come and sat on my lap and asked if we could talk. I remembered how bony she had felt and commented on the fact that she was losing weight.

'It's cos I can't sleep,' she'd said. 'I'm getting maybe two hours a night.'

Sleep can be a problem for lots of people in nightlife. Always going to bed when the sun comes up can really affect some people and they just can't get used to it. But in Joni's case, her insomnia was chemical. She'd been taking more and more speed because she was convinced she was fat and wanted to lose weight. Although she hadn't been a dancer, working with so many dancers who were so confident about their bodies had obviously had a big impact on Joni. It's just that none of us knew quite how big an impact. Nothing could stop me reliving that conversation and wishing I had said something different, something to comfort or encourage her. I felt truly wretched.

TJ was in bits. She kept saying that she should never have put

Joni in that environment and blamed herself for Joni's death. There was nothing Pete or I could say that would do anything to help. It was exactly the same when I got into work that evening. Everyone sat around wondering if they could have done something, *anything*, differently. I felt like I was everyone's mama that night. Even the toughest girls who had barely spoken to me for the past two years were asking me for hugs. There wasn't a single person who worked in that club who wasn't affected by Joni's death. Even Popeye.

For the next few nights, we couldn't stop talking about Joni, and we tried to piece together how long we thought she hadn't slept for, or when she had last taken some speed, or how much weight she had lost. None of us had ever suspected that she was considering taking her own life.

For the next few days, my phone didn't stop ringing. Girls just wanted to talk. A few of them came round to my place and we sat together going over every conversation we had ever had with Joni. I even got a phone call from a dancer's boyfriend: she wasn't saying anything and – as he'd heard so much about me – he was wondering if I could talk to her. I was really touched by that and was so emotional anyway that I burst into tears again: I hadn't known the girls felt that safe with me.

TJ got in touch with Joni's family and it was decided that a few of us would attend the funeral. It filtered back to us that her folks were struggling with paying for the funeral – it was costing over six grand – and Brad suggested that we could contribute.

'Sod that. The bar takes that amount of money in half an hour. We're just going to bloody well pay for it,' I told him.

The funeral was down on the south coast and although it was one of the saddest days of my life I couldn't help but see the funny side of things. At the front of the church was Joni's family, all in black, all looking a bit kicked in the shins by life. And at the back of the church was the posse from Liberty's. Now, I want you to understand that we tried to dress appropriately, but the thing is strippers don't really have clothes that most of the world would deem appropriate for funerals. When we 'dress down', we still look more made up than most catwalk models. It is just physically impossible to put a stripper entirely in black. The urge to accessorise is intense, un-ignorable, compelling. So, even though most of us found a sober pencil skirt and a sensible jacket, the shoes were a bit on the high side, the hair was a bit on the big side and the nails were definitely on the bright side. We might have thought we had left the house that morning disguised as civilians, but sitting in that church there was no pretending: we were nightlife through and through.

After the service, Brad gave the money we had all collected to Joni's mum. It came to about £12k in the end and you could tell from the look on her face that she was incredibly grateful. Aside from the grief and despair of losing her daughter – how much more intensely was she reliving the conversations she had had with Joni, trying to find out if there was something she should have done? – the cost of the funeral was clearly a big burden for her. We were all pleased that we could at least do that for Joni.

To Joni's mum, the six or seven grand it cost for the funeral was more than a year's worth of savings. Maybe it was even a lifetime's worth of savings. But to a dancer it was a couple of nights' work, or a couple of weeks' work if she couldn't quite get her hustle on. There would have been a time when I would have thought that made us smarter than Joni's relatives, that we were better than them. But the two years I had spent with Pete had made a difference. I was no longer as obsessed with money. I no longer felt that you should judge someone by how much money they made. The other people in that church hadn't been so different from my own family, and seeing them made me think about my own relatives and how I had judged them or ignored them in my quest for fast money. I felt ashamed of myself.

I had a godmother I hadn't spoken to for years. I had two little sisters whose childhoods I had missed out on. I had people in my life who had looked out for me and who I had never bothered to thank. With Pete's encouragement, I started to pick up the phone and try to make amends. There was a very long list of people I needed to apologise to.

Joni's death impacted on all of us at Liberty's in all sorts of unexpected ways. Some girls announced that they were leaving to set up their own businesses. A couple told me they had gone back to their studies. One girl used Joni's passing as the motivation to become the best at what she did: she entered international competitions for pole dancing and went on to compete in the world championships at Hedonism in Jamaica – I bet you didn't know there were world championships for pole dancing! – and ended up coming eighth. When I went round to her flat afterwards, I found out why: she had converted her entire studio flat into a pole dancer's gym. She had removed all the furniture except a bed roll and put mirrors down one wall and a pole in the middle: she had made dancing her life.

For me, I just wanted to go at everything full throttle and make every day, every hour, count. So when my friend Philippe came to me with a proposition, I was very ready to say yes.

You meet a lot of odd people in nightlife. When you leave work at 4 a.m. and go and grab a drink or a burger, you meet other people who also work at night and you always seem to bond because you have so much in common. Whether it's drug dealers, actors, detectives or nightclub promoters, you keep running into the same faces and eventually those people become your friends. Philippe was one of those people.

I reckon that at some point he had been a ballet dancer, then he must have moved into the West End doing chorus-line stuff before moving on to a bit of choreography and a bit of modelling. He was one of those truly beautiful people who you couldn't take your eyes off, in part because he wore so few clothes. Even in winter you'd find him in a pec-revealing vest and leather chaps that exposed his perfectly round buttocks. Oddly enough, given that description, Philippe is as straight as they come and had started earning a living as an escort. He had a reputation for having the biggest black cock in London, and there were a lot of older white women who paid a good deal of money to be 'serviced' by him.

'Are you still dancing, darling?' he said on the phone.

'I still got some moves. Why?'

'Well, I'm organising this really elite party and they only want one black girl, and I think you're it.'

Amongst my friends I am known as The Last Negro Standing because whenever someone wants one black girl for a job I am the black girl they want, presumably because I'm not as ghetto as some of my sisters. I had long been used to being the only black face in the room.

'OK. Sounds interesting. Tell me more.'

'I can't talk to you about it over the phone. You'll have to come and meet me.'

He explained that one of his clients was married to a very wealthy man. An extremely wealthy man, in fact.

'How wealthy?'

'Russian billionaire.'

'Keep talking.'

Apparently her husband knew all about her dates with Philippe and was very relaxed about it. As well as seeing escorts, the couple also arranged private sex parties and had asked Philippe to bring along some friends.

'You know I don't do extras, don't you?'

'I do, but you've got two options. They will pay you £10k to come to their villa for the weekend and take part in whatever they want you to take part in, or they will pay you £5k to go and be part of the cabaret. A few performances on the pole, look decorative by the pool . . .'

'There'll be a pool?'

'Honey. You have no idea. These people have so much money. Their place is dripping in gold.'

'OK. I'm in, I think. But I'd be much happier if I could take a friend.'

'I'll talk to them.'

A few days later, Philippe called with instructions of where to meet the wife, who had agreed that I could take another dancer with me. So TJ and I arrived at her hotel in Mayfair. This hotel is so exclusive that there is no sign outside. It is not listed in any directory. You cannot book a room there unless they already know you. Probably, you have to be in the Rich List or the royal family to get a booking. Just walking into the lobby made me nervous.

We took the lift up to her room and the doors opened directly into this massive, massive suite. It must have been the entire floor of the building. *What must this be costing her,* I thought – *£10k a night? £20k?* I felt that same old tug on my heartstrings that big money used to make me feel. *How do you get to be this rich?*

'You must be Sam?' A very smart-looking woman in a suit approached us and shook my hand. 'And you must be TJ?'

'Nice to meet you,' we both said.

'Come and sit with me. Shall we order drinks?'

Oh. This is the wife. She was so young – about 27 – and so pretty that I had assumed it must have been the PA, but she took us over to a table where she had photos of lots of beautiful people, including a picture of Philippe and the photos TJ and I had given him. She explained that she organised parties about twice a year for her and her husband and only invited a very select group of people. She met everyone beforehand to make sure they would fit in. I got the impression she wanted to make sure we weren't drug addicts, or mentally unstable, and that we were attractive enough, and clean enough, to make the grade. She told us there would be people at the party just to entertain, some strippers, some burlesque and drag acts; and there would be people there who would participate – basically the best and most expensive prostitutes from around the world.

'Are you sure you don't want to participate?' she asked in her thick Russian accent. 'I like you and I think my husband would like you as well.'

'I think I speak for both of us when I say that's not really what we're about. We're more than happy to come and entertain and be sexy and have fun, but we're not there to get fucked.'

'OK. I understand,' she said reluctantly.

TJ and I hung out with her for what we thought was a couple of hours, but when she called a taxi for us we realised we had been there for nearly six hours, just talking and drinking and ordering the most amazing meal from room service. Of course it wasn't really a taxi, it was her own private driver in her own private limousine. I thought to myself, *If this is a preview of how she is going to treat us, then I'm more than happy to take part.*

TJ and I were absolutely desperate to talk about her in the back of the car, but we knew that the driver would be listening in and telling the wife what we had said. Possibly our conversation was being recorded. This couple needed to be absolutely sure of who you were before they would let you into their world.

A few days later, Philippe called to say that the wife had liked us but wanted to ask again if we would be interested in taking part in the orgies. I repeated that I didn't do that.

'If there are some nice girls there, maybe I'll have a little play, but I'm not being paid for sex, OK?'

'OK, darling, it's just that she really likes you.'

'Well, that's very nice to hear. I'm happy to dance for her, but that's it, OK?'

It was another couple of days before Philippe got back to me and TJ and said that his client would like to hire us – as dancers – for the weekend. He also gave us the address of a clinic in Harley Street and told us an appointment had been made for everyone attending the party to be tested for HIV and other STDs. 'Just in case you get tempted on the night, darling, everyone needs to get the all clear.'

Obviously our tests must have come back fine, because a few weeks later we found ourselves in a VIP lounge at Heathrow waiting for a flight to the south of France: the sex party was taking place at the couple's villa overlooking Monte Carlo!

A bit like the first time Ali and I had flown to Denmark and spotted the other strippers on the flight, I instantly spotted the other party-goers in the lounge: a gorgeous guy with a mane of blond hair and muscles rippling under his tanned skin, drag queens, male-to-female transsexuals and the most beautiful man I have ever seen in my life, who not only turned out to be a woman but also one of the highest-paid hookers in the world. I was pretty sure that the man who started juggling with the fruit in the complimentary buffet would also be on our flight.

We were flown first class and met by a fleet of bullet-proof Porsche people-carriers that took us up a long and winding road into the hills above the sea. It was getting dark when we arrived, so we couldn't really see the house, but once we had gone through the massive entrance gates we spent another five minutes in the cars. Not many houses have five-minute-long driveways. This was a *big* place. That cost an awful lot of money. Kings and queens don't live in this much luxury.

We were put in a series of guest bungalows in the grounds. It was just like being at a luxury hotel – we had our own sauna, our own gym, a minibar (well, a maxibar), and there was even room service. The bungalow TJ and I were sharing was probably the nicest place I have ever spent a night – marble floors, handmade furniture, gorgeous bed linens and a walk-in shower that could probably have taken eight people at once.

'Wow.'

'Wow.'

'Wow again.'

'Double wow.'

We couldn't believe how absolutely fucking gorgeous the place was. When Philippe popped in to see us, he told us our pad was nothing compared to the bungalow he had been given.

'I wanna see it.'

'Not right now. It's showtime, darlings. Put your best outfit on and be ready in half an hour.'

'We can't get ready in half an hour!'

'You'll have to try.'

I put on my outfit – some little sailor shorts, a cute little sailor hat and pair of nipple tassels – and we all went up together to the main house. It was properly dark by this stage, so I couldn't see it all, but it was all glass and steel with marble floors. It was so cool and so polished it looked like the inside of a spaceship.

The buffet was in a marquee on the lawn outside, where there were chocolate fountains, cheese fountains, a girl making fresh sushi and another making crepes. It was like being inside Willy Wonka's chocolate factory. One half of me was just gobsmacked; the other half was – yet again –wondering what you have to do to be *that* rich.

The party took place in a vast hall in the main house, and in the middle of the hall was the wife. The man sitting next to her, I presumed, was her billionaire husband. I had imagined that she would be a trophy wife, a young bit of skirt making an old, fat, potato-faced man's fantasies come true. So when I saw him I was truly shocked: at first glance this man could have been George Clooney. He was gorgeous, but more importantly he looked like he had the money to pay us all.

They were sitting on a bed that was big enough for all 20 of us to get on, but Philippe explained that that wasn't where the action would take place. He pointed towards the back of the hall. 'That's where the boom-boom room is.'

'Boom-boom?'

'Oh yeah.'

There was a stage at one end of the hall that had a series of poles on it, some descending from the ceiling, others rising out of the floor. I looked at them and calculated it would be possible to move from pole to pole without touching the ground and tried to work out what moves I could incorporate to make the biggest impact.

Each of the performers was given a ticket saying what time they would be required on stage. I couldn't believe it: these people even had a floor manager! The lighting rig, the sound system – it could have all been used for a Broadway show. I was following a fire eater and a troupe of trapeze artists.

I took a little bit of speed before I got on stage. It had been four or five years since I had last worked a pole and I needed a little something to loosen me up. I'd practised a few moves at Liberty's after the club had shut, but I wasn't as fit as I used to be. I put my all into that performance, stretching every muscle and timing everything to the music. It felt so good to be back on stage again, but as soon as I had finished I realised I had done some damage. I really should have warmed up! Thankfully, I wasn't asked to perform again all weekend, because I really don't think I could have managed it.

When I came off stage, the waitresses starting doing the rounds with these silver trays piled up with all sorts of drugs. Sherbet, pills, ketamine . . . things I'd never heard of. It was at this point that George Clooney announced that those who wanted to were welcome to join them in the boom-boom room. At the flick of a switch, an entire wall at the end of the hall lifted up – it was like something from Austin Powers – and revealed the sumptuous orgy chamber beyond.

'TJ. Let's get outta here.'

We grabbed a bottle of Cristal and headed to our bungalow, where we downed the lot as we embarked on the lengthy process of taking off false eyelashes, removing make-up, taking out hair pieces – honestly, it can take as long to get undressed as it can to get ready.

We had been asleep for a couple of hours when the patio doors to our bungalow were thrown open and a group of about seven people stumbled in. They saw a bed and headed for it and continued with the orgy they had probably been having on the lawn. Unfortunately, that bed already had me and TJ in it.

'What the fuck?'

'Hey, guys, get out of here.'

Their response was, 'Fantastic, more bodies!'

'Seriously, people, we're trying to sleep here.'

These were very drugged, very horny people and they didn't really care that TJ and I were underneath them while they fucked and sucked and poked and licked. They were hell-bent on having an orgy on top of us.

'Listen.' I had to really fight to get out from under them. 'This is not on. We are *sleeping*. You have to go.'

They were like sex zombies, not really making eye contact, not properly understanding, and were only interested in their next orgasm. They saw the other bed in the bungalow and all seven of them staggered over to it.

'No. No, that's not what I meant. You have to leave this room altogether. You have to go.'

We eventually got them to leave and then laughed ourselves to sleep. In the morning when we left our bungalow and walked up to the main house, it was like someone had done a drive-by. We were stepping over bodies. Wrecks of bodies. Transvestites with wigs on backwards, naked women, semi-aroused men, make-up down their faces, clothes ripped off their bodies, all littering the gardens of the most amazing house I had ever seen. In the daylight, I saw the Russians' villa for the first time and it looked like the Sydney Opera House. Bright white angles and gleaming glass. It was breathtaking.

TJ and I picked our way over the bodies and made our way to the marquee, where a cook was quietly making pancakes and chopping up strawberries. *What must she be thinking? What has she seen? How often does she see this?* She just smiled at us and nodded out towards the swimming pool, where we saw the rest of the party-goers sprawled out in different stages of undress on sun loungers. I was so pleased that we had gone to bed when we did.

We were heading back to the marquee to get some breakfast when behind us we heard clang, clang, clang. We turned to see Philippe stomping behind us in a chainmail thong that was swinging between his thighs as he walked. He had the biggest smile on his face. Behind him was the wife, covered in leaves. She looked exhausted. Like she'd walked through a jungle for 15 days without any food or water.

'Boom-boom room?' she said to us.

We shook our heads, and she and Philippe carried on towards the house.

TJ and I spent the day lounging round the pool and taking a walk through the grounds. This place was so massive that it had its own pine forest, and in the middle of the trees we came across a log cabin. There were more naked people inside there.

In the afternoon, TJ and I were the only people – apart from the staff – who were awake, so we went into the house and decided we would take a look inside the boom-boom room. Oh. My. God. I can still smell it to this day. The place stank of sex and sweat and debauchery. I mean *reeked*. It was so pungent, so potent, that it almost made me gag. If you had licked the walls, you would have been crazy for four days. You really knew something had gone down in that room.

At dinner that night, when the participants surfaced, we started to hear some of the stories of what had gone on while we'd been in bed. Apparently one of the porn stars had bragged that she could do the splits standing up, like one of those extreme yoga poses. Then another girl said that she could do it too. Can you imagine: you think you're the only person in the world who can do this and then someone pipes up that they can do it too! So the pair of them were thrilled and did it in unison, pressing their pussies together as Philippe got on his knees and started licking them. Now that's something you don't see very often.

There were tales of one of the porn stars getting DP'd on the lawn, of clusterfucks in the pool . . . probably the whole time we were having dinner there were people fingering each other under the table.

The second night was a bit more tame, and most of the action centred around George Clooney, who shared his wife's interest in black men. Philippe didn't do boys, but the Russians had flown in a couple of beautiful guys from Holland who definitely did. I had a little play with some of the girls by the pool, but after the previous night no one had much energy. Some people were just too sore to be touched.

On the Sunday morning, the Russians called us in individually to their boudoir to pay us. They had all these little piles of money and they clearly got a kick out of counting it and handing it over. I was handed my envelope – which had a £400 tip on top of the fee because they had enjoyed my performance so much – and then we were all taken in the black people-carriers back to the airport and back to normality.

Pete was very pleased when I got home. Although he had met Philippe and knew that I would never sleep with someone for money, I suppose there is always that anxiety that if there is enough money on the table, or enough drugs, none of us really know what we are capable of. A few months later, Philippe asked if I would like to do it again and I said no, partly for Pete, but mostly because once-in-a-lifetime experiences lose their magic if you have them twice.

The feminists are coming!

I was coming into work one night and noticed a small group of women standing outside. I'm the only person I know who doesn't swerve those clipboard people, because I'm always curious to know what makes people stand out on the street, and as I walked towards them one of them rushed over and handed me a leaflet.

'There are places you can go. There are people you can reach out to. If you need to escape, call the number on here and we will come and get you.'

I was so stunned that I didn't know what to say, and it takes a lot to shut me up.

'If someone is forcing you to be here, that's illegal and we can take action against them.'

It was quite a verbal onslaught, and she believed so passionately in what she was saying there was no way of interrupting her.

'We can be discreet, we can take you away and you won't have to give your money to a pimp any more.'

'You don't know what you're talking about, do you? What do you really believe is going on here?'

'Well, I know there's a certain number of you that are forced to be here.'

'Why do you think that? What are you basing this on?'

'It's the laws of probability. I've counted fifteen girls go into the club so far and at least one is going to be trafficked or forced.'

Whoa! Hold those horses! This woman needed some new information.

'Let me tell you something. I'm the House Mother here. It is my job to look after our dancers and to enforce strict rules and

255

regulations. I don't know what you've heard, but our girls need to come to us with passports, with proof of address, they have employment contracts.'

She looked genuinely surprised.

'And they come in of their own free will.'

'No they don't.'

'Would you like to come in and see for yourself?'

'I would never go in a place like that, a den of sin.'

'Then how can you possibly know what you are talking about?'

I would have really respected her if she had taken me up on my offer, and I could see that she was genuinely concerned for girls' welfare, but she had mistaken a well-run licensed operation with a sordid room above a chip shop where girls are locked up for days on end.

'Well, if you would come in with me, do you know what you would see?'

'Sin.'

'Well, if you call sitting around and having a chat sinful, then that's exactly what you'd see. Girls who work in here might be sitting around for more than half the night waiting for customers to come in. They might not earn anything tonight. So ask yourself this: if you are a trafficker, are you going to put a girl in this kind of situation, or are you going to lock her in a room and send as many men in to see her as you can find in a night where you are guaranteed to make money? Whatever you think of what we do here, it is legal, it is consensual and it is not sinful.'

'I don't believe you.'

'Well then, tell me, of the 15 girls you say you've seen enter the club tonight, how many were marched here by men, how many of them looked like they were in fear and dreading what the night may hold? None. And if you stay here all night, you will not see pimps waiting to collect them and steal their money from them. You have got it all wrong. The women you want to help don't work here.'

She almost looked heartbroken. She was so sure of what she believed that having someone pick apart her beliefs clearly upset her.

'Well, it's still degrading to women, it's still sinful.'

'I don't know how you can say that if you've never seen it. If you change your mind, tell the boys on the door to call the House Mother and I'll give you a tour.'

Of course, she never did come in that night, but a few weeks later we got wind that a bigger protest was being planned for the following Friday. Just in case things got out of hand, we planned to put the club in a full lock-down from 10.30 p.m. onwards: no one in, no one out, doors bolted and locked.

It was actually quite exciting and there was a real buzz about the place that night – possibly because the customers couldn't leave, so the girls knew they would make some money. If the protesters had realised they were actually helping us, maybe they would have changed strategy.

I went into the security room to watch the protest on the cameras. We could see them as they turned off Oxford Street and marched towards the club. I guess there were around 150 of them, all wearing sensible shoes and all waving placards. And then – above the music in the club and the noise from the floor and through the doors – we could actually hear them chanting. They must have been making a right old racket.

As they got closer, the security boys in with me started to take the piss.

'She's fat.'

'She's bald.'

'She's only outside because she could never get inside.'

They were quite happy watching it all on camera, but I just had to go out and see it for myself.

'We're in a lock-down, Sam. You're not going anywhere.'

'Oh yes, I am. I just have to know what it is that makes these people leave their house on a cold autumn night, get together with 100 other people and take to the streets to wave placards. Don't you want to know?'

Dennis agreed to go with me. We should have gone out the back door, because as soon as we unbolted the door onto the street and those double doors creaked open, 150 faces turned and stared at me. I guess they thought I must be the spokesperson for Liberty Steel and were expecting me to say something, but I just wanted to gawp. For a few seconds, they stared at me and I stared at them.

I was stunned by how much noise they were making. They had these little chants and rhymes, and they were banging them out. They were holding up placards that said things like 'Stop Trafficking', and I was kind of blown away by their passion. These women hated what we were doing so much that they had gone to the trouble of making up little songs and designing placards.

Two women approached me. One had a really short, butch haircut and the other looked liked she was about to do a spot of weeding in the garden – all corduroy and wellies.

'Excuse me,' I said to them, 'I just want you to know that my name is Sam, I'm the House Mother here. There's a reason I work here, I'm the buffer between the dancers and the men.'

'You should be ashamed of yourself,' the corduroy woman shouted as the entire mass of protestors moved in. 'You pimp off other women, shame on you.'

'I'm not a fucking madam. I'm the House Mother. Do you even know the difference?' My curiosity was mutating into anger.

'Shame on you! Shame on you!'

'Listen,' I shouted to make myself heard. 'Listen!' There was no point. They were all chanting in my face and I could barely hear myself. 'Do you know what? None of you could get in here. If you came to audition, I wouldn't let you in . . .'

It was at this point that Dennis came up behind me, picked me up and carried me back inside. He bolted the door before he even put me down.

'That is the last time I ever let you do something so fucking stupid, Sam. They would have lynched you. What the hell were you saying?'

'I know. I know I shouldn't have said it, but I couldn't help myself. The words just came out. Should I go out there and apologise?'

'Don't be so fucking daft. If they see you again, they'll tear your hair out.'

I had a Brazilian weave at the time. About £900 worth. I wasn't risking that!

Those women stayed outside till after midnight but dispersed before the last Tubes stopped running. By the time we all left, it was quiet on the street. I kept expecting them to come back, but perhaps something of what I said had made a difference, perhaps they could now see that strip clubs were completely different from brothels.

Having said that, a few months later there was talk of exactly that happening. We'd read stories in the papers that the Government wanted to change the terms of all strip clubs' licences and rename them 'sexual encounter clubs'. We all thought that we worked in the entertainment business. Our dancers were already dealing with the stigma of words like 'stripper' and 'lap dancer'; to throw in the words 'sexual encounter' as well was just too much. Those women who had been protesting outside the club would have thought their prejudices and suspicions had been confirmed.

We worried that men would start coming into the club expecting something that was not on offer. We feared the kinds of situations such a change in the law would put our dancers in. We clearly had to do something: it was now our turn to take to the streets in protest.

Brad, Popeye and every man in the club felt the same way too. So we picked a date and agreed that we would march from the club to the Houses of Parliament and hand in a petition. Brad got in touch with the other clubs in London, and it turned out there was a suspicion that the new licences were just an excuse to charge each establishment more money. This protest was turning into a really big deal.

Dancers from about six other clubs arrived at Liberty's at 11 o'clock one morning and we all got to work making placards. We based them on the ones the feminists had made, except instead of saying 'Stop trafficking', ours said 'We stop the traffic'. Watching 50 strippers make placards was hilarious. We all have innate dressmaking and alteration skills, and they were all on their hands and knees with their little tongues poking out because they were concentrating so hard with their crepe paper and Pritt Stick.

Instead of using militant black felt tip, we wrote in glitter and got very Blue Peter about it. One of the girls ripped up her dress to make fabric strips to create letters.

'This is made out of authentic stripper sweat. They need to know that I have sacrificed my sweat for this!'

For the previous couple of weeks there had been endless chatter about what to wear on the march. Some girls came in evening wear, some in little stripper outfits, and the tequila girls came in their cat suits. We were the prettiest, cutest marchers the world has ever seen!

About 100 of us left Liberty's and marched down Oxford Street, then down to Trafalgar Square and on to Parliament Square. It's maybe a mile and a half, which is a very long way in seven-inch heels, but we had to go so slowly anyway because people kept stopping us and offering support. Car horns were being beeped, shoppers were cheering, and it was like a carnival. It was the first time anyone had seen that many strippers awake, alert and together at that time of day, and it really felt like it was our world walking through daylife, showing civilians what we were really like.

We made up some silly little chants, but as that repetition gets into your head you really start to mean it. Chanting in unison with other people makes you feel connected to them, and the closer we got to Parliament Square the more passionate we all felt about it and there was a real camaraderie going on.

'You know what this reminds me of, Brad?'

'The old days?'

'You bet. It's great, isn't it?'

I guess it's only when something is threatened that you realise how much it means to you. I think we all enjoyed feeling like we were a part of something, that we belonged to something. When we got to the Houses of Parliament, we stood there singing for a bit, attracted the attention of some of the press photographers who are always hanging around, and posed for a few pictures. Brad then handed in our petition and called the drivers – the club had a few limos for stag parties and VIPs – who came to collect us and take us back to the club. We had such a feeling of achievement, and that night the club was a complete party house. Everyone made money and it really was one of the best days of my whole career.

The Americans

The first I knew that the club had been sold was when I came into work and found Brad sitting at my desk in the changing room.

'Do you need to talk to me about something?'

'No, I just needed to use your computer.'

'Is yours on the blink?'

'Not exactly.'

The consortium that owned Liberty's had accepted an offer from one of the big American chains that ran massive clubs in places like Las Vegas and Atlantic City. Brad explained that two executives had just turned up and told him that his office was now their office.

As far as I was concerned, the fact that Brad didn't seem to be man enough to argue for keeping his office was a sure sign that the club needed someone else in charge. As the whispers started to circulate about what the Americans would do and the changes that were on their way, I was actually pretty relaxed about the situation because I felt things couldn't really get any worse.

The atmosphere wasn't helped by the fact that the Americans were arseholes. The pair of them strutted around the club as if they were famous: their body language was constantly saying, 'Don't you know who I am?' and 'Don't come near me because I'm special and you're trash.' And as they never actually spoke to anyone, body language was their only form of communication.

We learnt that their names were Arnie and Donny. Arnie had been a college football player (American football, that is) and it showed: he was 6 ft 5 in. with biceps the size of my head. Donny reminded me of Michael J. Fox: tiny, wiry and ridiculously youthful. He was probably close to 50 but could have passed for 35. I know it's a cliché, but he really did have short-man syndrome and he took every opportunity to show us what a big and important man he really was. It was interesting to see how the dancers responded to their arrival, and most of them jumped ship quicker than a Somalian pirate, switching their attention to Arnie and Donny in the hope that they would survive whatever axe was about to be wielded. Arnie and Donny, of course, were only too happy about that, and rumours soon started that they had slept with this girl, or that dancer, or maybe both of them, possibly at the same time.

The atmosphere in the club was appalling. Everyone was in fear of losing their jobs and the gossipmongers were only too happy to stir things up. The initial changes the Americans made to tighten up the way the club was run and make it more professional seemed to make sense, but other changes hurt the people I cared about. I received a memo – an actual meeting with actual conversation was out of the question – telling me that Terry and Jackie were no longer allowed to sell clothes in the club. From now on, the club would sell its own clothes to dancers and I was asked to look into the possibility of setting up a shop inside the changing room stocking everything a dancer might need.

TJ also told me that her tequila contract had been cancelled, and, to make it worse, some of her girls had gone to work directly with the club. TJ had no contract and no staff with which to win other contracts. She very nearly went out of business. It was starting to feel like the end of an era.

I wasn't letting the ship go down without a fight, so I walked into the Americans' office and asked for a meeting.

'You've been here two weeks and you haven't even said hello to me, so I have come to introduce myself. My name is Sam, I am the House Mother and you ignore me at your peril.'

'Hi, Sam, we know who you are. Take a seat.'

Well, that was unexpected. I really thought they hadn't noticed me. But now that I had their attention, I wasn't going to waste it.

'You have got a club full of scared people at the moment. How the hell do you expect these girls to charm customers when they are worried they might not have a job tomorrow?'

'Do you have any suggestions?'

'You bet I do!'

It turned out that they were only too happy to talk and had just been waiting for someone to approach them. In the meantime, they had been lying low, observing and making plans. They had sussed out that Brad was a doormat and were planning to replace him with Popeye.

'You do that and I walk. And if I go, you'll lose all of your best dancers. I told them about all the issues I had with Barry, some more serious to my mind than others.

They were stunned as they hadn't seen any problems with Popeye and agreed to keep a closer eye on him before they made up their minds. Obviously something I had said hit home, because in the following couple of weeks Barry was so nice to me. Holding open doors, asking about my clothes, buying me drinks. I was furious: knowing that he had the capacity to be a nice human being and that he *chose* to be a bully and a thug made him sink even further in my estimation. He had a choice, and he chose to intimidate and threaten. I didn't know I could detest him any more than I already did, but it got to the stage that I could barely look at him.

I told Brad that I thought they had it in for him, but he didn't seem that bothered. At first I thought it was because he was still bruised from his split with Sandy, but he later told me he had a watertight contract. 'They can't get rid of me because they can't afford to.' He had a clause that meant he was due five years' salary if he was made redundant. So long as he wasn't actually negligent or did anything that would justify sacking him, he only had to keep turning up and he would keep getting paid.

'How can you work like that?' I asked. What I really wanted to say was, 'Haven't you got any self-respect?'

'Truth is, Sam, where else would have me?'

It was true for almost everyone who worked at Liberty's. They had been crooked and lazy for so long that they wouldn't be able to get jobs anywhere else. They were stuck with the club, and the club was lumbered with them.

For a while, Arnie and Donny did make some positive changes. They insisted that everyone brought in their work permits, which created a huge stir among the Argentinian busboys and Venezuelan dancers. I had always suspected that some of them probably didn't have the right paperwork, but I was amazed at just how many people left and never returned. They also made sure the terms of our licence were properly enforced and customers like Blue Shirt were given formal warnings. It would have meant a lot to the girls if they had just banned him, but they had instructions from their bosses in America to maximise profits wherever and however they could.

One sure way of boosting profits was to get more dancers on the floor. Why collect 130 house fees a night when you could collect 150? I was told to get as many girls on shift as I could. When I couldn't hire dancers quickly enough, Arnie started sitting in on the auditions with me.

'What's wrong with that one?'

'She can't dance, Arnie. She has no rhythm whatsoever.'

'Doesn't matter, put her on the floor.'

I rejected another girl because I thought her level of grooming was so low that she would never look like a Liberty Steel girl.

'You can teach her, put her on the floor.'

'Arnie, she hasn't even bothered to shave her legs for her audition.'

'So what?'

He didn't care if a girl couldn't speak the language or hadn't combed her hair; so long as she had a pair of breasts and the £85 house fee, he was happy to let any girl go on shift. After what had happened to Joni, I fought with him to keep vulnerable girls out of the club, but he didn't seem to care.

'Who are you to judge if a girl can handle it? Give them a chance.'

'Arnie, I can't believe you just said that. I have worked in clubs since I was 17. I have been House Mother to hundreds of girls. That's who I am to say that, and when I tell you that a certain girl does not have what it takes to survive in this environment, I think you have a responsibility to listen to me. I know what I'm saying.'

'Put her on the floor.'

I was devastated. For a couple of blissful weeks I had thought that the new American owners were going to clean the place up, bring back standards of etiquette that Brad had been too detached from reality to enforce and make it a place where I would be proud to work. But it was now becoming clear that the Americans only cared about the profits. I knew what was coming: if there were more girls per punter, then each girl would have to do more to get a dance. Men would come in expecting to be able to do more than look, and the entire management would be forced to turn a blind eye. I knew I couldn't stay.

Their obsession with maximising profit made it inevitable that questions along the lines of 'What does a House Mother do anyway?' or 'What value does Sam add?' would come up – the opportunity to get me off the payroll was too tempting. From then on, I was basically micromanaged out of the place and when I made an error on my float there was a discplinary meeting. It was a farce that ended with me telling Brad that I quit.

The look on his face told me the old Brad was still in there somewhere, but he was too deeply buried, too shat on over the years to make any difference. He wasn't going to say or do anything to stop me. That really made me want to cry.

'Right, then. I'll empty my locker.'

The contents of my locker were as follows: the world's largest ever bag of make-up (a House Mother has to have just the right shade for any occasion/outfit/disaster), a big bag of humbugs (a House Mother should always have a treat for any occasion/outfit/disaster/triumph) and a PVC maid's outfit (well, you never know when it might come in handy). I put everything in a plastic bag and sat on the bench for a few moments. In a couple of hours, the girls would start coming in, strip off from their civilian clothes and slip into their stripper gear. Some of the best friendships of my life had been formed in a changing room. I pictured the scene later that night – boobs, perfume, shaving cream, pussies, tampons, hairspray. I could hear the gaggle of accents. I could see them all fighting for space at the mirror and checking out the competition while they applied mascara.

I was more than a little surprised to find out that I wasn't as upset as I had expected. The tears that had threatened to come streaming out of my eyes had retreated: I was going to be OK. In fact, I was going to be just fine. Never again would I have to tell a dancer to ditch her loser boyfriend, or prise her phone off her to make her go back on the stage while he was still shouting. I would never hear another gripe or another moan about what so-and-so had done. I wouldn't have to mop up anyone's sick. I wouldn't have to lend anyone their taxi fare home. There would be no more rows about whether the full house fee had been paid or not. It was over. And that was OK.

The double doors were locked, so I left by the back door, up the fire escape and into a little car park. It was still light. Everything looked different, even the daytime smells were different. From the car park at the back of Liberty's you could see the back entrance to the warehouse at Next where I'd once worked. I stood there for a few minutes wondering what would have happened if Alison had said something else when I'd told her about Denmark. What if she'd said it wasn't for her, or that she thought girls who did that kind of thing weren't worth knowing? Would I have listened to her? Or would I still have gone? And if I'd stayed, would I have become a manager in retail? Would that have been my fate? The thought turned me cold. Dancing might not have ended the way I would have liked, but I was still incredibly thankful for the adventures it had thrown my way.

I walked on to Oxford Street and hailed a cab. I gave the driver Pete's address. He wouldn't know what to do with me at 8 p.m. in the evening. Maybe we could go to dinner like a normal couple.

Or watch TV. Or go for a drink. They all sounded like brilliant options to me. As the taxi left the West End, I started to feel like someone had saved me. I thought about Brad, sitting in the club having shafted one of his oldest friends. He hadn't even tried to stop me leaving because he couldn't. In the end, nightlife gets you. Even the strong ones, even the good guys.

I was overwhelmed by the feeling that I had got out just in time.

Acknowledgements

First and foremost, I'd like to thank my Auntie Nya and Theresa. They taught me etiquette and sophistication (not to mention a few little tricks!) during the time we spent together. Without these two exceptional women, my dancing story would have been very different.

I'm grateful to Ben Anderson for believing in my story from the beginning and for setting me up with my agent, Melissa Pimentel at Curtis Brown. Everything Ben said about Melissa was true and within ten minutes of meeting her I knew my story was in safe hands.

Jo Monroe, the ghostwriter for this book, was the icing on the cake. We got on like a house on fire and she was able to get the best out of me during our very funny sessions. I really feel she's captured my essence in this book and I'm so thankful for that.

Finally, huge thanks to Bill Campbell, Fiona Atherton, Graeme Blaikie, Ailsa Bathgate and everyone at Mainstream Publishing for taking a chance on me and for doing such a wonderful job with the book.

Thanks all!